HUMANITARIAN ARCHITECTURE

||||||||||||||||||||||||||||||||||||

Never has the demand been so urgent for architects to respond to the design and planning challenges of rebuilding post-disaster sites and cities. In 2011, more people were displaced by natural disasters (42 million) than by wars and armed conflicts. And yet the number of architects equipped to deal with rebuilding the aftermath of these floods, fires, earthquakes, typhoons and tsunamis is chronically short.

This book documents and analyses the expanding role for architects in designing projects for communities after the event of a natural disaster. The fifteen case studies featured in the body of the book illustrate how architects can use spatial sensibility and integrated problem-solving skills to help alleviate both human and natural disasters. The cases include:

Lizzie Babister – Department of International Development, UK

Shigeru Ban – Winner of the Pritzker Architecture Prize 2014, Shigeru Ban Architects and Voluntary Architects' Network, Japan

Eric Cesal – Disaster Reconstruction and Resiliency Studio and Architecture for Humanity, Japan

Hsieh Ying Chun – Atelier 3, Taiwan

Nathaniel Corum – Education Outreach and Architecture for Humanity, USA

Sandra D'Urzo – Shelter and Settlements and International Federation of the Red Cross and Red Crescent Societies, Switzerland

Brett Moore – World Vision International, Australia

Michael Murphy – MASS Design Group, USA

David Perkes – Gulf Coast Community Design Studio, USA

Paul Pholeros – Healthabitat, Australia

Patama Roonrakwit – Community Architects for Shelter and Environment, Thailand

Graham Saunders – International Federation of Red Cross and Red Crescent Societies, Switzerland

Kirtee Shah – Ahmedabad Study Action Group, India

Maggie Stephenson – UN-Habitat, Haiti

Anna Wachtmeister – Catholic Organisation for Relief and Redevelopment Aid, the Netherlands

The interviews and supporting essays show built environment professionals collaborating with post-disaster communities as facilitators, collaborators and negotiators of land, space and shelter, rather than as 'save the world' modernists, as often portrayed in the design media. The goal is social and physical reconstruction, as a collaborative process involving a damaged community and its local culture, environment and economy; not just shelter 'projects' that 'build' houses but leave no economic footprint or longer-term community infrastructure. What defines and unites the architects interviewed for *Humanitarian Architecture* is their collective belief that through a consultative process of spatial problem solving, the design profession can contribute in a significant way to the complex post-disaster challenge of rebuilding a city and its community.

ESTHER CHARLESWORTH is the Founding Director of Architects without Frontiers (Australia), a design non-profit organization committed to working with communities in need. She is Associate Professor in Architecture and Design at RMIT University, Melbourne, Australia.

HUMANITARIAN ARCHITECTURE

||||||||||||||||||||||||||||||||||

15 STORIES OF ARCHITECTS WORKING AFTER DISASTER

ESTHER CHARLESWORTH

Routledge
Taylor & Francis Group

LONDON AND NEW YORK

First edition published 2014
by Routledge
2 Park Square, Milton Park, Abingdon,
Oxon OX14 4RN

and by Routledge
711 Third Avenue, New York, NY 10017

Routledge is an imprint of the
Taylor & Francis Group, an informa business

British Library Cataloguing in Publication Data
A catalogue record for this book is available from the
British Library

Library of Congress Cataloging-in-Publication Data
Humanitarian architecture : 15 stories of architects
working after natural disasters / edited by Esther
Charlesworth.
    pages cm
Includes bibliographical references and index.
1. Architecture–Human factors. 2. Architectural
practice–Moral and ethical aspects. 3. Humanitarian
assistance. 4. Natural disasters. 5. Architects–
Interviews. I. Charlesworth, Esther Ruth.
    NA2542.4.H86 2014
    720.1'08–dc23
    2013047753

ISBN13: 978-0-415-81866-7 (hbk)
ISBN13: 978-0-415-81867-4 (pbk)
ISBN13: 978-1-315-77654-5 (ebk)

Typeset by Alex Lazarou in Akzidenz Grotesk

Printed by Bell & Bain Ltd, Glasgow

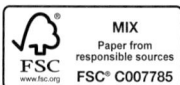

MIX
Paper from
responsible sources
FSC
www.fsc.org   FSC® C007785

|||||||||||||||||||||||||||||||||||||

This book is dedicated to the
memory of Ross Langdon (1980–2013):
a truly humanitarian architect

FOREWORD

INTRODUCTION

PART ONE

PRIVATE PRACTICE-
BASED HUMANITARIAN
ARCHITECTS

||||||||||||||||||||||||||||||||||

FOREWORD

MICHAEL SORKIN

PRINCIPAL
**MICHAEL SORKIN STUDIO,
NEW YORK CITY**

PROFESSOR OF URBAN DESIGN
**CITY COLLEGE OF NEW YORK
(CCNY)**

There is something more than a little tragic about the need to produce a book about 'humanitarian' architecture. That this should be a special category within the field of building speaks volumes about the condition of the design profession. What architecture, after all, isn't humanitarian, engaged with that most primal activity: the provision of shelter?

Of course, what is evoked is not this fundamental idea of use, but one of distributive justice. The practices represented in this important volume, *Humanitarian Architecture*, offer a variety of approaches to basic concepts of equity, for bridging the gap between the decently housed and the desperate. While none can be said to make a quantitative dent in the scale of problems that affect literally billions, their importance is that *people in need are helped*, that inventive precedents for amelioration in serious numbers are set, and that the propaganda of image and deed is spread by and to agents who can act in their individual ways for the public good. And, given that virtually all the architects included in this compilation operate from the site of privilege, their examples define that character of conscience that can and must influence others.

Although most of those gathered in this book focus their practices on the execution of particular projects, the idea of humanitarian architecture is much more capacious. The task of not simply housing, but *changing*, the way the world proceeds along many paths. If one thing is established by the work here, it is that although the desperation is general, it is not for lack of design capacity and it is surely a virtue of much of what is included that it so often exceeds commodity to aspire to the beautiful. Just now in New York and our region, we are living in the aftermath of Hurricane Sandy, and the level of response – not just from the design community but from the neighbourhoods, politicians and institutions, large and small – has been concerted and uncharacteristically efficient. Certified as a problem, redress is authorized. To be sure, part of the reason for the immediacy of the response is that the storm struck at the heart of power and organization.

Which goes to the core of the problem of humanitarian architecture. Who wants it? Architecture that will save the tremendous costs incurred by hurricanes and sea-level change has become desirable in places where the costs can be compellingly monetized: Manhattan will surely be protected. What about Bangladesh? For the desperate poor in harm's way, for billions in slums and refugee camps, we feel no such imperative. So, the first duty of humanitarian architecture is to establish the terrain of its own existence. At one end, the idea that an individual simply appears at the scene of a disaster to pitch in is effective, if in a limited way. However, the combination of *all of us* pitching in to help could go miles to help at the true scales of necessity. The idea that we are each responsible for reducing the level of harm in the world is at the core of any ethical system and there is so much harm to be removed.

How to make this imperative general? What is needed for it to be a professional ethic? More specifically, what can architects do – *as architects* – to lever a world more humane? Action is not without risk. On the one hand, creating a professional category of 'humanitarian' architects allows these exemplary practitioners to provide a kind of cover for everyone else: just as Brangelina and Bono are dealing with it for their profession (and getting damn good PR!). On the other hand, the idea of a tithe universally made as part of a designer's oath of practice would help establish the idea of a community responsibility, not just fingers-crossed voluntarism on the part of people of special conscience or capacity.

One of the things this book reveals is that participation in the project of ameliorating the environments of those with the least power to do so themselves can take many forms, that the idea of the architect jetting in with a hammer is far from the only paradigm. While most would agree that local empowerment is crucial, it is also clear that this must come from many directions, including the spread of wealth, education and rights. Humanitarian architecture can play a part in all of this and its success will be measured in the way in which resources are applied to best produce results at once sound and just.

At the most conceptual end of the humanitarian scale, the task of imagining and promoting alternative arrangements is a crucial task. While we have moved beyond the modernist – one-size-fits-all – paradigm of uniform housing in well-clipped green fields, there is much to learn from the ambition of that global programme, as well as from its focus on logical economies of means and the provision of decent infrastructure for all, including not simply space and hygiene but a rich repertoire of social and educational opportunities. The discourse of final outcomes is critical not simply for physical recovery from sudden disasters, but to describe a more general pattern for social recovery from poverty, injustice and neglect. The task of mating such visions with the particulars of locality should precede the urgent improvisations of renewal.

A focus on the short term – though obviously crucial in many circumstances – does have some conceptual downsides. We know that the temporary has a way of becoming permanent and that this contributes not simply to a mode of reproduction of slum housing in the wake of disasters, but also sets up the problematic sequence that dogs so many emergency operations, with their division into three phases: immediate, intermediate and permanent solutions. This schema grows more from the logics of social and organizational inefficiency and from issues of property and location than from sound planning and architectural practice. One of the key jobs for a comprehensive humanitarian architecture is to help prepare the ground – through pre-planning, technical innovation, capacity development and localized design – for realizing positive transformations following crises.

But it's also crucial that 'humanitarian' practice not be so uniformly associated with conditions of emergency. The slow task of improving cities, settlements, institutions and infrastructure should also be at the core of the work of architects seeking to redress both sudden and long-term issues of inequality and scarcity. While not wanting to get into the many strategic disputes about questions of informality and slum upgrading, it remains clear that the environments of those billions of our fellow citizens who live in conditions that deprive them of opportunities for health and happiness must be the object of an architecture of conscience.

MICHAEL
SORKIN

◁
Design for a self-financing, inhabited
levee for Far Rockaway, Queens,
proposed as a protective strategy
following Hurricane Sandy
by Michael Sorkin Studio.

△
Inflatable emergency shelter for group
gatherings designed for a temporary
community near Fukushima
by Michael Sorkin Studio.

MICHAEL
SORKIN

This means confronting the problem at every scale, from the design of entirely new cities to the rehabilitation of neighbourhoods, to the improvement and the construction of houses, to a light on a dark lane.

Surely, too, for those of us who genuinely believe in the *cause* of architecture, bringing building of quality to places that haven't had access to it, that haven't even imagined it, is of huge importance. A beautiful hospital in Rwanda or a magnificent library perched in the hills of Medellin is not simply a service but a signal. They assert a right to architecture for all and help form the shape of aspiration. Again, the strategy of bread and circuses must be watchfully, sceptically, critiqued and avoided – but the idea that every architect should struggle to make spaces that are inspirational, that improve life and raise expectations is at the core of our duty.

The testimony of the fifteen architects included in this necessary book should inspire us all to a practice predicated on the urgency of compassion and the eternity of kindness.

Michael Sorkin

is the principal of the Michael Sorkin Studio, a design practice devoted to both practical and theoretical projects at all scales and with a special interest in the city. He is Director of the Graduate Urban Design Program at the City College of New York, and has previously been professor at numerous schools of architecture, including the Institute of Urbanism at the Academy of Fine Arts in Vienna, Cooper Union, Columbia, Yale, Harvard, Cornell, Nebraska, Illinois, Pennsylvania, Texas and Minnesota. He lectures widely and is contributing editor at *Architectural record* and *Metropolis*. His books include *Variations on a theme park*, *Exquisite corpse*, *Local code*, *Giving ground* (edited with Joan Copjec), *Wiggle* (a monograph of the studio's work), *Some assembly required*, *Other plans*, *The next Jerusalem*, and *After the Trade Center* (edited with Sharon Zukin). He was born in Washington, DC, and received his architectural training at Harvard and MIT.

ACKNOWLEDGEMENTS

ESTHER CHARLESWORTH

Working on *Humanitarian Architecture* has been an extraordinary odyssey and opportunity. Many people have contributed their time, effort and patience in bringing this project and book to fruition, including the inspiring group of fifteen architects interviewed here.

I would like first like to thank the Australian Research Council (ARC), which provided the funds for undertaking the background research, interviews and associated travel. Without the dedication of the skilled and committed editorial team at Routledge Press, led by Fran Ford and then Laura Williamson and Emma Gadsden, the idea of collecting the personal and professional journeys of these humanitarian architects would have never come to print. I am also very grateful to Melissa Kinnear for introducing to me so many of the key figures working in the humanitarian architecture field.

I would like to thank Megan Nethercote for her skilled input into collating the images and interview material, and especially Adrian Marshall, who over the last two years has pulled the book together as a whole, from a series of initial fragments of interviews and images, in a professional, caring and persistent manner. Hilary and Max Charlesworth also acted as very gracious editors at key points in the book's finalization, for which I thank their enduring commitment enormously.

Finally, without John Fien's inspiration, comments and, most importantly, love, when many roadblocks and distractions were crossing my path, this book never might have reached its conclusion. To dearest Isobel: your smile made all the hard work and late-night and early-morning Skype interviews worthwhile!

△
Temporary housing, Croix-des-Bouquets,
Haiti (photo: Esther Charlesworth).

||||||||||||||||||||||||||||||||||||

INTRODUCTION

A world of disasters:
the rise and rise of humanitarian

ESTHER CHARLESWORTH

FOUNDING DIRECTOR
**ARCHITECTS WITHOUT
FRONTIERS**

ASSOCIATE PROFESSOR
OF ARCHITECTURE
RMIT UNIVERSITY

When on field research in New Orleans for this book during 2012, I was trying to buy a cell phone from a vendor called Miguel in a bulk phone shop in the downtown area. Miguel questioned why I was in New Orleans and, when I mentioned my next destination was Haiti, he commented, 'That place, Haiti, had a terrible disaster. Why on earth would you want to go there?' The memory of his own city under water, without food and shelter, only seven years earlier, had clearly faded. So though the catastrophic disasters of New Orleans and Port-au-Prince were once front-page news, the processes of rebuilding the social and physical capital of these cities quickly ceased to be newsworthy for either the mainstream – or the design – media.

Why should architects be involved in humanitarian work and the projects needed to deal with post-disaster emergencies and recovery? How can they contribute effectively to the long-term reconstruction processes needed to ensure the rebuilding of vulnerable communities?

This book explores these questions through the emerging movement of 'humanitarian architecture' by profiling the personal and professional journeys of fifteen architects engaged in working after natural disasters. From Australia, Haiti, India, Japan, Pakistan, Sri Lanka, Switzerland, Taiwan, Thailand and the USA, we hear narratives of the immense opportunities, challenges and frustrations of working in an emergency mode of humanitarian practice framed by uncertainty and ill-defined or non-existent project briefs. The architects interviewed for this book are defined and united by a collective belief that the processes of spatial problem-solving, and viewing the design management of projects as an iterative process, can contribute in a significant way to the challenges of rebuilding a city and its community following a natural disaster. Listening to these professionals, who have committed their careers to working in humanitarian and development fields, also reveals the ways in which many current models of architectural education and practice marginalize this field of design work into an 'alternative' box – as if it has little place in the 'true' hierarchy and DNA of the architectural profession. The time has now come to radically rethink the future role of design educators and professionals amidst such fragile times.

Global crises

Never has the demand been so urgent for architects to respond to the design and planning challenges of rebuilding post-disaster sites and cities. In 2010, approximately 42 million people were forced to leave their homes due to natural disasters across the globe, nearly twice the number of displacements during 2009 (*Huffington Post*, 2011). Yet the number of architects and built-environment professionals equipped to deal with rebuilding in the aftermath of these floods, fires, earthquakes, typhoons and tsunamis is chronically low. Indeed, if the design of human shelter and infrastructure is a key role of architecture, then it could be said to have failed miserably, as less than 10 per cent of houses and civic infrastructure in the Western world are actually designed by architects (van Schaik, 2011); their role in post-disaster reconstruction, especially in the Global South, is significantly less again.

Along with injury and loss of life, the most serious impact of vulnerability – whether it is from poverty, natural disasters or conflict – is the deterioration and destruction of built environments. For example, the December 2004 Indian Ocean tsunami killed 200,000 people, and displaced over one million people living in destroyed coastal areas, in Sri Lanka alone. During 2005, in New Orleans, Louisiana, Mississippi and Alabama, Hurricane Katrina killed more than 2,000 people and destroyed 275,000 homes – nearly ten times as many as in any previous natural disaster in US history. Storms in central China in May 2007 resulted in more than 1,000 deaths and the destruction of 243,000 homes. The 2010 earthquake in Haiti killed 200,000 people and left more than one million people homeless. More recently, in March 2011, a catastrophic earthquake and tsunami in Japan caused more than 20,000 deaths and damaged or destroyed over 125,000 buildings. As well as the human catastrophe of these events, the economic and ecological impact on a nation's economy after an earthquake or flood can be debilitating. For example, natural disasters in Australia, New Zealand, Japan and the USA made the first half of 2011 the costliest six-month period in the international insurance market's 323-year history (Economic and Social Commission for Asia and the Pacific and the United Nations Office for Disaster Risk Reduction, 2012; Harmeling, 2009; Munich RE, 2013; International Federation of Red Cross and Red Crescent Societies, 2012). Indeed, 2011 has been called 'the year that shook the rich' (Ferris and Petz, 2012).

However, while the emergency fields of medicine, law and engineering have been actively helping repair and rebuild devastated communities, generally there has been a marked absence of strategic spatial problem-solving and design-led solutions for longer-term recovery. This is the role of architecture and the profession is now beginning to ask how post-disaster recovery and reconstruction (and the systemic global problems of poverty, mass migration and the future impacts of climate change) can be addressed through design for the people who most need it but who have little chance of ever affording it given the political economy of conventional architectural practice (Schneider and Till, 2009).

ESTHER
CHARLESWORTH

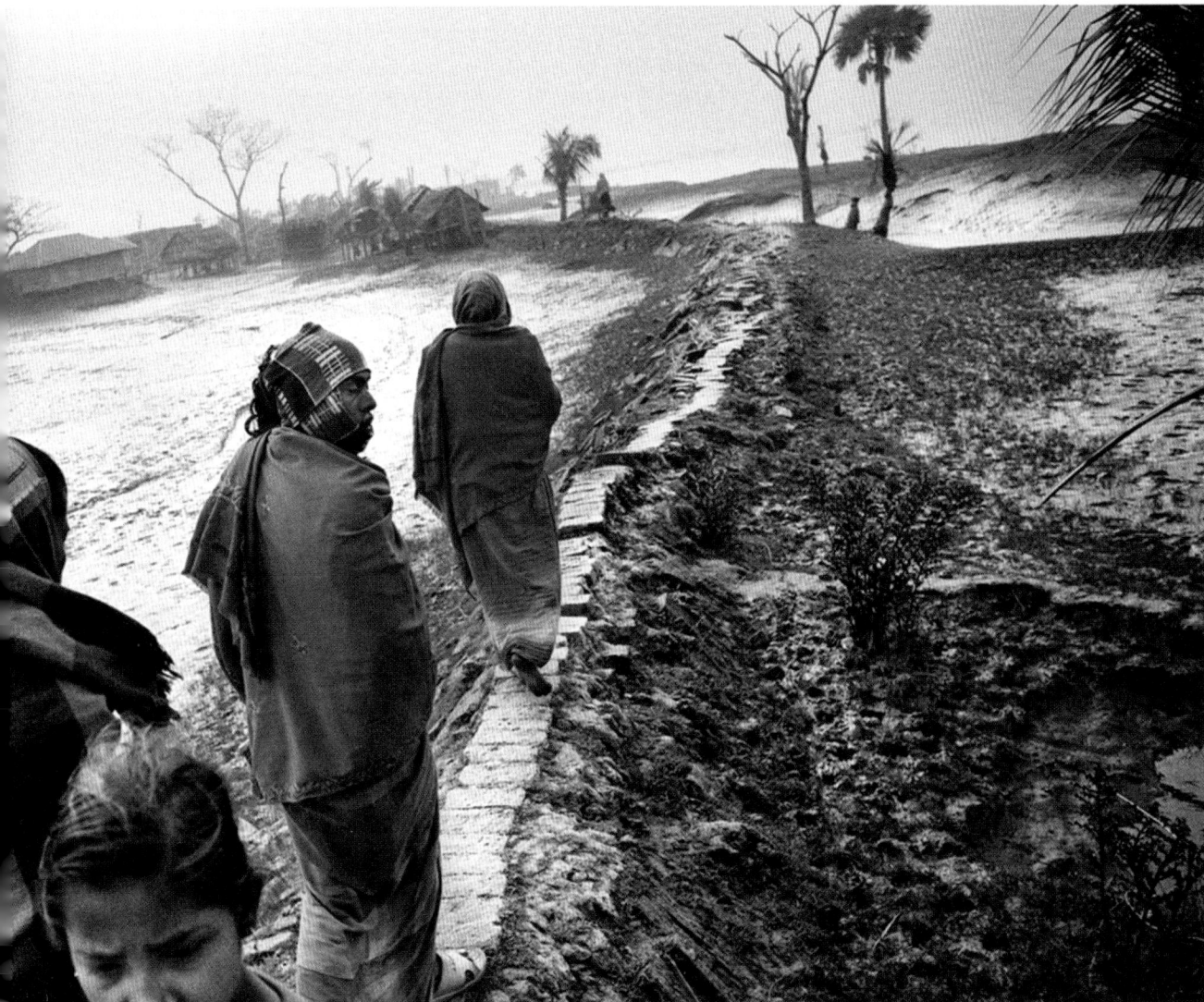

Fifteen humanitarian architects – fifteen projects

What if architecture also looked at its market as including the two billion people on Earth who have substandard housing, schools, health clinics, etc.? Now, not one of the two billion people actually has the assets themselves to pay even our fees, let alone a private sector architect's fees. But what we can do is make the argument to governments, to non-profits, to institutions, that good design is worth investing in.

(Eric Cesal)

The architects profiled in this book are a small sample of built-environment professionals working globally after disaster. Architects working more broadly within the development sector (from

△
Homeless climate refugees,
after cyclone Alia, Bangladesh
(photo: Kadir van Lohuizen – NOOR).

slum-upgrading projects and post-conflict reconstruction to working with marginalized Indigenous communities) form a larger cohort again. Many more books could be devoted to profiling the extraordinary design projects and processes now being undertaken in these fields.

Is 'humanitarian' the most appropriate word to describe this diverse group of architects? Many of the interviewees and external commentators in this collection, including Ian Davis, Michael Murphy and Paul Pholeros, challenged my use of the 'humanitarian' label during our lengthy conversations. Their position is that all architecture is – or at least should be – humanitarian in the way it posits design solutions for a range of community groups and related problems. Murphy, for example, in his interview for this book, argues that, 'We have to remember that all architecture is political. Besides, it's not as if I'm meeting people in Haiti who are calling themselves humanitarian architects. I think they would call themselves architects working in the humanitarian sector.' It is not only architects who critique the 'humanitarian' approach. Journalist David Rieff (2003) has questioned 'the hazard of charity' in international development organizations trying to solve the complex global problems of war and poverty. Rieff also writes that 'in the absence of critical contextual analysis and hard political decisions, there can be no humanitarian solution to humanitarian problems' (Rieff, 2003).

My intention with the 'humanitarian' framing of this typology of design practice is

to acknowledge architectural work that has really only begun to be noticed as a movement in its own right in recent years, particularly since the Indian Ocean tsunami of 2004. Many architects and engineers have been working in this space for a much longer period, as Ian Davis' classic book *Shelter after disaster* (Davis, 1978) points out so well. However, their role in the aid and development fields has been more recognized as logistical and technical rather than part of the larger process of design thinking that might contribute to the physical and social reconstruction of devastated communities, cities and landscapes.

One of the key figures in developing a more interdisciplinary approach to disaster management was Texan engineer Fred Cuny. Cuny worked in Iraq, Bosnia and Somalia in the 1970s and 1980s before tragically disappearing in Chechnya in 1995. Cuny challenged the professional silos of the post-disaster field as he sought to discover how innovative disaster management planning and health practices could better benefit the lives of survivors. His work with his previous company, InterTect, still informs practice in the aid and development field today (PBS, 2013).
The stories and lessons emerging from the fifteen interviews in this book position design as a long-term, transdisciplinary and collaborative process for rebuilding a damaged community, its local culture, environment and economy. This is in contrast to the more typical disaster response of designing shelter 'projects' that build 'houses' that are 'turned over' to residents and then left behind when the development

agency exits the scene; or what I have previously discussed as the 'design parachute' approach (Charlesworth, 2006). This parachute analogy describes the common process of fly-in–fly-out architects, donors and contractors 'dropping' into a post-disaster area with a pet project, building it quickly and then getting out to await the next disaster elsewhere. While the initial 'roof overhead' may provide temporary shelter, this approach rarely uses local construction techniques, materials or contractors to facilitate ongoing community resilience and economy.

From post-disaster projects in Gujarat to working with cardboard log temporary housing for refugee camps in Rwanda, the architects interviewed in this book illustrate ways in which the spatial sensibilities and the integrated problem-solving skills of architects can be applied after the human and natural disaster of floods, fires, hurricanes, earthquakes and typhoons. As Arup engineer Jo Da Silva comments, 'Architects can draw. Everyone else in the development sector writes' (Charlesworth, 2012). These fifteen narratives provide examples of built-environment professionals collaborating with post-disaster communities – as facilitators, collaborators and negotiators of land, space and shelter rather than as 'save the world' modernists, as often portrayed in the design media. The fifteen projects selected to illustrate the interviews involve temporary, transitional and permanent housing projects, as well as community infrastructure structures. While most of the architects profiled in the book work exclusively in the

△
MASS Design Group's Butaro Hospital,
Rwanda (photo: Iwan Baan).

of humanitarian architecture connotes using design skills to assist vulnerable communities, particularly after the crises of war and natural disaster. This definition sees architecture as much more than just drawing conceptual designs, resolving technical issues and building complex structures. Humanitarian architects work with a variety of donors, stakeholders and communities on site-specific projects that require strategic solutions to a wide range of issues such as the resolution of land tenure disputes, community relocation issues installing power, water and sewerage systems, and preparing masterplans for rebuilding entire cities after natural disaster. Alongside politicians, planners, construction managers, environmentalists and community leaders, architects also have a significant role to play in disaster mitigation. For example, how can we better prepare for the likely perilous impacts of climate change-related disasters through more ecologically based planning strategies, stronger building codes, flexible and climate-resilient floor plans and designs, and the testing of robust construction materials?

The rise of the humanitarian architect parallels the emergence of 'public-interest architecture'. Defined by Bryan Bell as design that seeks to address 'issues of social justice, allow individuals and communities to plan and celebrate their own lives, and serve a much larger percentage of the population than it has in the past' (Bell and Wakeford, 2008), public-interest architecture has expanded the definition of what constitutes a design problem

post-disaster zone, several of the projects chosen (for example, the MASS Group's hospital work in Rwanda, and Paul Pholeros' sanitation programme in Nepal, cross over into the 'development' sector. The lessons from all projects, however, are similar with regards to the level of community consultation taken to develop the project and the complex web of stakeholders needed to bring these much-needed projects to fruition. As well as looking outwards to how the architectural profession can better serve society, the interviews and supporting essays also look inwards at the design profession to understand the transformative processes necessary for establishing an alternative architectural discourse and praxis.

Reframing humanitarian architecture

I started feeling – and subsequently expressing – that I did not want to be *that* kind of architect practising *that* type of architecture. I wanted to work in the villages for the non-rich. I wanted to serve not the conventional but the alternative client, the un-served client: the villager, the slum dweller, the poor, the marginalized.

(Kirtee Shah)

The word 'humanitarian' implies having a concern for, and wanting to help improve the welfare of, people in need. Comparable in intent with the fields of humanitarian law and medicine, the emerging field and a design solution, and has widened the range of audiences served by the profession. This trend is also extending the traditional roles of the architect from that of a 'design guru' or 'artistic hero' to also include roles as a 'social reformer', 'community educator/facilitator' and 'peace-maker'. Nathaniel Corum expanded on this idea in his interview:

If you're a doctor you're hopefully able to heal someone directly, but how do you do this as an architect? Humanitarian architecture is our profession's healing gesture: a growing frontier in architecture that is increasingly inclusive.

Architects are now to be found, for example, working alongside doctors and nurses from Médecins Sans Frontières (MSF), sanitation engineers from Engineers Without Borders

(EWB), human rights lawyers in UNHCR refugee camps, on post-conflict reconstruction projects, and in areas affected by cyclones, bushfires and earthquakes.

The business of rebuilding cities and communities after disaster has a long history of its own, however, beginning before the volcanic eruption at Pompeii in AD 79, right through to the recent 2011 earthquake and tsunami in Japan. However, the rise of the design not-for-profit sector has been a

△
Development workshop, France, post-flood housing project in Gia Lai Province, Vietnam (photo: Tuan Anh).

very recent one. While the better known Médecins Sans Frontières was established in 1971, RedR in 1980, and EWB in 1990, it has only been really in the last decade that we have seen the rise and recognition of agencies such as Architecture for Humanity (AFH), Article 25, Architects Without Frontiers and its global network Architectes Sans Frontières (ASF), Architects for Peace, and Emergency Architects (EA). While these design agencies differ in their geographic and organizational modes, all share a common goal of working with vulnerable communities to ensure a long-term and sustainable reconstruction process that contributes to rebuilding destroyed housing, villages, cities and livelihoods.

Creating more harm than good?
Many writers and architects have questioned the role, motives and effectiveness of architects in rebuilding after disasters. It cannot be automatically assumed that the architectural discipline, working in its traditional mode of 'meet client – draw up design scheme – get necessary approvals – get project built – and then hopefully get it published and awarded' will be able to deal with the complex challenges that the post-disaster scene presents. Even Samuel Mockbee's seductive mantra of 'proceed and be bold' (Dean and Hursley, 2005) implies that a design intervention is the *right* solution to reducing social marginalization or fixing poverty. Working in the emergency setting after an earthquake, storm or tsunami often includes tackling a myriad of seemingly unsolvable challenges, as evidenced through the fifteen interviews in this book. The challenges include:

not knowing quite who the client is (the affected community? The donor? The reconstruction authority?); being unsure of what sort of project is actually needed first (temporary housing? Water and sanitation? Community infrastructure?); and how to decide the most appropriate processes for ensuring these projects actually lead to some level of livelihood reconstruction. Without employment or some semblance of hope for the future, the prospects for many survivors of disasters can seem very bleak; simply providing temporary housing solutions is but one part of the reconstruction jigsaw.

David Sanderson has suggested that 'Architects are often the last people needed in disaster reconstruction' (Sanderson, 2010). He argues that architects are rarely taught the skills needed to work in the aftermath of an emergency and, unlike other humanitarian practitioners who focus on the people processes involved in recovery and reconstruction, architects are socialized into making personal marks through their own design projects. Sanderson also argues that many post-disaster shelter programmes have lacked 'genuine participation by affected people' (Sanderson, 2010). Likewise, Dana Cuff argues that architects in the USA have failed in the areas of civic engagement and urgency, despite their valiant work after the country's two greatest urban catastrophes – New Orleans and Lower Manhattan (Cuff, 2009). She relates these failures in approach to the modernist discourse of *tabula rasa* – of erasure and renewal – that attracts architects to the post-disaster space. Cuff references

Naomi Klein's theory of 'disaster capitalism' (Klein, 2007) that links profitable business to the political opportunities that come from certain approaches to reconstruction after a disaster, often to the exclusion of concern for the long-term welfare of the disaster survivors.

However, to blame architects entirely for such short-term and inappropriate shelter solutions is far too easy. Architects are only part of the reconstruction conundrum that is, ultimately, far more affected by the scale of the disaster, the political capability of the national government where the disaster has struck, the motivations of donors and the impact of the recent entry of large multinational construction and engineering conglomerates into the reconstruction field.

Why build a Ferrari when all you need is a moped?
(Pollard, personal communication)

> We need to keep our fingerprints off the product as much as we can. Ironically, as an architect you are often aiming to make sure your fingerprints are very visible, to clearly have an impact through the design and construction and the resulting product. You want people to be aware of what you have contributed.
> (Graham Saunders)

It is easy to agree with both Sanderson and Cuff that there are too many badly designed, poorly built and wrongly sited examples of prefab(ricated) design experiments in the post-disaster field. I have witnessed on site the folly of experimental design solutions – from inflatable octagonal tents to polyurethane

ESTHER
CHARLESWORTH

△
42 degrees inside! Igloo-style temporary
housing, Port-au-Prince, Haiti
(photo: Esther Charlesworth).

igloos and funky shipping container housing – in southern Sri Lanka, New Orleans, Port-au-Prince and, more recently, Sendai. We have also too often seen the impact of the mentality of the 'universal solution' in the field of emergency housing. As Nathaniel Corum comments:

> These are [post-disaster] projects that can't go sideways. These designs need to work. I dislike the word 'prototype' within humanitarian architecture; if you're going to build something in this space, make it right. Be your own guinea pig; test new ideas closer to home. Humanitarian design responses should be *less* experimental since we're typically working in more challenging environments with community members who cannot afford failure.

Ian Davis also argues: 'These concepts are generally

prohibitively expensive; their exotic forms are usually ill-suited to local conditions … Emergency housing sounds compelling, but it almost never works!' (Davis, 1978). Shigeru Ban, known for his more *boutique* approach to shelter reconstruction, suggests in his interview that:

> We cannot make a universal prototype for temporary shelter like the universal solutions that the medical profession has for different diseases. That's why I think it's easier to send a doctor over there to help the people, but in architecture there is no universal solution. You must have the local people working, local architects.

While I visited Haiti in 2012, a construction manager working with a large international development organization based in Port-au-Prince explained to me that his experience working with

architects commissioned to design a transitional shelter structure had been 'torturous'. Six architects had worked for six months to come up with an appropriate design for temporary shelter. He said that while the time frame was bad enough, none of the architects has bothered to observe local methods of construction or spoken to local builders or communities while coming up with their 'unusable theoretical designs'. This experience led him to conclude that, 'I could have come up with a better design on the plane on the way over here!'.

Again, it is too simple to criticize architects alone for badly designed settlement layouts or for housing projects that were rushed in order to shelter disaster-affected communities. As most of the interviews in this book reveal, being an architect in the post-disaster field is far from what is taught in undergraduate design

◁ RMIT students working on a project for transitional housing in Hoi An, Vietnam, 2008 (photo: Esther Charlesworth).

▽ RMIT student diagram for community consultation techniques, Hoi An, Vietnam, 2011 (photo: Esther Charlesworth).

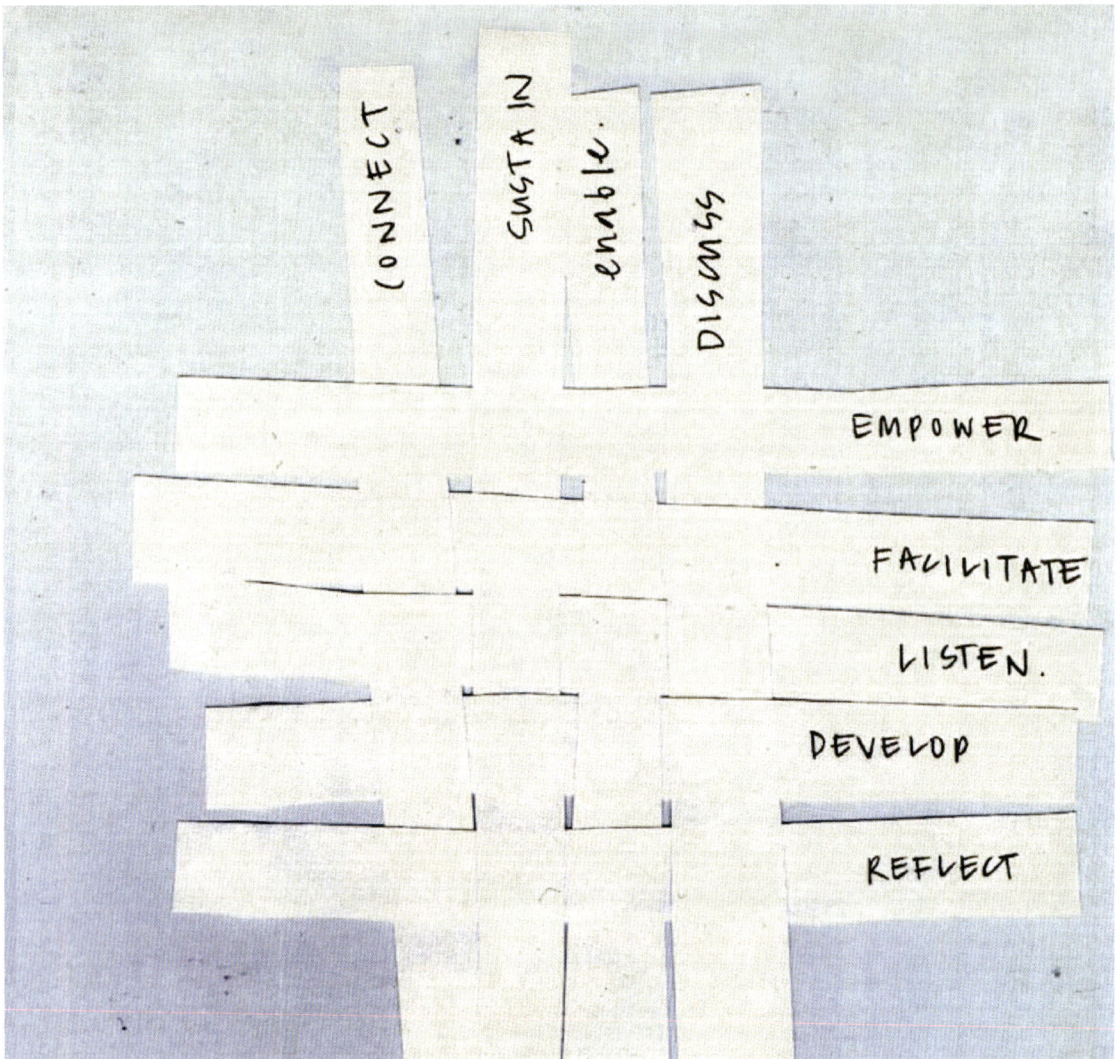

CONNECT SUSTAIN enable. DISCUSS

EMPOWER

FACILITATE

LISTEN.

DEVELOP

REFLECT

degrees or experienced working in a corporate or residential design firm. Examples of an individual architect coming up with an innovative, cost-effective and culturally appropriate design project and working alone in the disaster field are very rare. The reality is far more one of working through a systematic process of developing a project and donor brief, undertaking extensive community consultation with a wide range of project stakeholders and beneficiaries, working with health, logistics and education specialists, and ensuring that any project has ongoing funding to provide training and maintenance for the housing or infrastructure project. Despite these commonly accepted norms of development practice, design fantasies about appropriate shelter responses still abound when, in fact, budgets are incredibly modest. Graham Saunders from the International Federation of the Red Cross (IFRC) talks about these budget issues:

> About a year ago we analysed the total expenditure on shelter across all major emergencies. This indicated that the average spend per affected household per shelter was $50. The implication of this is that sophisticated, cutting-edge or innovative shelter solutions are very welcome but, due to the limited financial assistance made available for shelter and the scale of the need, such shelter solutions should cost no more than $50. Although different disasters do result in different needs, and the resources available also vary significantly, there clearly is a 'reality gap' between the aspirations and solutions provided by the

innovators and the possibilities at country level in a given emergency. The $2,000 solution is very desirable, but it will be the $50 version that is utilized at scale.

Implications for architectural education

Perhaps the chief factor behind the relative lack of architects involved in humanitarian architecture is the lack of training for post-disaster design problem-solving in design and architecture schools. While new postgraduate programmes in the area of humanitarian architecture are emerging in the UK, Spain and France, Marie Aquilino writes in *Beyond shelter*:

> There is still no career path that prepares students to work as *urgentistes* – design professionals who intervene at a crucial moment in the recovery process to produce enduring solutions.
>
> (Aquilino *et al.*, 2011, p. 7)

Many of the architects interviewed for this book found that their architectural education and initial work experiences in a design practice had not prepared them in any way to consult with communities, consider a non-corporate architectural career or to work in a non-Western context. My own education, completed in the 1980s, encouraged students to align themselves with a celebrity architect *du jour* or to latch onto arcane theories of postmodernism, post-structuralism and deconstruction in order to prove our mettle as intellectually *bona fide* architects. While learning architecture comprised a great deal of fun, 'all-nighters' and

assiduously following the paths of our then heroes – Richard Meier, Peter Eisenmann and Zaha Hadid – this education generally failed to equip students for even the next stage of their careers working in a traditional architectural practice as a junior designer.

British architect Lizzie Babister describes her experience in this way: 'The education of architects in the UK is very narrow. It is almost entirely focused on working in the UK and the developed world.' Shigeru Ban also comments: 'After working as an architect for a while, I became disappointed in the way that the profession was working only for privileged people, rich people. corporations.' Sandra D'Urzo adds to this discussion:

> Universities, of both the North and the South, are not equipping us well enough to be able to say, 'Yes, I want to go into development. Architecture is needed even more by the needy than the rich.' It's still very conventional the way we're taught architecture for rich and wealthy clients and socialized into wanting to be one the 'top ten' star architects.

Thus, one of the aims of this book is to investigate the alternative humanitarian career paths that can be supported by the architectural profession for future generations of students – similar to the strands of public health and legal aid in the medical and legal professions. How do you pursue a career in international development and aid as a designer? The avenues for doing so have been remarkably slim to date, and many assume that you volunteer with a large aid agency for many years before

△
Straw bale house under construction,
an example of Corum's work with Native
Americans (photo: Skip Baumhower).

eventually securing one of the rare contracts with international development agencies such as the UN, Red Cross or World Vision. This book presents the professional journeys that these fifteen architects took to be working full-time in the disaster and development fields. Their journeys were not predictable or linear career paths, and many remarked that until very recently in the post-disaster shelter sector there had been a 'cowboy culture'

at play among international development agencies and indiscriminate hiring of casual building contractors, rather than qualified built-environment experts working in the humanitarian field. As evidenced through the interviews, no professional journey in the humanitarian sector was the same; each architect pursued their passions to connect issues of social justice with a career in architecture.

Implications for architectural practice

What is most interesting is how humanitarian architecture has changed since the Global Financial Crisis. It prompted a re-examination of the purpose of the profession and forced people into asking larger questions. Why do we do this? Why do we spend so much time acquiring these skills? Why do we put so much passion into our work? Is it

ESTHER
CHARLESWORTH

worth it just to be in a magazine or to have an article written about you? Is it worth it just to have a very beautiful portfolio? Or is there some higher level of satisfaction that can be gained out of directing our architectural efforts elsewhere?

(Eric Cesal)

Today, the architectural profession is facing significant problems of perceived irrelevance and marginalization. It has largely stood outside the major global concerns arising from the twinned economic and ecological crises that define the second decade of the twenty-first century. In Spain and Portugal, 80 per cent of architects are now unemployed; a whole generation of designers is being forced to shift careers and move countries to seek employment. Many critics attribute this market failure of our discipline to the apolitical, pragmatic discourses that often shape commercial architectural practice (Gamez and Rogers, 2008). With a general focus on profit, design media, architectural awards and aesthetics, these discourses have helped create livelihoods for a relatively small number of professional designers compelled to work for the proverbial 2 per cent whom Bryan Bell describes as 'the very few, the elite, the highest income bracket served to excess by market forces' (Bell and Wakeford, 2008) in order to generate enough fees to support even a modest architectural practice. Thus, Bell argues, market forces, not social need, are determining 'whom we serve, what issues we address and the shape of all our design'. This has contributed to a narrowing of the discipline from one of its possible central roles in society – designing

homes and civic infrastructure for communities in need, for those whom, one might argue, need spatial innovation and ingenuity the most. The possibilities, however, for using the core skills of the architectural discipline for a much larger group of 'clients', or in Cynthia Smith's phrase 'the other ninety-eight per cent' (Smith and Unies, 2011), is well within our reach. Graham Saunders comments:

Architecture is one of those … few disciplines that actually combines the need for a real management rigour, careful planning and organization with an understanding of science, materials, technology and engineering. Architecture requires spatial awareness and the art of design. But it also requires the ability to put stuff into practice, to problem-solve and work with people with different skills and expertise, to plan and schedule a series of activities that all need to interlink.

Brett Moore argues that the 'value add' of the architecture profession in the disaster relief scene is significant, through the challenge of having to produce a tangible product among the chaos that ensues after a natural catastrophe:

I think that some of the skills that architects have, not just in design, but of being a facilitator, an organizer, an analyser, these skills are very important in the emergency field. These are not skills that human rights lawyers and others who have had a humanitarian education necessarily have. Architects are one of the few professional groups that are educated in how

to manage projects, to look at a problem and think of a succinct, rational solution with budget, materials, people involved, that also addresses a human rights issue – in this case, the right to safe and dignified shelter.

A road map for reading humanitarian architecture

The stories of the fifteen humanitarian architects in this book explore the transition of these designers from a traditional architectural career to engagement with the complexity of working with communities after a natural disaster. Each conversation is illustrated by a reconstruction project selected by the architect to demonstrate the ethics and principles of the agency or practice that the architect works within. In order to frame the diversity of practice employed within the humanitarian architecture field, the fifteen interviews are presented in three groups:

1. private architectural practice-based humanitarian architects;
2. university research-based humanitarian architects; and
3. NGO/international aid-based humanitarian architects.

Many of the fifteen architects straddle more than one of these categories. For example, when asked about his 'Robin Hood' model of design practice, Paul Pholeros answered:

People tend to forget the fact that I still practise as an architect. They see my Healthabitat 'hat' and assume that's what I do all the time. Well I don't. I still work as a 'traditional' architect. Why? Well, first, it pays the bills and, second, it's what I was educated to be. It's what I was trained to do, and most importantly, I still enjoy it. Yes, if the 'Robin Hood' analogy is about using some of my earnings from the wealthier clients and the time it buys working for poorer clients – clients that may never ring my office – then that's true.

This book aims to survey a wide range of individual architects who are working nearly full-time in the post-disaster field. While several of the architects such as Ban and Pholeros maintain mainstream architectural practices, it is interesting that it is their post-disaster and development work that has placed them in a media spotlight. Ban comments about his dual design practice:

> People would commonly say to me, 'Why are you involved in that disaster stuff? Why aren't you doing real architecture?' I do both. I run a private architectural practice doing houses and other typical architectural projects. I also work a lot after disasters. It's very important for me to do both. The bigger buildings help me do the disaster relief projects. I hope to do both sorts of project simultaneously. I always tell my students, 'You have to get experience first, before working in a disaster area. Otherwise you'll never get any experience as an architect.'

This book is intended to capture the extraordinary range and spirit of a small sample of architects working in the challenging environment of the post-disaster field. Humanitarian architecture (or whatever we call it) is expanding rapidly in response to the global rise of disasters and related issues of displacement, migration and poverty. We do need to be realistic. In any form of design practice, there will be good and bad projects. The same is true in the aftermath of a disaster. Nevertheless, with skilled consultation and the development of short- and long-term strategies for reconstruction, the architectural discipline has a critical role to play – alongside other international development professionals – in designing and implementing strategic spatial solutions for the shelter and infrastructure destroyed by disaster.

After a catastrophe, there is still a role for beauty, innovation and humility. Indeed, it is more important than ever.

References

Aquilino, M., Brillembourg, A., Coulombel, P., & Klumpner, H. (2011). *Beyond shelter*: Metropolis Books.

Bell, B., & Wakeford, K. (Eds) (2008). *Expanding architecture: Design as activism*: Metropolis Books.

Charlesworth, E. (2006). *Architects without frontiers: War, reconstruction and design responsibility*: Routledge.

Charlesworth, E. (2012). Interview with Jo Da Silva, founding director of Arup International Development, London, 15 April. Unpublished.

Cuff, D. (2009). Design after disaster. *Places, 21*(1): 4–7.

Davis, I. (1978). *Shelter after disaster*: Oxford Polytechnic.

Dean, A.O., & Hursley, T. (2005). *Proceed and be bold: Rural studio after Samuel Mockbee*: Princeton Architectural Press.

Economic and Social Commission for Asia and the Pacific and the United Nations Office for Disaster Risk Reduction (2012). *Reducing vulnerability and exposure to disasters: The Asia-Pacific disaster report 2012*.

Ferris, E., & Petz, D. (2012). *The year that shook the rich: A review of natural disasters in 2011*: Brookings Institution – London School of Economics Project on Internal Displacement.

Gamez, J., & Rogers, S. (2008). Architecture of change, in B. Bell & K. Wakeford (Eds), *Expanding architecture: Design as activism*: Metropolis Books.

Harmeling, S. (2009). *Global climate risk index 2010: Who is most vulnerable?; Weather-related loss events since 1990 and how Copenhagen needs to respond*: Germanwatch. Available online at www.germanwatch.org; accessed 20 February 2012.

Huffington Post (2011). Natural disasters displaced 42 million in 2010; climate change could be factor, experts say. Available online at www.huffingtonpost.com/2011/06/06/natural-disasters-displaced-persons_n_871664.html; accessed 4 February 2014.

International Federation of Red Cross and Red Crescent Societies (2012). *World disasters report 2012: Focus on forced migration and displacement*: International Federation of Red Cross and Red Crescent Societies. Available online at www.ifrc.org/publications-and-reports/world-disasters-report; accessed 20 September 2013.

Klein, N. (2007). *The shock doctrine: The rise of disaster capitalism*: Macmillan.

Munich RE (2013). *Topics geo: Natural catastrophes 2012: Analyses, assessments, positions*: Munchener Ruckversichereungs-Gesellschaft. Available online at www.munichre.com/publications/302-07742_en.pdf; accessed 20 September 2013.

PBS (2013). *Intectect: The international disaster specialists*. Available online at www.pbs.org/wgbh/pages/frontline/shows/cuny/bio/intertect.html; accessed 4 February 2014.

Rieff, D. (2003). *A bed for the night: Humanitarianism in crisis*: Simon and Schuster.

Sanderson, D. (2010, 3 March). Architects are often the last people needed in disaster reconstruction. *The Guardian*.

Schneider, T., & Till, J. (2009). Beyond discourse: Notes on spatial agency. *Footprint, 4*, 97–111.

Smith, C.E., & Unies, N. (2011). *Design with the other 90%: CITIES*: Cooper-Hewitt, National Design Museum.

van Schaik, L. (2011). Architecture and a sustainable city: Overview. In E. Charlesworth & R. Adams (Eds), *The EcoEdge: Urgent design challenges in building sustainable cities*: Routledge.

Dr Esther Charlesworth

is an Associate Professor in the School of Architecture and Design at RMIT University, Melbourne. After completing her Masters of Architecture and Design at Harvard University in 1995 and a PhD at the University of York, she was Visiting Assistant Professor of Architecture and Urban Design at the American University of Beirut between 2000 and 2002. Between 1995 and 1999, Esther was Senior Urban Designer with the City of Melbourne, leading the redevelopment of the city square, among other significant urban design projects. She is the Founding Director of Architects Without Frontiers (AWF). Since 2002, AWF has undertaken over 32 projects in 12 countries and AWF has been described by ABC radio broadcaster Phillip Adams as 'destined to develop into one of the greater forces of good on this battered planet'. She has published widely on the theme of social justice and architecture, including *CityEdge: Contemporary case studies in urbanism* (2005), *Architects without Frontiers: War, reconstruction and design responsibility* (2006), *Divided cities* (2009) *The EcoEdge* (2011) and *Live projects* (2012).

PART ONE

||||||||||||||||||||||||||||||||||||||||||||||||||||||||||||||||

PRIVATE PRACTICE-BASED HUMANITARIAN ARCHITECTS

||||||||||||||||||||||||||||||||||||||||||||||||||||||||||||||||||||||||||||

This section discusses the practices of a range of architects working across disaster zones in Taiwan, India, Japan, Haiti, Rwanda, Nepal and Australia. These architects combine the challenging task of running a traditional design firm with undertaking not-for-profit work in the post-disaster and community rebuilding arenas.

Ban

I was a little bit disappointed that we, as architects, were not working for society.

Chun

Post-disaster reconstruction indeed is a big challenge. It brings out the passion and righteousness of architects who usually work in air-conditioned rooms.

Murphy

If we bifurcate 'humanitarian architecture' from 'architecture' we fail to demand of architecture its responsibility to the public.

Pholeros

I think part of the job we have as [architectural] professionals is an obligation to fire arrows to try and break down orthodoxy.

Roonrakwit

I don't do 'Robin Hood'. I don't steal. But I do try to get a share from the rich or from the middle and then give it to the poor.

SHIGERU BAN

FOUNDING DIRECTOR
**SHIGERU BAN ARCHITECTS
& VOLUNTARY ARCHITECTS' NETWORK**
www.shigerubanarchitects.com

Shigeru Ban

is internationally renowned for his innovative
use of paper, and for his activist work
within disaster zones around the world.
As an accomplished Japanese architect,
with offices in Tokyo and Paris, Shigeru
has become famous for projects such
as his Curtain Wall House, the Japanese
Exhibition Hall at EXPO 2000 in Hannover,
the Nicolas G. Hayek Center and the Centre
Pompidou – Metz. Increasingly, however,
Shigeru has gained a reputation for his
designs of emergency relief housing for
disaster areas. His innovative work with
paper, especially recycled cardboard paper
tubes, has effectively housed victims of
disasters in Japan, Rwanda, New Zealand,
Haiti and Sri Lanka. In 1995, Shigeru began
work as a consultant to the United Nations
High Commissioners for Refugees and
established the NGO, Voluntary Architects'
Network. Shigeru Ban was recently
named the 2014 laureate of the Pritzker
Architecture Prize.

> I was a little bit disappointed that we, as architects, were not working for society.

||||||||||||||||||||||||||||||||||||||

SHIGERU BAN

SHIGERU BAN ARCHITECTS
& VOLUNTARY ARCHITECTS'
NETWORK

Mr Ban, I believe you did a lot of your graduate studies in the USA. What were your career aspirations when you graduated? Did you have any skills to know how to work in disaster areas? ▶ I didn't have any knowledge and skill to work as an architect in the disaster area; undergraduate education in architecture in my experience is not very practical. I was planning to go to graduate school in the USA, but my mother asked me to design a small building for her office when I graduated from university. So I decided to go back to Tokyo to complete my mother's building and then return to graduate school. That was my plan. However, working on my mother's building required experience and I didn't have that. I missed the chance to go back to Japan; so I started my practice by accident in Brooklyn.

After working as an architect for a while I became disappointed in the way that the profession was working only for privileged people, rich people, corporations. And what we were doing was helping them represent their power

△
Shipping containers are stacked in a chequerboard pattern up to three storeys in the temporary housing project in Onagawa, Japan.

and money with monumental architecture. Power and money are invisible; so they needed our buildings for show. I was a little bit disappointed that we, as architects, were not working for society.

I started developing a cardboard tube system which I knew would make a very strong temporary structure and I was looking for some opportunity to use this for temporary shelter, such as after a disaster.

When I saw the terrible genocide in Rwanda in 1994, a terrible war in which over two million people became refugees, and when I saw the photos of the very poor tents provided by the UN, I knew the people were suffering. This was not enough to keep them warm during the rainy season; so I went to the United Nations High Commission in Geneva to propose a better shelter using paper structures.

I was really lucky to be accepted as a consultant because, at that time, the UN was not interested in making a better shelter. But they did want to stop people from cutting down trees. The UN provided refugees with only a plastic sheet and the refugees had to cut down trees to make the frame. The UN started providing aluminium pipes but the refugees saw the pipes as quite valuable and sold them. So the UN couldn't find any suitable material to provide to stop the refugees cutting trees. That was when I happened to propose using recycled paper. It was accepted and they started developing this structure as a consequence. This is the beginning.

Have you been disappointed that no other international agencies have scaled up any of your proposals? ▶ I spent three or four years with the UN and, at that time, I was very lucky to have a very good German architect as my boss. He was interested in my ideas, but it's very difficult to have a continuous medium- to long-term project in the UN because people are always moving and changing and, of course, everyone wanted to stay in Geneva instead of refugee camps. So, as soon as my boss was sent to somewhere else, my post-disaster shelter project was finished.

I did my undergraduate degree in Australia, my Masters in America and my PhD in the UK and there wasn't much discussion about the connections between architecture and social justice in any of those degrees. People would commonly say to me, 'Why are you involved in that disaster stuff? Why aren't you doing real architecture?' ▶ I do both. I run a private architectural practice doing houses and other typical architectural projects. I also work a lot after disasters. It's very important for me to do both. The bigger buildings help me do the disaster relief projects. I hope to do both sorts of project simultaneously. I always tell my students, 'You have to get experience first, before working in a disaster area. Otherwise you'll never get any experience as an architect.'

△
An atelier built using paper tubes and shipping containers forms part of the temporary housing project at Onagawa, Japan.

And what about your background, your parents, even before you started studying architecture? Was there something about a family connection to social justice? ▶ No, nothing.

So what sparked this interest in working in the post-disaster field? Why Rwanda? ▶ I wanted to use my knowledge and experience for the people who need housing, because I was quite tired of working for rich people. Even though I was happy working with expensive housing, it was not really enough to make me satisfied with architecture. Also, the year after Rwanda, in 1995, a major earthquake struck Kobe in Japan. Obviously, being Japanese, I wanted to do something there. I started with building a temporary shelter for former Vietnamese refugees in Kobe and I built a temporary church. It was an opportunity for me to start my own Voluntary Architects' Network because there are many disasters in Japan, almost every year.

And in all these situations from Rwanda to Kobe – and later to Sri Lanka to Haiti – how do you consult with the people who are going to be using your structures? Obviously what was suitable in Kobe may not be suitable in Haiti. ▶ Oh, I am not trying to push my structure in isolation. I go to an area and develop something appropriate to the situation. For example, when I was in Sri Lanka, I used the local rock that was available. Paper tubes are one material I normally use because paper is available everywhere. While the surface material is usually easy to get, the framing material is very difficult to get.

> I knew the people were suffering… So I went to the United Nations High Commission in Geneva to propose a better shelter using paper structure.

When I built a temporary house in India, a local textile factory was making its own paper tubes to put the textile up. So, I used them. When I was working in Haiti – there's nothing available in Haiti – we could get the paper tube in Santo Domingo. When I built a temporary school in China, big tubes were available locally.

When you go to the post-disaster site, what is your technique or method for finding out what's needed in terms of speaking to the authorities, speaking to the people who are going to be using your building? ▶ The situation is different depending on the disaster. For example, in Kobe I went there by myself and I went to the priest of the Catholic church who was helping the Vietnamese refugees. He had a budget so I could use this money. When I worked in Turkey in 1999 a local venture company representing a very popular Swiss venture invited me to organize a project. In India a rich lady saw an article on one of my refugee projects and she

△
Opening party at the temporary housing project, Onagawa, Japan.

SHIGERU
BAN

just invited me. Also, a young American businessman knew about me and he has many friends who help.

In China in 2008 I started communicating with the School of Architecture. They arranged for me to share my experience with their students and other architects, and so I got asked to design the local temporary school. It was really all by chance.

Do you get the chance to evaluate these projects, to find out whether they're still standing two, five, ten years on, that people are happy, that they're still using them? Do you get the opportunity to do this? ▶ Wherever I work, I always find good local architects to collaborate with me. When I was working in India I had good local architects who went back to the local village quite often to see what is happening. Also, the church I built in Kobe, it was supposed to be there for three years but it stayed for eleven years because people love it. Somebody in Taiwan asked us to donate it. So we disassembled it and it was rebuilt in Taiwan as a permanent church. It's still there.

What do you think are the challenges architecture faces compared to other professions when it comes to humanitarian work? ▶ Well, compared to, for example, the medical profession, the solutions to housing crises vary greatly depending on the country, depending on the crime rate and so on. We cannot make a universal prototype for temporary shelter like the universal solutions that the medical profession has for different diseases. That's why I think it's easier to send a doctor

over there to help the people, but in architecture there is no universal solution. You must have the local people working, local architects.

Little by little, architects are starting to be interested in doing this. Even famous architects have started doing something. When I was in Kobe I didn't see any architects there. But I think architects are now starting to be interested in working in this area.

What do you think are the main characteristics of providing a good shelter – say, three essential characteristics? ▶ Every shelter must be dependent on the country. Some countries don't make temporary shelters. Like when I was working in Italy three years ago, I was very amazed that the local authority was providing tents, like an army tent, immediately for every family and they then built a permanent apartment for everyone in four months. For everyone! Without any transitional shelter! It was an interesting solution.

In Japan it was totally different. They put the victims in the gymnasium and people stayed

there for six months until temporary housing was ready. It was a terrible situation with no privacy. So I designed a partition system to give people privacy. It was very successful.

In Haiti the temporary shelters will become permanent homes.

△
The temporary housing project in Onagawa, Japan, provides much-needed housing for an earthquake-devastated community.

> I wanted to use my [design] knowledge and experience for the people who need housing, because I was quite tired of working for rich people… It was not really enough to make me satisfied with architecture.

So depending on the country the solution will be different and I respect and work within the local government's solutions.

Do you think the internal partition system that you've developed for Japan's earthquake victims is more in the direction you might go next time working in the post-disaster field? ▶ I'm hoping not to do this after the next earthquake in Japan. In Japan they shouldn't have such a terrible evacuee situation for so long. And the temporary houses were too poor. I'm hoping the government will do something different. I don't want to keep doing this by myself. That's why this time, after the 2011 earthquake and tsunami in Japan, I made a good proposal for three-storey temporary housing to the government. And this time, I was invited by the government to give a lecture to politicians and leaders to show the examples. So I feel something is changing a little bit there.

So it's up to the government and local community to provide shelter solutions? ▶ My solution was good for this situation but I don't know what I should do for the next situation.

And what about Haiti? How do you work there in that very difficult situation? ▶ Before I went to Haiti I looked for locals in the Dominican Republic to work with me; and because of my activities now it's easy to find some professor who is interested in working with me. At that time I was teaching at Harvard. So I made a prototype with my students at Harvard and I brought it to a school in Santo Domingo where they designed a project by themselves according to the prototype. I raised money and sent it over. They used all student labour to prepare the first of fifty shelter projects. Then, I went

back there when they were ready, rented a truck for the materials, and we built it ourselves during a weekend.

So how many structures were built? ▶ We built only fifty. That was as many as I could afford.

Have you worked with many other design not-for-profit organizations because each situation is very particular? ▶ No. For me, it's important to go to the place of the disaster quickly. Working with other organizations takes time to discuss something. And when I was working in Sri Lanka, one of the organizations there – I don't want to say which one – said, 'Oh that is the area you are working in! Unless you collaborate with us you're going to have some problems.' It's very territorial. I didn't want to listen.

It's been said that reconstruction can actually be a third disaster. For example, you have the natural disaster, then the political disaster caused by the lack of preparation and planning, and then the disaster of slow or inappropriate reconstruction. Is it better that we're not there because we might cause more harm than good? ▶ I'm not too involved in the reconstruction phase. Even in Japan I'm not doing it. There are so many local architects looking for projects, waiting for projects. There are good architects, and local contractors are waiting for the projects. I don't want to be involved with any of that.

◁
Atelier made with paper tubes and container shipping facades as part of the housing reconstruction project at Onagawa, Japan.

> The medical profession has universal solutions. That's why I think it's easier to send a doctor over there to help the people, but in architecture there is no universal solution.

Regarding your involvement in the New Orleans 'Make It Right' project, a lot of effort was made by twenty-five different architects. How was that process working with a whole group of architects? ▶ I didn't have a lot of problems with the other architects but, in the beginning, it was very, very slow. I was a little bit frustrated. I thought they spent too much time on the publicity but it turned out to be a good project. It was built and I went back there on completion and we gave the key to the new owners and they were very happy.

How many of your designs were built in New Orleans? ▶ Only one. They said they want to build more but I didn't hear anything after that. So I don't know.

When you were commissioned to design the Christchurch Cathedral, didn't some New Zealand architects ask 'Why isn't a New Zealand architect involved?' ▶ They were wrong. New Zealand architects are my local architects.

Your local partner? ▶ Yes. And also the engineer is always local.

So did you go to Christchurch immediately after the disaster? ▶ No, because the 2011 Japanese earthquake happened. However, I was invited by the Christchurch Anglican Church to propose a design. So I said, 'Because this is a disaster project I will do it pro bono.' So they asked me to come immediately. I found a local contractor in Christchurch who was eager to get started immediately, but finalizing the site took much longer than expected.

And how do we best equip or train young architects to be useful, humanitarian architects? ▶ Well, as I said before, you have to be a good architect first because even a temporary house is hard and it has to be beautiful; and you have to know the materials and the construction system. You have to know how to deal with the local architects and local engineers, and you need enough training to work in disaster areas because it's a more difficult situation there.

You must have experience as a proper architect first. If you have only been trained for one situation you are not very useful. Every time the situation is different and you have to be very flexible. So you have to have experience working in many different areas.

What is the biggest challenge people will face? ▶ First of all, you cannot work financially as just a disaster architect; you have to have a proper job otherwise you cannot continue. You can do it once, but you find it difficult to continue and run a viable architectural practice.

How do you see your career evolving in this area or will you just respond where you feel it's appropriate? Has your thinking shifted after fifteen, twenty years of working in this disaster area? ▶ I have no big desire to make my organization bigger because once your organization becomes big you have to think about politics. You have to think about financial things and it becomes very complicated and you are not free any more.

So how does the Voluntary Architects' Network work? If it's just day-to-day volunteers, who organizes the volunteers? ▶ I do. I'm teaching in Japan. And in Japan there's an interesting situation. Each teacher has students from first year to PhD level who assist them. So, in my studio even if I'm in Australia, I could call them to start preparing and fundraising. Even as students they're already trained and have been to disaster areas so they know what they're doing. So they'll start preparing for me and then we'll go to a disaster area together. And then we find more people locally, I contact the local university, the professors, to join us. Always we need local people to be involved; each time we make a team with local people and the leader is always my student. I don't want to hire people to join my organization.

How do you switch mentally, I mean, coming from a disaster zone and then doing a very big house for somebody with a lot of money? How does this work? ▶ When I started, originally, I wanted to have a balance between working for rich and working for disasters; but little by little there is no bother any more. No difference any more. The house has to be beautiful. My satisfaction comes when people move into either the big house or the temporary house. It's just the same; the only difference is if I'm paid or not.

Why have you chosen the Temporary Container Housing project in Onagawa, Japan, to demonstrate the ethos of your work in the post-disaster field? ▶ This project came about in response to the devastation of the 2011 earthquake in Japan. This project highlights the importance of good design for temporary housing to avoid having a terrible evacuee situation for too long. It provides a three-storey temporary housing design based upon shipping containers. I hope in the future that the government invests in these kind of solutions. As I said, I do think there are small changes happening there: I was invited to lecture government on the benefits of such approaches.

> You have to be a good architect first, because even a temporary house is hard and it has to be beautiful, and you have to know the materials and the construction system. You have to know how to deal with the local architects and local engineers.

SHIGERU
BAN

SHIGERU BAN

Temporary container housing
Onagawa, Miyagi, Japan

△
Shipping containers provide temporary
medium-density housing.

Project type	End client
Transitional housing	**Onagawa community**
Number of apartments	Location of project
189	**Onagawa, Japan**
Architectural firm	Size
Shigeru Ban Architects	**12,320 m²**
Design team	Date completed
Voluntary Architects' Network	**November 2011**
Donors	Cost
Niebaum-Coppola Estate Winery, Hong Kong Ambassadors of Design Limited, Hiroshi Senjyu Suruga Bank, Japan Eri Logona Japan Inc., Ryuichi Sakamoto, Grace Farms Foundation Inc., Perolini Baumanagement AG, Parfums Givenchy, Jeff Spiritos and Klemens Gasser, S-G Investment, Yoshihisa Ejiri, Lo Chung Wing Victor, Nami Ogata and private donors	**$465,000**

Temporary container housing
Onagawa, Miyagi, Japan

Following the 2011 Japan earthquake, the town of Onagawa was struggling to construct enough temporary housing due to a lack of flat land. Voluntary Architects' Network proposed three-storey temporary housing made from shipping containers. By stacking these containers in a chequerboard pattern, the system creates bright, open living spaces between the containers. In the belief that the standard temporary houses issued by the government were poorly made with insufficient storage space, Voluntary Architects' Network installed built-in cupboards and shelving in all of our houses with the help of volunteers and through a donation fund. Voluntary Architects' Network hopes this will become the benchmark for new government standards of evacuation facilities and temporary housing.

◁
Interior, shipping container housing, Onagawa, Japan.

▷
Exploded axonometric. This drawing demonstrates how the container housing project overcomes the problem of insufficient level terrain for reconstruction by offering a housing solution with multiple storeys to increase residential density on the available land. Shipping containers are stacked in chequerboard patterns up to three storeys. This approach offers multiple benefits: a shorter construction period through the reuse of containers; wide intervals provide parking areas, a location for community facilities, privacy for families, open living spaces between containers; excellent seismic performance and potential for permanent use.

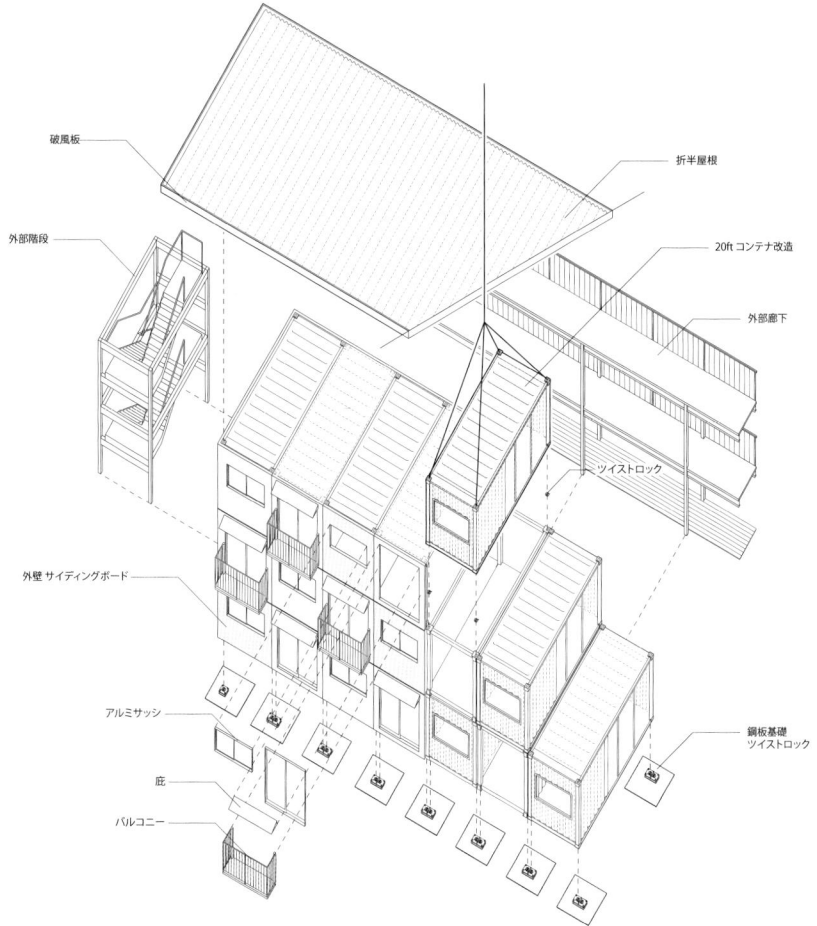

▽
Apartment plans. Three house plans are offered in this project based on the arrangement of the shipping containers: apartments of 19.8 m² designed for one or two residents; apartments of 29.7 m², designed for three or four residents, and apartments of 39.6 m², designed for more than four residents.

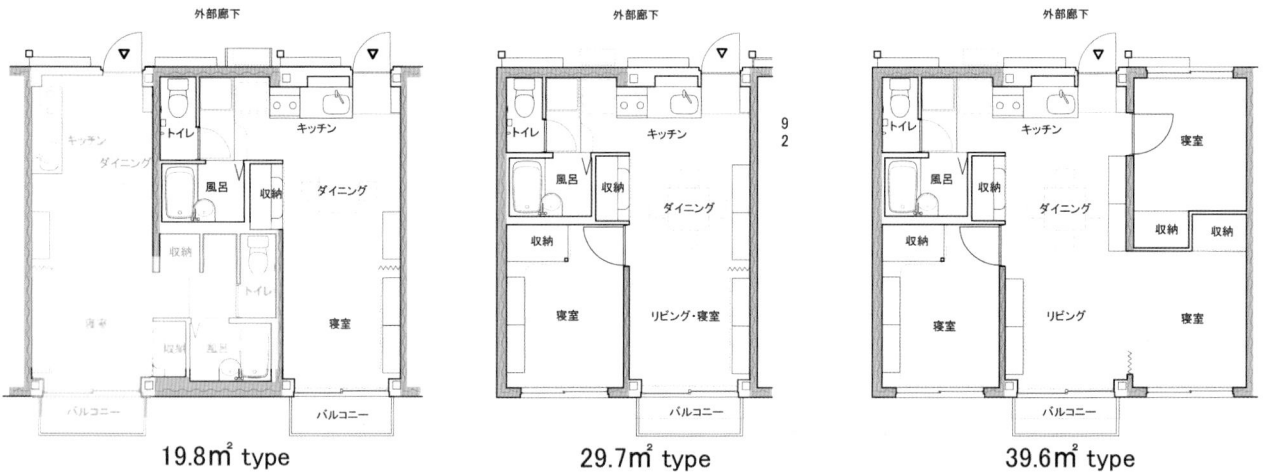

破風板

外部階段

外壁 サイディングボード

アルミサッシ

庇

バルコニー

折半屋根

20ft コンテナ改造

外部廊下

ツイストロック

鋼板基礎
ツイストロック

アクソノメトリック

外部廊下

トイレ　キッチン
風呂　ダイニング
収納
トイレ　寝室

19.8㎡ type

外部廊下

トイレ　キッチン
風呂　収納
収納　ダイニング
寝室　リビング・寝室

9
2

29.7㎡ type

外部廊下

トイレ　キッチン
風呂　収納
収納　寝室
ダイニング
収納　収納
寝室　リビング　寝室

39.6㎡ type

HSIEH YING CHUN

DIRECTOR
ATELIER 3
www.atelier-3.com

Hsieh Ying Chun,

founder of Atelier 3, moved his studio to rural Taiwan in the wake of the devastating earthquake of 1999. Since this time, his studio has been involved in the reconstruction of housing and communities in disaster zones, such as in projects with victims of the South-East Asian Tsunami. In 2004, Hsieh Ying Chun set up Rural Architecture Studio, which carries out similar work in rural China, including work on the reconstruction effort following the Sichuan earthquake. Atelier 3 proposed an architecture that was long-lasting, ecologically sound, culturally sensitive and could be built at a fraction of the cost, typically 25–50 per cent below the standard. In 2011, Chun was awarded the Curry Stone Design Prize in recognition of his social design impact through the construction of more than 3,000 homes with local people in natural disaster zones in Taiwan and Mainland China.

It's the same all over the world – academic training in architecture does not include these basic [social] issues, which means that the dwellings of 70 per cent of the world's population are irrelevant to architectural professionals today.

||||||||||||||||||||||||||||||||||||||||||||

HSIEH YING CHUN
ATELIER 3

Hsieh, how did your original architecture studies train you for the disaster reconstruction work you are involved in now? ▶ Sadly, it's the same all over the world – academic training in architecture does not include these basic issues, which means the dwellings of 70 per cent of the world's population are irrelevant to architectural professionals today. Our experience in reconstruction is based upon what we have learnt over many years in rebuilding housing after disasters.

You work as both a constructor and contractor. Has this helped you in the development and emergency fields? ▶ It would be difficult to progress if one confined oneself to design with only drawings, without thinking and organizing from a broader perspective and exploring related subjects such as construction techniques and the tools involved. Many topics need to be taken into consideration; for example, construction tools need to be simplified so that disaster victims without professional building skills can take part in

the reconstruction, and so that the reliance on capital can be minimized.

What does the term 'humanitarian architecture' mean to you? ▶ What we are now confronting is the most urgent issue faced by disaster victims, the question of their survival. This is different from the design work that we have done in the past, and different from the work of most architects. For us and for the disaster victims every part of the process immediately reflects whether it's good or bad, right or wrong. There is no room for ambiguity. Through this process I have experienced a strong sense of responsibility and self-expectation.

Our work can truly benefit disaster victims, people living in rural areas and the average person. It is done quietly and it is unknown to most, in contrast to the general conception of high-end environmentally friendly architecture. We never deliberately put the emphasis on 'humanitarianism'.

After the most destructive earthquake in modern Taiwan, on 21 September 1999, you worked on the reconstruction of the Thao Aboriginal village. Could you tell me about this experience? Did it make you rethink your role as an architect?
▶ The Thao Aborigines comprise the smallest population of Taiwan's recognized Indigenous minority groups. They have unique cultural traditions and customs, a unique language, well-maintained beliefs based on ancestor-worship and rich seasonal rituals. Most of the Thao population is concentrated in Brawbaw Village on the banks of Sun Moon Lake. On 21 September 1999, a massive earthquake damaged or destroyed 80 per cent of Thao homes in the area. To provide a base for recovering and preserving Thao culture, a resettlement community was constructed, with support from Taiwan's Academia Sinica, as well

as domestic and foreign NGOs and civic groups.

The plan for the resettlement community was organized with the ceremonial spaces as the main axis, and developed in accordance with the underlying topography of the land as well as the local environment. A system of 'work instead of charity' was invoked to allow tribal members to contribute collectively to the labour of rebuilding the community, address the question of economic livelihoods, and most importantly resolidify tribal consciousness through collective labour.

When did you set up Atelier 3? Was it after this reconstruction project? What are the aims of your practice? ▶ No, we set up Atelier 3 in 1987 and were not engaged with any reconstruction projects at the time. Our aim was to find the third path in contrast

with the prevailing dualism of 'Western modernization' and 'Eastern traditionalism'. We were seeking a more realistic approach.

Building on the founding aims of Atelier 3, what do you see as the connection between architecture and social justice? ▶ Architecture is the largest cultural accumulation of humanity. It is a collective social behaviour, and individuality is barely recognized. Ego and individuality have no place. It would be difficult to change the state of injustice if we don't peel away the basic layers of architecture and society and find a way to restructure the livelihood and architectural production system. For example, without the design of an autonomous community construction scheme, it is rather impossible to stop relying on the mega-capitalist architectural production system.

Working as an architect, how do you deal with the trauma of the aftermath of natural disasters? At some point do you become immune to it all?
▶ You have to look at disasters as natural phenomena. Most of humanity's building experience evolves from tackling natural disasters. Reconstruction is different from the temporary disaster relief. We work towards solving problems accumulated over the years; therefore, our work is not specifically aimed at the post-disaster area, but rather at livelihoods and homes for all the common people.

What do your colleagues in mainstream architecture think about the shelter and reconstruction area you are involved in now? ▶ We are not only engaged in the

△
The New Yangliu Village Community in China, following the post-earthquake reconstruction project by Atelier 3.

△
Sichuan Yangliu Village reconstruction: villagers erect the lightweight steel structure with manpower and handtools.

general design of the building, but also of the materials, tools, construction methods, organization and regulations. This is beyond the experience of most of our peers and it is hard for them to understand its value and importance. They usually understand our work at the humanitarian level, but have difficulties with their aesthetic judgement of our work. Even when they want to try, they often give up. What we get most often is 'Very good, very much in agreement, and may God bless you. See you.'

Why are there so few architects working in both emergency and long-term recovery planning after disasters? ▶   Most architects today are helpless when they go to post-disaster areas. As I said earlier, reconstruction is different from short-term disaster relief. We try to solve problems that have developed over years and made communities vulnerable and reduced their abilities to respond effectively themselves. No architect's education touches on these matters. This subject

requires contemplation of many issues, such as production, economics and culture. It takes much more than simply building a house.

Are architects well equipped to work in chaotic situations, such as after a disaster? ▶   In the professional division of labour, architects can only assume part of the responsibility. With the fragmentation of professional knowledge, it's hard for any one profession to appreciate the complete system, and so many of us are often unable to address issues in a disaster area comprehensively.

What do you think are the main characteristics of good practice in your shelter field? How do you move effectively between the emergency, transitional and permanent shelter phases?
▶   The general practice in the disaster area is to use emergency tents for six months and then simple transitional shelters for two to five years while waiting for the completion of permanent houses. During this process, the transitional shelter is extremely costly and mostly uses non-sustainable petrochemical materials, such as benzene board, or steel that is difficult to recycle.

> What we are now confronting is the most urgent issue faced by disaster victims, the question of their survival. This is different from the design work that we have done in the past, and different from the work of most architects.

Sichuan Yangliu Village reconstruction: earthquake disaster victims rebuild their homes.

> Architecture is the largest cultural accumulation of humanity. It is a collective social behaviour, and individuality is barely recognized.

We have designed a lightweight, sustainable and economical steel framing system that is applicable in all three phrases. Building materials can be sourced locally, such as grass, adobe, bamboo, wood and rubble. The structure is movable and construction can be done incrementally. It doesn't rely on professional contractors; people can build the shelters themselves.

Please tell me about your work after the Sichuan earthquake. I believe you helped Yangliu Village construct fifty-six new homes for 350 people?
▶ On 12 May 2008, Sichuan experienced an earthquake of magnitude 8.0 on the Richter Scale. More than two million rural homes needed to be rebuilt. We

The New Yangliu Village community in China following the post-earthquake reconstruction project by Atelier 3.

began work in June, developing, constructing and promoting waste-separating toilet facilities. By the end of July, the first model of a lightweight steel-frame adobe home had been finished. By the end of September, rural homes in villages across Qingchuan, Wenchuan and Maoxian Counties had been successfully constructed.

Yangliu Village is one of the few Qiang tribal minority villages to maintain Qiang cultural and linguistic traditions. Through the use of mutual aid and labour-sharing methods among the villagers, the reconstruction of fifty-six homes was successfully completed within the first year.

Light steel frames were used in combination with traditional local building techniques. Ground-floor walls were built from locally sourced and salvaged stone, the next storey's walls used reinforced concrete, and on the top floor construction used wood. Work began from a basic 'open' structural layout, giving individual families a great deal of freedom to adjust plans based on their particular circumstances and requirements. Ultimately, this strategy created a harmonious balance between standardization and diversity in the overall appearance of the rebuilt village.

Do architects always have a role in emergencies? If so, what is it? How has this role shifted in recent years? ▶ Architectural expertise is very important for disaster reconstructions, but it needs to be reviewed and transformed. The main thing we have to abandon is the ego of the architect. The less he or she does the better. We should only work on the irreplaceable parts so that local techniques and traditions can blend in. Promoting one's own values and preferences usually results in failure.

What other professional groups do you typically work with on shelter projects? Engineers, logisticians? Do you keep your architect's hat on? ▶ We do most of the tasks ourselves, except for structural calculations, for which we consult the structural engineer.

What is the lightweight construction system you have developed for use after a disaster? Is it suitable for every disaster? ▶ It is similar to the Chuandou wood structural system that has been practised for more than 5,000 years in China. We replace the wood structure with lightweight steel and use nuts and bolts instead of mortise and tenon joints. Material production and construction methods are simplified so that low-skilled local people can participate in the construction. This way, mass production can be achieved. The open and parametric design allows integration with traditional craftsmanship and local materials. It solves the contradiction between the uniformity of industrial production systems and the need for variety. The cost of long-distance transport is relatively low for lightweight steel. This makes it all very appropriate for post-disaster reconstruction.

How important is community-based construction after disasters? ▶ In most places, especially rural areas in the Third World, building houses is not an individual act. Moreover, funds are insufficient to commission professional construction teams. When houses need to be rebuilt in villages or communities, the best results are achieved by collaborative efforts of the workforce. This means that the construction methods need to be simple enough so that villagers without professional building skills are able to participate in the process.

This process can help to address the common issue of unemployment in disaster areas. Working together can also promote a new sense of community, and strengthen relationships between people through mutual assistance. This means that we are not just involved in physical reconstruction, but also helping to console the spirit. Rebuilding the village or community in this way transforms the construction site into something like a carnival, an experience filled with joy.

Why do architects typically assume that post-disaster design is a chance to

experiment with new design techniques, digital production or prefabricated solutions?
▶ Post-disaster reconstruction indeed is a big challenge. It brings out the passion and righteousness of architects who usually work in air-conditioned rooms and it also brings out all sorts of unusual ideas. There's no harm in having ideas and building some experimental houses. However, caution needs to be exercised when it comes to the real situation because no one has the right to treat disaster victims as experimental objects.

It is extremely dangerous to draw schemes directly from the designer or architect's subjective point of view without first considering the creativity and skills of disaster victims, as well as local materials and construction systems.

How do you evaluate the success of your reconstruction projects? ▶ We have helped to rebuild more than 2,000 family houses over the past thirteen years. With numerous try-outs on construction methods, we have confidence in both design and construction aspects of our projects; especially in the field of 'autonomous construction'. We have also received a lot of pressure from various parties for promoting low-price housing; it is somewhat revolutionary in the business.

> Post-disaster reconstruction indeed is a big challenge. It brings out the passion and righteousness of architects who usually work in air-conditioned rooms and it also brings out all sorts of unusual ideas.

Many young architects graduate with the aspiration that they will work for the next Frank Gehry or I.M. Pei. Is this your experience? How do we best equip/train young architects to get involved in the humanitarian field? ▶ The task and challenge of the dwellings of 70 per cent of mankind is the main issue; post-disaster reconstruction forces us to face this inescapable issue. Like a black hole, it is an area untouched by modern architecture. It surpasses the aura of the masters and even the demands of humanitarianism. It is an unlimited world full of hope for ambitious young people and architects.

Which project have you chosen to represent the work of Atelier 3 and why? ▶ We designed an 'Open System Structure' that inherits the rules of the traditional Chuandou system of post-and-beam wood frame construction. It is flexible and allows us to integrate local materials and skills. The simplified construction method allows villagers to collaboratively rebuild their homes by themselves. It is a chance for them to exercise their labour and creativity. This project also overcomes the many contradictions between the uniformity of mass production and the beauty of variety. It helps us solve the puzzle of how to integrate industrialization and traditional handcrafts.

HSIEH YING CHUN

Post-earthquake reconstruction project
Yangliu Village, Sichuan, China

△
View of the New Yangliu Village, Sichuan,
China.

Project type	Location of project
Permanent housing	**Abzhou, Taiping Township, Sichuan, China**
Architectural firm	Date completed
Atelier 3	**2009**
Design team	Cost
Hsieh Ying Chun, Nie Cheng	**$70.52/m²**
Donors	Total cost
Autodesk, Red Cross, Nandu Foundation	**$1,005,524**
End client	
Yangliu Village residents	

Post-earthquake reconstruction project
Yangliu Village, Sichuan, China

Yangliu Village is one of the few Qiang tribal minority villages to maintain Qiang cultural and linguistic traditions. Through the use of mutual aid and labour-sharing methods among the villagers, reconstruction of fifty-six houses was successfully completed within one year. Light-gauge steel frames were used in combination with traditional local building techniques; ground-floor walls were built from locally sourced and salvaged stone, the next storey's walls used reinforced concrete, and on the top floor construction used wood. Work began from a basic 'open' structural layout, giving individual families a great deal of freedom to adjust plans based on their particular circumstances and requirements. Ultimately, this strategy created a harmonious balance in the overall appearance of the rebuilt village between standardization and diversity.

◁
View of the New Yangliu Village, Sichuan, China.

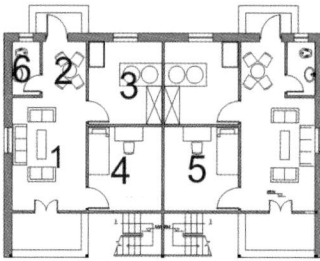

Ground Floor

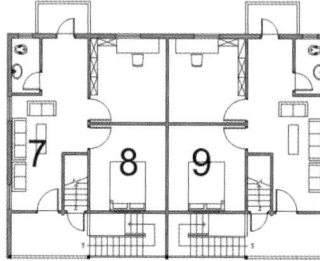

First Floor

1. Living Room
2. Dining Room
3. Kitchen
4. Bedroom
5. Bedroom
6. Bathroom
7. Recreation Area
8. Bedroom
9. Bedroom
10. Study
11. Storage

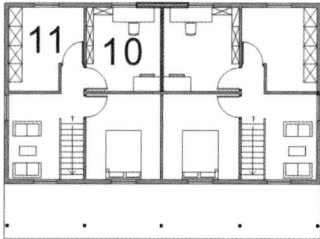

Second Floor

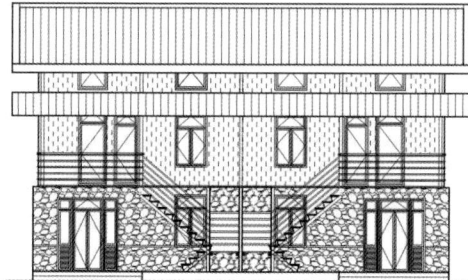

Elevation

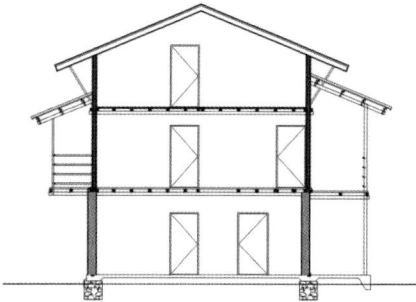

Section

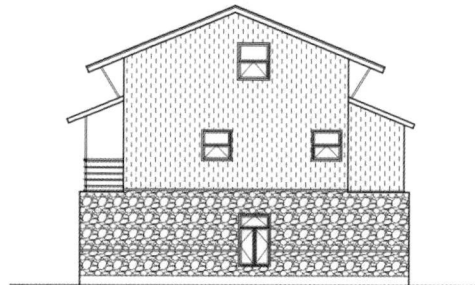

Side Elevation

△
Sichuan Yangliu Village reconstruction:
technical drawings.

HSIEH
YING CHUN

MICHAEL MURPHY

CO-FOUNDER AND EXECUTIVE DIRECTOR
MASS DESIGN GROUP
www.massdesigngroup.org

Michael Murphy

co-founded the award-winning MASS Design Group with Alan Ricks to improve social equity and health outcomes through design innovation. As Executive Director, he oversees MASS's business development and marketing efforts, cultivating new partnerships with donors, NGOs, business leaders and governments to lead design projects that enable the built environment to solve health challenges. Michael has taught courses on design for infection control at Harvard University's School of Public Health, has served as Entrepreneur in Residence at Clark University and serves on the advisory board for the Master of Professional Studies for the New York School of Interior Design as well as for the TED Prize 2013. He holds a BA in English Literature from the University of Chicago and a Masters in Architecture from Harvard University Graduate School of Design.

Architectural education does prepare you to be quite a generalist and able to assess problems from a multiplicity of scales and perspectives.

||||||||||||||||||||||||||||||||||||||

MICHAEL MURPHY
MASS DESIGN GROUP

Michael, how did your original architectural studies train you for the public health architecture work you are involved in at the moment?
▶ Architectural education does prepare you to be quite a generalist and able to assess problems from a multiplicity of scales and perspectives. That skill set is pretty unique to design and architecture. With the right amount of time and commitment, it allows for significant problem-solving in addressing global challenges. It is this application of design that we bring into settings that may not have benefited from architectural services before.

Tell me about your work with Partners in Health when you were at the Harvard University Graduate School of Design (GSD), which was really the origin of MASS Design Group.
▶ When I met Dr Paul Farmer, founder of Partners in Health, he was talking mostly about the health infrastructure, the buildings, that they had constructed across Africa. He mentioned how architects had rarely reached out to see how they could help and I wondered if he

could benefit from having architects and designers assist his building teams on the ground.

There weren't really many architecture groups, such as MASS, focusing on the intersection of architecture and public health at that time, were there? ▶ I was not aware of any design groups focusing particularly on public health and architecture. I would say, however, that a lot of organizations that are working on questions of housing, infrastructure and access to key resources like education, by proxy, are working at the intersections of health and environment. What's interesting about Partners in Health is that they claim that in order to deliver appropriate and complete health care, we also need to approach issues of shelter, education and infrastructure. This is because access to care is inhibited by any number of social and political factors, not just financial limitations.

Does the term 'humanitarian architecture' have meaning for you? ▶ I would like to see us stop referring to architecture as 'humanitarianism'. We have to remember that all architecture is political. Besides, it's not as if I'm meeting people in Haiti who are calling themselves humanitarian architects. I think they would call themselves architects working in the humanitarian sector.

Yes, I understand. Can you tell me more about this? ▶ I'm very excited about the increasing number of architects working on issues of poverty reduction, health care and access to education. I think this shift is important for the discipline and for the re-creation of architecture's value. I think the resistance I have to the label 'humanitarian architecture' is that I think architecture should always have had a responsibility to the public. Too many architects seem to have forgotten that they are not only responsible to their client, they must also represent the public. If we bifurcate 'humanitarian architecture' from 'architecture' we fail to demand of architecture its responsibility to the public. If we maintain that link, then it allows an architect to choose between humanitarian architecture and regular architecture – as if there is such a thing – or one could choose political architecture versus apolitical architecture. We have to invert the question and ask: if you say there is such a thing as humanitarian architecture, then what is non-humanitarian

architecture? What does that say about the buildings that are apolitical? What does that say about the architects who choose not to engage in politics or not to engage in the issues around the people that the buildings are serving?

What would you say about the fact that there was not really an emergency architecture discipline until after the Indian Ocean tsunami? That the rebuilding work after that disaster was mainly lead by logisticians and engineers? ▶ I think we have to look at what has changed in relief organizations and the multinational funding around disasters over the last 30 years. Architects deserve credit for some successes, but we must also acknowledge that there were a lot more architects and engineers on the payroll of multilateral agencies and international development organizations than there are now. A lot of architects were let go as development contracting became increasingly privatized. Infrastructure became less

a priority and architects and engineers left many of these organizations. Neoliberalism has seen aid and disaster funding transition towards an economy that favours cost and efficiency over human development. A lot of architects are now responding on their own to fill in the gaps this policy shift has left behind.

Tell me about the first time you went to Rwanda and tried to understand the health issues of the communities you were working with. I imagine that this work was far more complex than the design projects you'd worked on until then. ▶ I was very lucky to be with the organization Partners in Health, who had taken on challenges at the scale of the nation, not just the scale of the hospital. They were asking questions like 'What causes one community to get better health care than others, and how could the entire state get better health care?' I not only had a support system made of people who were asking those challenging questions, but one

▷
David Saladik, a MASS Director, leads efforts on the ground to build efficient, effective and empowering health infrastructure. Pictured here, he is working with GBS, the Haitian architect of record for the GHESKIO Tuberculosis Hospital, and the construction team to review foundation designs.

that made it possible to ask those questions and to try to implement bigger solutions. Thus when it came to the Buturo hospital project, the question wasn't simply 'How do we build this hospital?' It was also, 'How do we build something unique that can actually address some of these bigger issues that are not only relevant to Rwanda, but relevant globally?'

Has the desire to ask such political questions and do the work you do been influenced by your family background? Was there something in your upbringing that inspired you to get involved in this more socially oriented aspect of design work, or was it just an awakening when you met Dr Paul Farmer? ▶ I really got involved in architecture because of my parents. My father was in local politics and worked in government, in upstate New York, for most of his life. He was a very inspiring figure. My mom is a nurse, and the two of them have devoted their lives to public service. I think I always was interested in, and asking questions about, justice.

Did you have the opportunity when you were studying architecture to ask those questions? ▶ Studying architecture is partly a technical degree and partly an engagement in systemic thinking. You go from the scale of the building to the scale of the urban environment, and it trains you to put hard questions into context and see examples where others have asked and addressed similar concerns. Certainly, urbanism is alive and vibrant and being dissected in many different ways in academia. The challenge is that we don't often get the opportunity to

> If we bifurcate 'humanitarian architecture' from 'architecture' we fail to demand of architecture its responsibility to the public.

practise and test these ideas, and it's in practice that we actually get to see the ideas that work, the ideas on which you can compromise and those you can't.

At the same time, there are a lot of architects in the field who see the post-disaster area as a chance to experiment, and I guess we all know about the cardboard logs, prefab temporary housing containers, and so on. What inspires the idea that a prefab solution is the right way to go? ▶ I think these depend on the context. It's a lot to ask of an architecture course to solve the challenges of Haiti's housing by sending an architecture student for a week to Port-au-Prince. Students are not deeply experienced in the complex social, economic, racial and political history of Haiti. But I also don't want to delude myself into thinking that it's really the architect's fault. A prefabricated solution for housing is being pushed not simply by architects, but by a huge global financial infrastructure that has already prefabricated these houses and whose mission is to sell them. There is a massive, multinational construction industry based around disaster relief and more resources to influence what happens and, ultimately, more agency than any groups of architects. So, I think architects can suggest good solutions and try to come up with better alternatives; but unless we're

engaging with and affecting practices in the construction industry, we're not going to have any impact at all.

Tell me more about the work you're currently doing in Haiti? ▶ We're working with two really exciting projects in Haiti with the non-profit GHESKIO, who are engaged deeply within the Haitian community. They work with the poorest of the poor and provide free comprehensive health care. We've been asked to support their infrastructure on two projects and have worked to involve the production of different materials as well as the design of the facilities to directly improve health outcomes. We are building a tuberculosis clinic and a cholera centre with GHESKIO in order to better heal patients and to reduce infection between patients, nurses and doctors – a goal we believe can be achieved through the layout and design of the building.

Apart from the hospitals and the medical centres that seem to be what the MASS Design Group is mostly focused on, have you been involved in housing reconstruction at all? ▶ We have worked on housing in Rwanda around the Butaro Hospital. In collaboration with Partners in Health and its partners we sought to further grow the health care network of the Butaro District by providing housing for the doctors and staff. The project was designed to provide

△
The GHESKIO Tuberculosis Hospital
in Port-au-Prince seeks to model more
resilient infrastructure in facing both
disease outbreaks and natural disaster.

◁ △
The 140-bed Butaro Hospital in the Burera District, Rwanda, 2011
(photo: Iwan Ban).

construction training and capacity building in the community, as well as the quality of homes that would encourage the best doctors and nurses to stay and work in the area.

What would you say to a young architect who wants to get involved in this area of work that intersects public health and natural and long-term systemic political disasters? ▶ Ambition – naive or informed – is probably fundamental. The blind commitment to accomplishing and implementing is what is missing from the field. I tell people who really want to do their own project to just do it. I also tell them not to quit when it's really bad. Sticking it out is really the hardest part. We have to commit our lives to it. If you have two weeks of vacation and you want to do something, then I think it is better to link in with an organization that can accommodate that minimal impact. If you want to start your own company, then I recommend really going deep and going big. Of course, I try to manage ambitions too. There is a lot of assuming you have more expertise than you do if you're out in the field. So humility is the second most important part of this process. On the other hand, there is something to be said for trying to 'make it work' and being an entrepreneur. Getting out there by yourself and trying to figure out how the system works is, in itself, a skill that I think is missing from architectural education.

In five years' time what would be the portrait you'd paint of the MASS Design Group? What would be the substantial differences to where you are now? ▶ I think in five years' time we will see the scale of work we're getting into becoming more national, and I think that it's really exciting to be thinking about bigger issues around policy and engaging at a planning level. I see ourselves maintaining the work that we do, but extending into a lot of different discussions in a lot of different places and advancing the dialogue of the role of architecture in improving health outcomes.

Why have you chosen the GHESKIO project to illustrate the work and ethics of the MASS Design Group? ▶ GHESKIO's MDR-TB facility at Signeau was destroyed in the 2010 earthquake. Patients currently reside in disaster-relief tents. MASS has partnered with GHESKIO to build a seismic, sustainable and dignified building that will provide effective infection control as well as a more permanent means to grow the country's health care to provide for better Haitian health.

> We are trying to think about architecture as a process, not an object. Our role likely has to be more long-term than a client who wants simply a building [designed by an architect]; that requires a different engagement, a different relationship, and a different business model.

48

MICHAEL MURPHY

GHESKIO Tuberculosis Hospital
Port-au-Prince, Haiti

△
The lush landscaped courtyard and
open-air gathering spaces provide
opportunities for social engagement
among patients undergoing long courses
of treatment in open-air environments
where the risk of transmission is
low. Dr Jean William Pape, founder
of GHESKIO, worked with MASS
to develop a unique concept for
consultation patios outside patient
rooms, where doctors and patients can
meet in the open air and thus further
reduce risk.

Project type
Medical facility

Architectural firm
MASS Design Group

Donors
**Individual donor
(name undisclosed) and USAID**

End client
**GHESKIO (le Groupe Haïtien
d'Etude du Sarcome de Kaposi et
des Infections Opportunistes)**

Location of project
Port-au-Prince, Haiti

Size
14,000 m²

Date completed
**Ongoing, estimated completion,
Autumn 2013**

Cost
$1,000/m²

Total cost
$1.8 million

GHESKIO Tuberculosis Hospital
Port-au-Prince, Haiti

The new state-of-the-art GHESKIO Tuberculosis Hospital will replace the previously earthquake-destroyed MDR-TB facility at Signeau and will provide TB patients, who are still being housed in temporary tents, an effective and dignified place to stay for the duration of their long-term treatment. Simple but effective methods of passive ventilation and infection control are used to reduce in-hospital transmission of TB in this high-risk population, as well as to reduce energy costs for the facility. Through involving local labour and building a facility focused on long-term health outcomes, MASS seeks to model a sustainable means to reduce community vulnerability and build greater resilience during disease outbreak and natural disaster.

◁

The GHESKIO Tuberculosis Hospital, due to be completed in 2014, is innovatively designed to deliver both optimal infection control and dignity to the patients and staff who will use the facility. Leveraging low-cost passive systems to create airflow and dissipate heat gain, the design also integrates unique metal details that highlight the Haitian metalworking tradition.

EXTERIOR CORRIDOR
open-air circulation
decreases incubation
of infected airborne
particles

CONSULTATION PATIO
open-air consultation
with mobile patients
diminishes risk of
infection for doctors

RESTROOM DOOR
cleaning staff may
access toilets without
passing through
infected space

IN-ROOM SINK
doctor may wash hands
after consultation
without entering
patient restroom

EXTERIOR FINS
exhaust from restroom
in-wall vents is
directed away from
windows

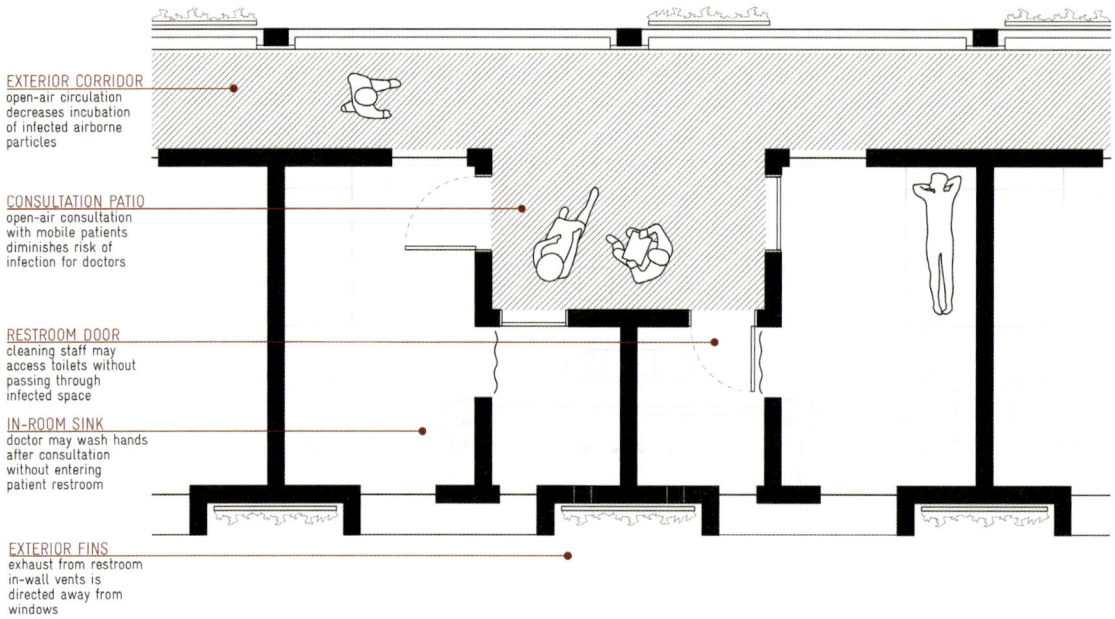

△
Floor plan, GHESKIO
Tuberculosis Hospital.
Layout of patient rooms was
designed in collaboration
with Dr Jean William Pape,
recipient of the Gates
Foundation Global Health
Prize and founder of
GHESKIO.

▷
Site plan of GHESKIO
Tuberculosis Hospital.
Strategies for simple and
effective infection control
include isolation rooms with
negative pressure systems,
and open-air circulation and
waiting areas.

PAUL PHOLEROS

DIRECTOR
HEALTHABITAT
www.healthabitat.com

Paul Pholeros

trained as an architect at the University of Sydney and, since 1984, has directed a private architectural practice working on urban, rural and remote area projects throughout Australia and internationally. He is a former director of Emergency Architects Australia and a partner of Healthabitat, along with a medical doctor and an anthropologist/public health officer. For over twenty-five years Healthabitat has worked to improve the health of Aboriginal people, particularly children, by making healthier living environments in many remote and, more recently, rural and suburban areas of Australia and in Nepal and some major cities in the USA. In 2011 Healthabitat was awarded the UN-Habitat's World Habitat Award and also the Australian Institute of Architects national Leadership in Sustainability prize for sustaining the lives of people. In 2007 Paul received an Order of Australia for services to architecture, Indigenous housing and health.

> I think part of the job we have as [architectural] professionals is an obligation to fire arrows to try and break down orthodoxy.

||||||||||||||||||||||||||||||||||||||||

PAUL PHOLEROS
HEALTHABITAT

Paul, this term 'humanitarian architecture' or 'humanitarian design'. Does it have any meaning for you? ▶ I do not favour any 'qualifiers' of architecture, such as 'community' architect, 'solar' architect or 'sustainability' architect. You are either an architect or you're not; and to me, architecture implies that all of those parts should be covered in the work we do. So, I hope that all architecture is humanitarian architecture. I think architecture should include and use more areas of knowledge rather than be segmented by these tags.

The development work we do at Healthabitat is undertaken in a disaster zone. The extent of house failure in remote Indigenous Australia is so extreme in many places you would think a flood or an earthquake or cyclone had happened. Therefore, how we can actually get some improvement to houses on the first day of a project is essential. So we prioritize on the basis of safety and health, in a very detailed way, to fix the most important things first. That's not very glamorous, it's certainly not spatial or about form; it's all about function.

Our work grows from that approach. Just like after a natural disaster, you need social reconstruction as well as physical reconstruction. You get this by ensuring employment, by integrating local people into the works at every level – and not just the tools level but at the planning level, and the thinking level is most important. And, if ongoing maintenance work keeps going, then I think you will see social reconstruction.

Much more slowly, you see a psychological reconstruction. It probably takes five years in the development work we do – but you certainly see a change in attitude. If the house functions, if work can be maintained, and if people are actively involved in a project for a period of time, then you see change.

What led you to work in Australian Indigenous communities and the development sector more generally? ▶ We had some very inspiring lecturers at Sydney

University in the 1970s. A lot of what we were taught wasn't specifically about Indigenous people or humanitarian issues, but it certainly was a broadening education and that was a critical starting point for what I would be able to do later.

More directly, about seven years after graduation I'd taken on work upgrading a small clinic in central Australia for an Aboriginal medical service. They had the money, but couldn't get the government architect from South Australia to come and actually do the work. So I took it on as a 'straight' commercial architectural project, doing design work for a small building.

It was very humble and very small-scale, but they were good clients. They paid their bills. They did what they said they'd do. Everything went fine, and then a nearby community asked if I would do the same clinic design work for them. So in 1983 I started as an architect working for Indigenous clients. I did a service; they paid me. But it was in 1985 that a serious change in the work happened.

Yami Lester was a charismatic Aboriginal leader. He ran a health service and knew of me because some of the small design work I had been doing was for some of his clinics. One day, Yami put me in a room with a medical doctor who had worked for the health service for a year, and an anthropologist who had retrained as an environmental health officer and who had worked in the region for ten years and spoke the local Aboriginal language fluently. Yami explained that he had observed that some people and families were going to a clinic more often

than others. He said that this made him realize that just treating people was not actually making them better. So, he came up with a one-line brief for us: 'to stop getting sick'. Simple but yet so profound!

That was really the commencement on our serious work in Indigenous Australia and that's what has led to all the work I have done from that point to this.

Paul, was there anything about the sort of professional lives of your parents that influenced the areas of work you are involved in today? ▶ My parents weren't professionals. My dad was a migrant. The classic story of someone who came to a new country to try and make good.

My parents lived well, but they lived very simply. They made things rather than bought things and that was a strong influence. Also, I grew up in a mixed culture of Greek and Australian (my mother) and, as a kid, I learnt a lot from that mixed environment. The 'Greek other'! In my case it was a pretty mild 'other' but it meant a different language, different habits, different food and a different view of the world. It became an important part of my life that the 'other' was never a threat.

The most important gift from my parents was that they had no expectations of what I should do. University wasn't a goal; initially it wasn't even an option. That changed when I received a government scholarship to go to university. This was neither a great achievement nor a negative. It was just another path. No one quite knew what to expect because there was no experience of

university in my family. I'm always very grateful for both that lack of expectation and unconditional support from my parents. That was a great gift.

Thank you Paul, but just going back to your studies again. You said you studied in the 1970s. That was a decade ahead of me. When I was studying architecture in the 1980s, it was consumed by postmodernism and then deconstruction. There was a lot of criticism of the modernist ideals around social reform and social housing. So, did architecture school in the 1970s imbue you with a concern for social justice? ▶ It probably took me twenty years to realize how important those university years were. The Head of School where I studied, Professor Peter Johnson, said that he couldn't predict the world in which we would be practising architecture. He was very open about this. And he thought that we had to be 'educated' not 'trained'. Therefore, his aim was to provide us with a broad-based education that would equip us with skills for the world well beyond Sydney University, beyond Australia, and beyond the requirements of the architecture profession in the 1970s.

In hindsight I think that's quite a profound idea, and it wasn't just 'all talk'. In my first year we had courses in anthropology, ecology, ethnology, sociology and environment studies. Names like Marr Grounds, Harry Recher, Amos Rappaport, Liz Fell, Guy Warren, Jennifer Taylor, Steve King, Ric Mohr and many more became common to us – and I have not met too many architects since for whom these names are all that familiar.

None of these courses were taught by architects pretending to be an anthropologist or a sociologist. They were taught by people who were experts in the disciplines, and many of them went on to become some of the most respected in their field. I am embarrassed to say it but, before our first ecology lecture in 1971, there wasn't one person in our class of seventy that even knew what ecology meant. So, we were being pushed and prodded in all sorts of directions right from the beginning.

For example, the anthropologist who taught us said, 'Look, the study of anthropology is really all that matters. So I don't know why you are studying architecture.' We had someone teaching sociology who, at the time, seemed like a radical feminist. She started the course by saying to all the young men in the class, 'You are the problem!' – which was both true and was a great way to start off a course. The ecologist put it in even more blunt terms: 'Do you want to be one of those people who will destroy the planet through thoughtless architecture?'

All these people had the great conviction that the world was much bigger than architecture and I think that that was *the* critical point. They weren't as crazy as I'm making them out to be and they contributed a huge amount, but they wove these subjects into the fabric of the course and showed us that the concerns of architecture, the real guts of it, had to be broader than just buildings. Later, some great architects like Glenn Murcutt and Richard Leplastrier, who were also doing their early defining work at the time, taught us how the many complex parts of environment, culture and technology could be woven together.

So what do you think happened in the 1980s and 1990s?
▶ There was a reversal. Architects started pretending they were philosophers and anthropologists. I think the translation of a lot of these things, and how one could weave all of these ideas into the real world of architecture, became too hard for the profession – and people said 'Let's revert to what we do best: make shapes and develop styles … like postmodernism.'

Others said architects should work like sociologists or philosophers or anthropologists – and I think this was also a mistake. Over the last thirty years, architecture has tended to walk away from some of the most important but complex issues. So we have retreated to the more simple things we think we can better control – things like designing decorative buildings and the idea that every problem must have a building as a solution. Both tendencies are dead ends.

You run a mainstream architecture practice, work with Healthabitat and have been director of a design not-for-profit. My friend, Fred Schwartz, a New York architect, coined the term 'Robin Hood architects'. Would you put yourself in that camp? Or is that just a glib term? ▶ I liked Robin Hood. People tend to forget the fact that I still practise as an architect. They see my Healthabitat 'hat' and assume that's what I do all the time. Well I don't. I still work as a 'traditional' architect.

Why? Well, first, it pays the bills and, second, it's what I was educated to be. It's what I was trained to do, and most importantly, I still enjoy it. Yes, if the 'Robin Hood' analogy is about using some of my earnings from the wealthier clients and the time it buys working for poorer clients – clients that may never ring my office – then that's true. I choose all my clients carefully and I think I choose where I spend my time even more carefully. And that really isn't bounded by whether they are wealthy or poor. Time is the limiting factor and you have to be cautious where you spend it.

> The way I work should remain constant – whether it's for a client in a village in Nepal or an Aboriginal family in the centre of Australia or a corporate client in Sydney – I hope the level of skill and expertise is the same. I think that's the core.

Women and children in Bhattedande, Nepal, suffer most from the ill-health effects of smoke from poorly ventilated spaces.

and to improve the housing. So I'll take two parts of the Robin Hood mythology.

What do you see as the key difference between working as a commercial architect with traditional clients and then working in the disaster or development sector? ▶ That is a really good question. The more I think about it, it's actually one of the key questions.

The way I work should remain constant – whether it's for a client in a village in Nepal or an Aboriginal family in the centre of Australia or a corporate client in Sydney – I hope the level of skill and expertise is the same. I think that's the core. There's just no way we can avoid that in our 'development work' with Healthabitat. It's the urgency of work that is so fundamentally different.

If we can ensure a shower works for the first five years of a child's life anywhere in Australia, their chance of a better life will increase dramatically. They will hear better, see better, breathe better and, in thirty-five years' time, there is even a great chance of a reduction in kidney disease and the need for dialysis. Most of these positive outcomes of making sure a shower is working will happen well after I am dead and gone.

It's that urgency which I think is different. If I don't design a house for someone in the affluent suburbs of Sydney, so what? They will be able to get someone else to do it and I don't think their lives will be fundamentally any poorer.

Also, I think the collaboration involved in most of the work

Another part of the Robin Hood analogy that I like is that Robin Hood was able to shoot arrows very effectively. I think part of the job we have as professionals is an obligation to fire arrows to try and break down orthodoxy. In the Indigenous housing area in Australia, this is an important time to be firing many arrows.

Some of the worst housing built in the last thirty years is being built by governments who are spending more money on remote Indigenous housing than at any time in Australia's history. We, individually and as a profession, have an overriding responsibility to speak out in an attempt at exposing this

> I don't think there is a universal solution or architectural response, but I think it's equally frustrating to suggest returning to absolute base zero on every design project. We don't do it in our 'mainstream' work so I don't see why we do it in Indigenous or community design work.

TEDx talk was 'to reduce poverty through design'. I think that's really important. Eliminating or removing poverty is an aspirational goal, and you would have to be pretty arrogant to make the claim that any one piece of work could remove or eliminate poverty because poverty has many dimensions. All the work of Healthabitat is about improving health and, hopefully, reducing levels of poverty. But we try to remain humble about what we can and can't achieve.

of Healthabitat is far broader than in my commercial practice. Architecture is a good collaborative profession. We're taught to be collaborative and I think it is really important in the work we do. But the collaborations are narrower.

In Healthabitat we have medical doctors, a forensic entomologist, a doctor of dust, a statistician, engineers, a physicist, epidemiologists, environmental health specialists, educators, lawyers, plumbers, electricians, builders, industry experts, graphic designers, IT designers, industrial designers and a raft of other professionals that come in and assist. But it really is the actual communities who add their collaboration into the work that make the key contribution – and they collaborate in ways that are not common in commercial architecture.

Finally, I think the measurement of success is totally different. If we ask fifty architects what is their measure of success, we may find that a happy client is one measure. But what defines the 'happiness'? It may be that success is a beautiful building, but then, what is the beauty? Another measure they

will tell us is winning an award and professional recognition. But then, who is doing the recognizing? Or is it really the moment of fame that goes with the recognition?

My definition of success links back to the example of work given earlier: the child that doesn't have to go to the hospital in thirty-five years' time for dialysis every few days as a result of having a working shower during their first five years of life.

However, that has never been a notable success of Healthabitat's work in the last five years as it is invisible. It doesn't mean that it's not a success nor does it mean it is not important. It just means the measure of success needs to be different. And that's something, as a profession, we have to be constantly thinking about: the measures of what we consider professional success – and why.

This seems to relate to the themes in your TEDx talk in June 2013 [www.ted.com/ talks/paul_pholeros_how_to_ reduce_poverty_fix_homes. html] and the idea that design can help eliminate poverty. Could you expand on that?

▸ The expression I used in the

So where do the spatial thinking and creativity of the architect fit in? ▸ The spatial thinking skills we use as architects are just tools, means to an end, not the end in themselves. Our work at HealthHabitat always comes back to health and the question of how we can use our skills – as tools – to achieve health goals.

At the front end of any disaster or development work, there are about fifty things that cascade in terms of priority before you even begin to think about immediate shelter. How do you provide emergency lighting, security, emergency treatment, potable water, washing, waste systems and cooking? How do you get all these most basic systems there on day one?

You've had probably a lot more experience than most architects in working in transdisciplinary ways, for example with doctors and anthropologists. However, there is a fundamental difference in that a doctor working in the development and disaster sector can have a universal solution, for example in treating a disease or ensuring safe water. This is not the case in architecture even though generations of architects would

△ Healthabitat building works in Bhattedande, Nepal, to improve sanitation and health through new toilet and waste system.

argue that there is a universal solution. It's part of the problem of the post-disaster scene that people want to fly in with their 'one-size-fits-all' design – and I'm sure you've seen the same in the Indigenous sector. **Why do some design professionals like to hypothesize about other people's living conditions without really having experienced them?** ▶ Yes, Healthabitat gets about five prefab housing solutions a month and we are asked to comment on the latest design for a house that's going to solve all the problems of all Indigenous people. What that means I don't really know. The designs are based on myths – about costs, likes and dislikes, the universal client and reducing

damage and vandalism. All it means is that these people have absolutely no idea about the actual problems.

I don't think there is a universal solution or architectural response, but I think it's equally frustrating to suggest returning to absolute base zero on every design project. We don't do it in our 'mainstream' work so I don't see why we do it in community design work.

Healthabitat's work has developed and refined broad design principles. They relate to the safety, health and the well-being of people. They guide a wide range of architectural responses very specifically, but every design response has to vary for every

place. If it's Haiti, New York City or an Australian desert community, clearly the physical structure, the social structure, the people, the language – they are all different. However, the bugs harming the kids in New York City are very similar to the bugs doing damage to kids in Australia and Haiti. So some things are the same; but the response on the ground to how we solve the problem might be distinctly 'NYC'. The safety and health principles guide the response.

Even in very different settings we are still trying to measure how we have reduced a certain illness and that keeps the architectural or design response much more direct. It is not about the shape of the roof; it is not about the look of the building. It is about whether the number of people with a particular illness declines over a set period of time. This is a hard test of the work.

So, I keep a foot in each camp. I don't think everything is universal but similarly I don't think every new project starts from zero.

In the last decade there has been a very steep rise in the design not-for-profit sector. Groups like Architecture for Humanity, Architects for Peace and Emergency Architecture. Is this because architects are searching for more meaning in their work? ▶ You're absolutely right. I think a lot about this. The humanitarian architecture movement has come out of nowhere in a very short time. All of these groups appeared and there are lots of them, as you say. Not just in architecture either, but in engineering and medicine also.

I'm not sure how to explain it, but here are two possible reasons. We've been through a boom in architecture practice in Australia as much of the world went through a boom. Perhaps this allowed people the resources and time to think more broadly, to think beyond what they were doing in day-to-day practice work. That may be the starting point, but maybe the real trigger comes at times like now, when the architectural profession is in decline and you have the enforced time off to think about other ways to work. You've maybe heard of these groups, and you lend your support to them. So it might be a two-step process – lots of work and then no work.

The architectural profession could use this phenomenon to expand the scope of what we do. That to me is the exciting part – to expand the scope of what we do. And if the universities follow – changing what gets taught, how people are trained and educated – then it can become a long-term phenomenon.

You were recently invited to Christchurch to advise on methods of reconstructing the damaged city. What are your reflections about what has happened in Christchurch and what could reasonably be done by the design profession? ▶ The New Zealand Institute of Architects invited me and I've had a bit of time to think about my very short visit. The two earthquakes that did all the damage had a total duration of less than a minute. And in that less than that one minute it caused $500 billion worth of damage. If you ever want to bet on a competition between humans and nature it will be a clear result! I think that this event has to make us all a bit more humble about the world and our place within it.

The disaster immediately mobilized a community response, which I think in most disasters is normal. But New Zealand was well equipped to provide an even greater community response. I talked to many people and was shown examples of how they mobilized; this was a highlight of the post-quake time.

Two years on, the 'big end of town' is coming back. That means that the corporate sector and their re-imagining of the city is being well and truly pushed hard now – just like in New Orleans after Katrina. Unfortunately, many in the community who mobilized initially are now being seen as the 'kids at the table' and now it's time for the adults to eat. So I think that's going to be a tussle about how that plays out.

The big question is the role of people in the city. Those who intervened in the city fabric immediately after the quake

▽
Sketch section of new toilet system for Bhattedande in Nepal by Pholeros.

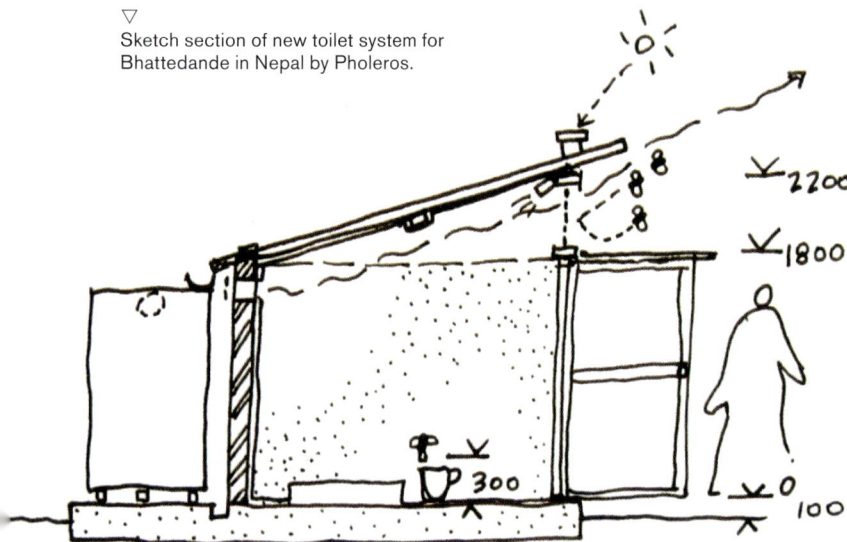

PAUL
PHOLEROS

have identified the larger issue: it isn't about just earthquake reconstruction, it's about the role of people in the city.

This is an exciting way to view it. What is the role of people in the city, in planning the city life, in deciding the way a city develops, the way a city is zoned? The final thing that just struck me in Christchurch, whether it was a formal meeting, over a meal or in casual meetings, was the extent of the human grief. Now the human grief will obviously continue for a long time. You realize the trauma that people have been through. That isn't going to go away quickly. It's a part of all development work. And this is a rich country like New Zealand! I think we probably underestimate what a big factor grief must be when people have had poor living conditions, have been dismissed, marginalized or abused, or been told they're stupid for generations.

In New Zealand's case, it was an earthquake and the loss of people, houses and a city. There has also been a loss of certainty, too. Lost certainty about the very place you put your feet; it might shake or might disappear tomorrow. So, big issues are all being played out in New Zealand right now.

And has the Christchurch earthquake galvanized the architecture profession there at all, in terms of what their role could be in even doing disaster risk reduction measures before the next earthquake? Has there been a shift in dialogue about the capacity of architects to respond to such disasters?
▶ I think it has. I was lucky to be shown around by David Sheppard, the president of the NZIA, and

he's got the pulse of practices around the country. He thinks that the earthquakes have really galvanized lots of branches of the profession, young and old, because there are risks in other cities in New Zealand. There is a lot of discussion and work related to earthquake damage mitigation.

It's also pushed the professions to look at how cities work in the event of disasters. Landscape architects that I met with have been saying that city parks and open space may have three different roles. On a nice spring day they are parks but, immediately after an earthquake – if trees are planted in a different pattern – they can also be the place where helicopters can land safely to evacuate people. And over the two years of reconstruction, the same park may be used for emergency accommodation or community meeting spaces. So a landscape design might need to have three overlays and this is having an impact on how the professions see the work.

The reason I was asked to Christchurch, interestingly, was that David Shepherd saw the work Healthabitat presented in Bangladesh earlier this year, and he remarked, 'Some of those principles could be applied to the city being remade in New Zealand.' That was a tenuous connection, I thought. But having been there, I can say that some of the health principles, and how our work engages people, in the remaking of places, could be used in a developed world context such as post-earthquake New Zealand.

Finally, with the global financial crisis hitting colleagues in the architectural profession in Australia, in fact, worldwide, what will this mean for the profession at large? ▶ It's probably the question of the moment. If I had to look at history, I would say that there is very little chance that we're going to change the way we work as a profession. I don't think there's a lot of evidence to show that happening in Australia. Now this conservatism is not what my heart would like to happen. But, think about this: over the last two or three decades, the entrenched conservatism of architectures has not only 'lost' us landscape to the landscape architect, but also, and worse I think, landscape concepts and processes been relegated from architecture. We lost interiors; we lost construction engineering. I think we lost the environment a while ago to environmental engineers. We've lost the digital revolution and we've lost the building of buildings to project managers.

We've lost most of the profession, and while we seem to have become expert at giving away things, at the same time, we look for more clients, greater recognition and new modes of working. It's very hard to see how we're going to be able to become more and more focused on less and less and then expect to see more clients turning up and working in a much more multi-disciplinary way.

When Healthabitat was representing Australia at the Venice Architectural Biennale in 2012, the main interest in our work was from the developing world or countries that aren't the most affluent. Without question, they were the people who stayed and talked and we have communicated with since. They identified with the work because it is the bulk of the work they have to do in their countries.

Even the smart media firms that were employed by the Institute of Architects to promote the exhibits in that Venice Biennale were stumped when they were trying to brand what Healthabitat does – and found it wasn't a building. They were looking for a picture of some sort of 'whiz-bang' new type of building that solved health issues. They couldn't quite understand why we were contacted separately by sustainability, and environmental and health journals saying, this is a health story, this is an environment story, or this is a sustainability or human story.

I will be so bold as to say that forging the link between health and environment is the last chance for our profession. I'm not sure we have too many more options left after that. Disasters bring this into crystal clear focus that should be understood by all. The well-being of people and how they survive in either a destroyed or disrupted environment should direct us to the well-being and health of people and the environment in general. So, for a suburban dweller in Sydney or Melbourne or Darwin, the focus of architecture should be on the well-being of people and the well-being of the places they live in.

They are interconnected and if we don't know that by now we never will. If we have the skills to reflect on architecture in these terms, then I think issues of natural disasters, the suburban challenge and the urban challenge will not look to be that different. Health and the environment will define the skills and partnerships we will need, as will the next generation of architects. If we miss this opportunity I'm not sure that we will change our clients or our mode of working or end up with a more multidisciplinary problem-solving approach.

You have made an interesting point because that interface between public health and architecture is such a critical one you would think it should be a core subject in an architectural education, but it is not even an elective in most design programmes. ▶ It's about the identification of the problem. When Healthabitat helped Colin James, a visionary architect and educator, set up a 'Housing for Health' elective between architecture and the health sciences school at Sydney University, he soon had the nursing faculty involved, and then he got the planners involved. He expanded the vision of architecture.

The core was health. The architecture students fronted on the first day saying, 'What they hell has health got to do with anything?' And the health students were saying, 'What the hell has architecture got to do with anything?' What a good starting point! It was a real stand-off on day one; but after a couple of weeks of the course they realized that both sides had a lot to contribute to solving complex problems. For starters, we have different ways of viewing the world. In a world of increasingly complex problems, we need a broader-skilled architectural profession with strong links to our friends in a range of varied professions, and we need a strong connection to every community in which we work: architecture focusing on the well-being of people and the places they need to survive. Is this humanitarian? Or simply human?

Why did you choose to feature the Nepal Sanitation Program to demonstrate your work? ▶ It was started relatively recently in the history of Healthabitat but shows concisely the impact of design on the living environment and health. What began as a project to construct toilets to remove human waste safely, quickly transformed into a project that addressed problems of smoke-related illness caused by cooking with green timber in enclosed houses. The design solution removes human waste and also provides free, smokeless cooking fuel from the combined human and animal waste. The work has also built a local team capable of carrying out all aspects of the work and is now training teams in new, participating villages.

PAUL PHOLEROS

The Nepal Sanitation Program
Nepal

△
The Nepal Sanitation Program aims
to improve community health through
infrastructure upgrades.

Project type
Sanitation programme

Architectural firm
Healthabitat

Design team
**Healthabitat, CHDS Nepal, Rotary
Club of Many Warringah and the
development committee from each
participating village**

Donors
**Each Nepali family contributed
cash and in-kind, supplemented by
international donations to specific
families**

End client
**Families in three villages (to date)
in Nepal**

Location of project
**Kathmandu Valley, Kavre District,
Nepal**

Size
**102 toilets and waste water
systems installed (as of June 2013)
for approximately 1,000 people**

Date completed
Commenced 2007 and ongoing

Cost
$153,000

PAUL PHOLEROS

The Nepal Sanitation Program
Nepal

The Nepal Sanitation Program constructs toilets to remove human waste safely, provides hand washing facilities and uses human waste, combined with animal waste, to provide 3–4 hours of free, smokeless cooking fuel daily. Working with a local partner, CHDS (Nepal), we have built a local team capable of carrying out all aspects of the work and which is now training teams in new, participating villages. To date over 100 toilets and waste systems have been completed in three villages and are being used by over 1,000 people.

◁
Bio-gas construction underway with community participation.

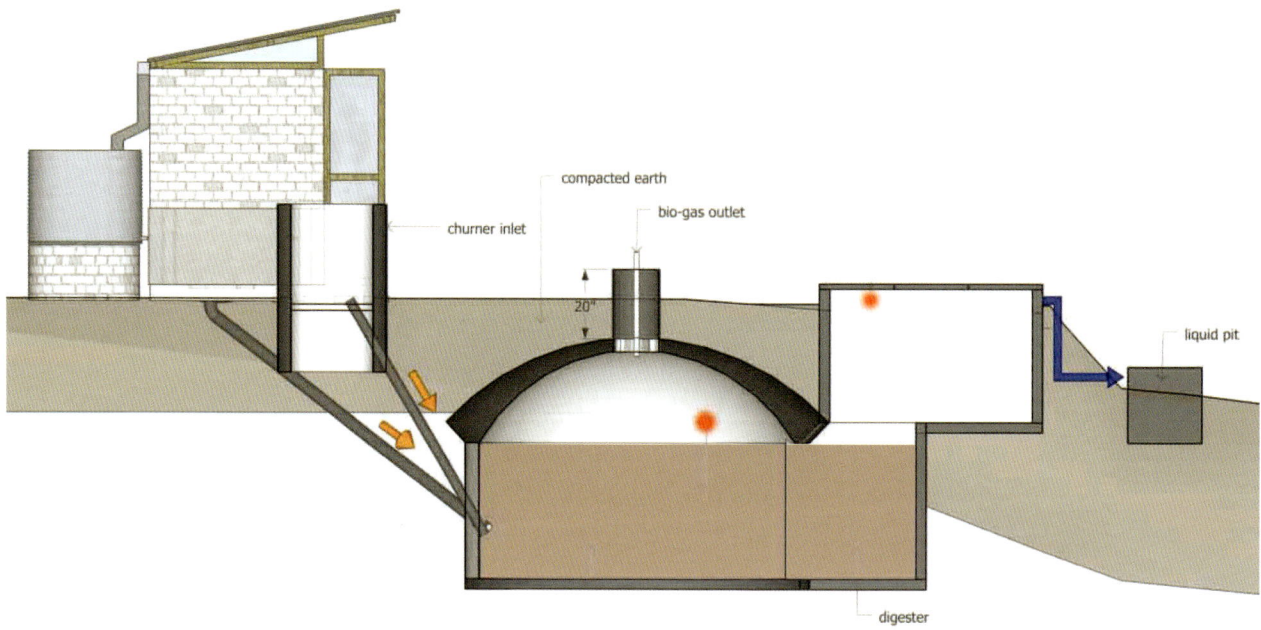

compacted earth

bio-gas outlet

churner inlet

20°

liquid pit

digester

△
Rendered section of toilet and waste
system design for the Nepali villages
sanitation upgrade project.

PATAMA ROONRAKWIT

MANAGING DIRECTOR
**COMMUNITY ARCHITECTS
FOR SHELTER AND ENVIRONMENT**
www.casestudio.info

Patama Roonrakwit

studied architecture at Silpakorn University, Bangkok, and at the Centre for Development and Emergency Practice at Oxford Brookes University. Roonrakwit is currently the Managing Director of Community Architects for Shelter and Environment (CASE), which she founded in 1997. The group works with a humanitarian and anthropological approach to creating appropriate housing for the urban poor in informal settlements. CASE projects involve community members as participants in the process of improving their shelter and environment – a process including surveying and mapping communities, group meetings and workshops, and the completion of new homes.

When you work with the poor you are not allowed to spend a lot. And when the poor have to spend their own money, it's even more important because you [as an architect] cannot make mistakes, they cannot afford mistakes.

||||||||||||||||||||||||||||||||||||||||||||

PATAMA ROONRAKWIT

COMMUNITY ARCHITECTS FOR
SHELTER AND ENVIRONMENT

Note: This interview was undertaken by Ifte Ahmed on behalf of Esther Charlesworth

Patama, you studied development and emergency practice at Oxford Brookes University, but where did you do your original architecture qualifications? ▸ I finished my first architecture degree twenty years ago at Silpakorn University in Bangkok. I then did my Masters at Oxford Brookes in 1994 and 1995. I then organized many courses for them in Bangkok, in Vietnam, in Cambodia and in Laos.

I once heard you say that architects are 'trained to be the recognized experts and to function more as a dictator when it comes to decision-making'. ▸ Most of the time, architects think that what they've learnt makes them an expert, that they always know better. That they know where and how people should live, in what or where they should be, what is the good environment. I think this is wrong because the architect will not always be there. I mean, after you design, you leave. I have the sense that for so many projects, after they are built, the owner has to knock down or add something, change this, change that. This is a waste of money. And it's not very healthy working this way, and especially when you work with the poor. They don't have that money to fix the architect's mistakes.

So it's better to think and work in another way. The architectural knowledge and skills I learnt are important, but they never taught me that the design process should be done by an architect in partnership with, and as a servant of, the owner of the place. Yet this saves cost and also makes the building more efficient. When you work with the poor you are not allowed to spend a lot. And when the poor have to spend their own money, it's even more important because you cannot make mistakes, they cannot afford mistakes.

Tell me about your work in the development and disaster field and how that relates to the skills learnt in your architecture degree. ▸ I use the discipline of architecture as a tool to communicate with people. At the moment, I am working on a market in the Min Buri district of Bangkok. In fact, we have been working with this community for almost seven years. It's a covered market, and it is being built little by little as they can afford it. This is a healthier way to work with people because we are not just changing the physical environment. The most important change is changing is … I don't know the word in English … the way of thinking. Yes, the perception. Unfortunately, poor people often find it difficult to believe in themselves, and so wait for someone to lead. Instead, I use architectural design thinking to encourage them to be more confident.

So my way of working is not about changing or improving the physical environment. To improve the physical you have to improve all your life. Life is a valuable but transient thing, after all. Once we can change our minds, we can see things in new ways. We can then know what we want, know how to plan for it, how to live longer and how to do things that last longer. This is a much better way than just improving the physical things.

In terms of the technical aspects, my studies help a lot. But the way of working on design with communities, not really. I had to develop a lot of my own techniques to work with people on the ground.

Many people would call this humanitarian architecture. Does this term have any relevance for you? ▶ Every architect should be focused on the needs of their client, whether we work for rich or poor people. Even if you build a rich and expensive house, that's for people as well. So I think you should be more concerned about this work, instead of asking 'Am I a normal architect or a company architect or a humanitarian architect?'

Can you tell us about the housing you designed for the homeless under the Bangkok Bridge? ▶ The government provided land so the homeless could be relocated from under the seventy-eight bridges in Bangkok, and the Asian Coalition for Housing Rights (ACHR) asked me to do the designs for these people. It was quite difficult because there was no budget, nothing. ACHR supported us through the UN's Young Professionals Program. I worked with two or three quite new young architects who joined me on this project.

We organized a meeting with the homeless people living under the bridges, and people came from around thirty bridges all over Bangkok, although they needed one or two days to come.

I didn't know what to do but I had to find out. So the first session was called 'Dream House'. I asked them to explain what their dream house would look like. This was to break the ice as well as to see what everyone was thinking. I found that it wasn't very difficult. And they were able to very quickly indicate that they didn't need something luxurious or fancy, they just need a space to sleep.

And then from that, I started to learn with them in order to summarize the design. I didn't have any idea about how much space they wanted or what the best layout would be. So we played design games and we found out what the kitchen size should be – this many square metres – and then we found out what the bedroom size should be.

△
CASE temporary housing as part of post-tsunami housing reconstruction in Bang Muang, Thailand (2004/2005).

We then played a game with paper and placed stickers on it, like a model. And I also marked out the real scale on the floor so we could all see. And then the task was to put it together to make a house. So they made a house from the bedrooms and kitchens. I did that because I have found that when you start thinking about a new house, many people just think of their own space. It is harder to think about the community. So once they all finished their houses, I asked them to put them together as a community – and it became a slum again and they saw that themselves. So they said, 'No. This is not right. We have to leave some space for this and for that.' And that played out as an agreement across community. And then we played with other designs until, finally, we got an affordable design. And it's not just affordable in terms that you can build it now. You don't have to complete it in one term. You can be incremental. You can build so much, leave it until you get some money and then fill in the rest.

Can you please tell me about Community Architects for Shelter and Environment (CASE)? ▶ I started CASE with a classmate from Oxford Brookes. After we had worked on some projects in Thailand, he said, 'Why don't we call ourselves something so people can recognize who we are?' So, we named our group CASE. And then more architects came to me, people who want to work in this field. They came to me and I said, 'I don't have much money.' We had a small budget from the ACHR's Young Professionals Program, but not enough money to hire anyone. However, that didn't matter and we started with one, two, three, four and then up to five staff, and we expanded to many projects. It was like a club that architects could join. During the week, they had full-time jobs and on Saturday or Sunday they could come to work with us. Also, every summer break and holiday we now accept architect students to be trained in the office. We get more than twenty trainees here and we send them to work in a community.

We had a lot of financial problems at first. So we decided to register CASE as a company so that we could earn some money from normal commercial projects as well. We retained our emphasis on housing, and did housing design mainly for the middle class. Middle class is what I call the 'informal urban poor'. They are poor and they have housing problems, but nobody helps them because they are not considered as poor as people in slums. So I started to work with this group as well and we earned some money.

Is this the kind of practice that all architects should be doing?
▶ I don't do Robin Hood. I don't steal. But I try to get a share from the rich or from the middle class and then give it to the poor. I work with the poor for free, but I need to survive myself. I've been thinking of the informal urban poor for quite a long time. I always say to my students or young architects, 'Look, once you are an architect, you can choose to serve everyone not just the rich.' Because I remember ten or fifteen years back when I started working with the poor, many architects asked me if was I crazy. 'You're not an architect', they would say, 'You're a social worker.' They didn't look at this group as clients at all.

I don't want to compete with housing estates or developers. I try to offer an option that allows people to have their own house the way they like with the budget that they have. And I think every architect can do this.

Getting back to your family background, can you talk a little bit about your parents? ▶ My father was a technical college teacher, more like an architect helper and that kind of thing. But I have two uncles who are architects. And my mom was a teacher at a primary school. And she likes doing handicraft, drawing things. When I was a child I didn't have many toys but something that I did have still stays in my mind. It was a big box of coloured pencils and paints. I was allowed to draw and paint on two walls in my house. All it takes is two walls; with two walls you can do anything.

When I came back from Oxford Brookes, I was working in the

> I don't do Robin Hood. I don't steal. But I try to get a share from the rich or from the middle class and then give it to the poor. I work with the poor for free, but I need to survive myself.

PATAMA
ROONRAKWIT

△
CASE information centre timber detailing and decking, Phang Nga, Thailand.

slums and my office was shared with an NGO. When my mom visited me at work, she was totally confused. She's like, 'I thought that you come back from England and you would do something better than this architecture for the poor. You can be a lecturer.' She didn't understand then but finally, little by little, she has come to understand.

What about your colleagues who are doing regular mainstream architecture, what do they think about your work? ▶ Now some understand. And I have been recognized for quite some time as an architect who has done a good job.

Architects are quite often missing in action in emergency, long-term post-disaster recovery and that kind of work. Why is it like that? ▶ In a country like Thailand if you work in this kind of architecture you don't

earn much. But for the Western architect, you can earn a lot from this, right? There are so many programmes that you can get money from. But here, it's not like that. I think architects still see this as charity work, not serious work that you can survive on.

So what kind of post-disaster work have you done?
▶ Thailand needed so many architects after the 2004 tsunami. Some CASE members went to this area, to that area, to so many places. We did a temporary shelter in Phang Nga province in the south of Thailand. And after that, I designed and built a knowledge centre for tsunami victims in Bang Muang, also in Phang Nga. My friends did schools.

Very early on I realized that people couldn't say what they wanted. Many were still shocked, they're looking for missing family

members. We got land from one temple in Phang Nga and we tried to think of what kind of temporary shelter we should make, but we realized that it wasn't only shelter that was needed. I mean after the state of shock, people needed to be in a very good place. So our idea was that it shouldn't be like a barracks. It should be something that's flexible, something that people can adapt by themselves, and that can happily fit in three or four or five or six family members.

And this temporary shelter should be a good example or model that people can go back to their own places and build affordable houses. So we designed a unit, 1.2 m × 2.4 m – that's the normal size of construction material in Thailand – that they could join together to make two or four or eight units, put together as modules. We built thirty and, when we came back, we found seventy-two that people had built by themselves. They were arranged in clusters so people can look at each other and become friends. After all, they were going to be there for years before going back to their own places. They're now growing their vegetables and things. It's like a village.

And you used a lot of recycled materials in your projects?
▶ Yes. We had to because there was no money. It wasn't that we necessarily wanted to be green. We do this because we don't have enough money, that's why we use recycled materials, reuse the grey water and try to use wind power. Materials collected from broken structures were free. We had to clean them, polish them and then fix them. And the labour was free. So the budget was zero.

You also work on flood issues in Bangkok. Has that been successful? ▶ After the terrible floods in 2011, I was asked by many clients to design a house that they can live in during a flood. So many people were concerned about this. This really was quite odd. I would ask them, 'Do you want to be in your house when it floods? You cannot just stay there. You need a boat.'

Everybody is like, 'Oh, we need this. We need that.' I got a grant from the Ministry of Culture to design a temporary shelter that can float and then be developed into a permanent house. But nobody used it. So I don't know. It's a trend or a fashion that just goes on endlessly and stops you from working on something serious.

Do architects always have a role in emergencies? Do they have a role at all? If so, what is it? ▶ They should have. I think many architects in Thailand are now becoming very concerned about this.

There are now many design not-for-profits – like Architects Without Frontiers or Architecture for Humanity – around the world. Are there many agencies like these in Thailand? ▶ No. From what I see, it's easier in a Western or developed country to find a sponsor or budget to work in this field, and you can survive as well. But here, it's not like that.

Some architects like to experiment after disasters. They design structures out of cardboard tubes or ones like igloos. Why do they do it? Is this design innovation? ▶ It's a toy to them. I mean, if they are happy doing that then let them. I like thinking about different designs. You know, 'What if you do this? Will it work or not?' Architects are like that. We like creating things, thinking of something new. It's fun to do that. So why architects keep doing this? Because it's fun.

Why have you chosen the tsunami reconstruction temporary housing and information centre project in Phang Nga Province, Thailand, to illustrate some of the principles you have been discussing in our interview? ▶ It was a very good example of people taking on a project. We built thirty housing units and left and then when we came back one day we found seventy-two more. The people had made them themselves, and arranged them so people can look at each other and become friends, like a village.

My Mum was totally confused. She's like, 'I thought that you come back from England and you would do something better than this architecture for the poor.'

PATAMA ROONRAKWIT

Tsunami reconstruction: Temporary housing and information centre
Bang Muang, Phang Nga Province, Thailand

△
Thirty-two CASE temporary housing
units were constructed with the
involvement of tsunami-devastated
communities in Phang Nga, Thailand.

Project type		Donors
Temporary housing		**CARE International**
Architectural firm		End client
Community Architects for Shelter and Environment (CASE)		**Victims of the 2004 tsunami in Phuket, Thailand**
Principal architect		Location of project
Patama Roonrakwit		**Bang Muang, Phang Nga Province, Thailand**
Design team		Date completed
Architects from CASE and young volunteer architects		**February 2005**

Tsunami reconstruction: Temporary housing and information centre
Bang Muang, Phang Nga Province, Thailand

Very soon after the tsunami the CASE team assisted tsunami victims to build temporary housing on land donated by a local Buddhist temple and funded by CARE International, and also an information centre with dormitories. Thirty-two housing units were designed and built in clusters, taking care not to cut down any trees on the site. The houses were simple, adjustable and could be replicated by the local people. The design was based on a 1.2 m × 2.4 m module derived from the dimensions of materials available in the local market, resulting in a typical 2.4 m × 2.4 m unit, which was adjusted to build houses of different forms such as square or L-shaped, according to the site conditions. Materials used included plywood, cement board, fibre-cement roofing and locally available pre-cast RC posts. Similar materials were used in the information centre and all the buildings were raised above the ground to avoid floods and future tsunamis. Even though the housing was supposed to be temporary, residents lived in them for many years after the tsunami as the houses were well built and durable.

◁
Temporary housing under construction in Bang Muang, Thailand.

◁ Some possible configurations of CASE's flexible temporary housing.

▽ Plan and section, temporary housing module for reconstruction project in Bang Muang, Thailand.

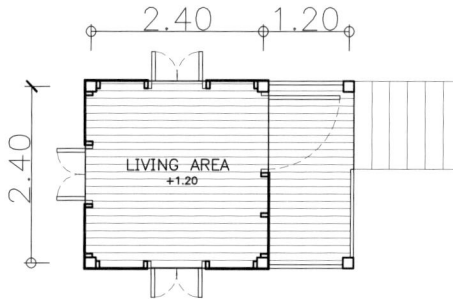

2.40   1.20

2.40

LIVING AREA
+1:20

PLAN
SCALE   1:100

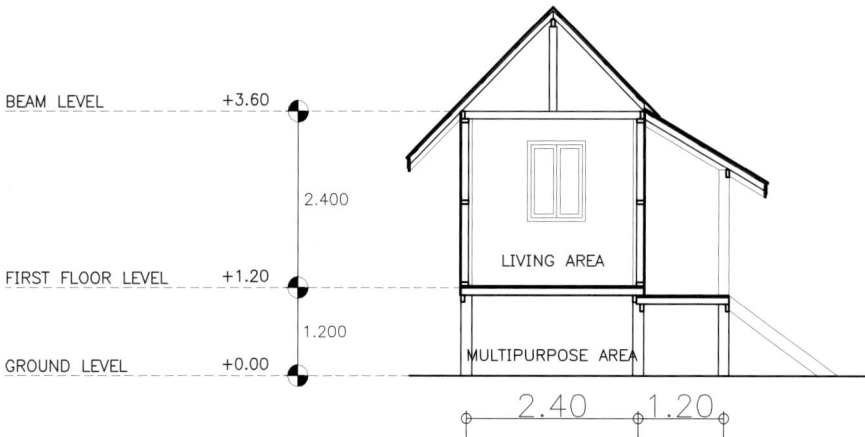

BEAM LEVEL   +3.60

2.400

FIRST FLOOR LEVEL   +1.20

1.200

GROUND LEVEL   +0.00

LIVING AREA

MULTIPURPOSE AREA

2.40   1.20

SECTION
SCALE   1:100

PATAMA
ROONRAKWIT

△
Typical housing cluster sketch, showing the grid developed to avoid cutting down trees on site.

▽
An information centre for victims of the tsunami is constructed, consisting of a group of five units slightly larger than the temporary housing units in Phang Nga, Thailand.

PART TWO

UNIVERSITY-BASED HUMANITARIAN ARCHITECTS

The two architects profiled in this second part both work and research in the post-disaster field. The role of universities and specialized student practice units operating both within and external to the university is critical in disseminating key lessons from the humanitarian design sector to students interested in expanding their future careers in the international development field.

Corum

I dislike the word 'prototype' within humanitarian architecture; if you're going to build something in this space, make it right.

Perkes

All architecture is public ... but not everyone has the same access to architecture and not everyone is treated the same way.

NATHANIEL CORUM

HEAD OF EDUCATION OUTREACH
ARCHITECTURE FOR HUMANITY
www.architectureforhumanity.org

Nathaniel Corum,

an architect with degrees from Stanford and the University of Texas at Austin, is the recipient of a Fulbright Scholarship and a Rose Architectural Fellowship. He collaborates with international teams and diverse communities on planning and design/build projects as the Head of Education Outreach at Architecture for Humanity and as a Senior ECPA Fellow under the auspices of the US Department of State (Energy and Climate Partnership of the Americas). Nathaniel is a member of the art collaborative SPURSE and the Sustainable Native Communities Collaborative. Corum is also author of *Building a straw bale house* from Princeton Architectural Press (2005).

I dislike the word 'prototype' within humanitarian architecture; if you're going to build something in this space, make it right.

|||||||||||||||||||||||||||||||||||||||

NATHANIEL CORUM
ARCHITECTURE FOR HUMANITY

Nathaniel, how did your original design studies prepare you for the kind of community reconstruction work you are involved in now? You trained as a product designer? ▶ At Stanford, I was able to pursue studies that connected the art and engineering faculties. We learnt directly, through making things, in both the studio art and product design departments, and absorbed a growing methodology for creative problem-solving. They'd put us on the spot and challenge us. 'Design something that will present an animated movie using only cardboard and rubber bands. You have two days.' That's the school's brand of design thinking: brainstorming, troubleshooting, problem-solving, rapid prototyping – a celebration of ideas and process. Stanford gave me a degree and a way of approaching diverse design challenges. After working with architects for several years in New York, in the course of an MArch [Master of Architecture] degree at the University of Texas at Austin, I began writing grants for international research work, learning to write my own ticket instead of waiting for the right project to arrive.

Were there courses on community rebuilding like the projects you're doing now in your architecture degree at UT? ▶ The sustainability focus at UT Austin remains strong. The programme influenced me, in that a part of the work now makes use of agricultural co-products and other locally sourced materials and technologies. The 'agri-tecture' practice and community design/build approach came out of my education and upbringing. It was early days in the green building movement. Now, there's a big shift to green building, but UT was in early and put us on a leading edge. Studios featured challenges such as an elder housing complex and a school in rural Africa. There was the feeling that these topics had importance, leading to the discussion and practice of *community design* and *participatory design*.

Where did your commitment to social justice come from? ▶ My parents both had a service mentality. My father was a teacher and my mother was a social worker. They thought it was important to impact people's lives directly and positively. My parents took our family back-to-the-land. We moved to a farm in Vermont where there were all kinds of chores: taking care of crops and trees and animals, and buildings to be built. That had a real effect in terms of making me aware and passionate about the natural world and the idea that I could do things with my own hands. We would make a building when we needed one. My parents went to Harvard, but they taught me that it was good to work with my hands as well as my mind.

How does your background in product design help you conceptualize appropriate solutions for communities in need, because your original design training would be more for the 'high end' of town? ▶ The Stanford design methodology is great, really applicable to architecture among other things. The problem-solving focus, together with a 'let's do it with what we have available right now' attitude, is instrumental to what we're doing today. A fair amount of new technology is being driven by humanitarian issues, whether it's a new vaccine or a water filter. Some of the best current architecture is made in this spirit. How little can you bring with you? What is the architectural equivalent of a Swiss army knife? I gravitate to condensed hardware and architectural pieces that connect and expand to become efficient and useful on the ground. This strategy allows building envelopes to be made with local materials using skills that already reside nearby. Many problems have been created by shipping entire buildings. That's not how to intervene. Asset-based process is the way: working with local people to amplify materials and methods already present on site is a path to replicable and resilient communities.

△
Example of straw bale houses built for Native Americans and undertaken by Corum (photo: Skip Baumhower).

△
AFH's workplace for ocean farmers seeks to revitalize an industry and a community devastated by a tsunami.

The high-end projects I took on early on were fun, learning how to draught by hand and build models. While it was good to have creative latitude and to be designing special projects, a yacht interior and amazing residences, I felt we were working just for wealthy clients, despite huge design needs in communities that hadn't worked with designers. Luckily my career timeline has synched up with a surge of interest in green building, humanitarian design and community design practice.

So, what is this whole humanitarian architecture movement? Does the phrase mean anything? You have said that there have been some ideas that could lead to architects proposing well-meaning but inappropriate solutions in developing countries. ▶ There are a lot of names for this movement; some needing definition. Community design is a funny term because to the lay person it may sound like we're in the practice of designing entire communities. Though it can sometimes amount to that, the concept is to design *with* community on crucial facilities. Ask people what they want and empower them, *the local experts*, to be primary members of the design team. Terms such as 'participatory design' or

'user-focused' design are probably clearer ways to describe the work. Architecture for Humanity pioneered several important parallel threads to empower social design: job creation programmes and micro-enterprise strategies, the concept of 'urban acupuncture' points. We're only able to build a few buildings so we start with key buildings: schools, community centres, business incubators. These buildings are useful for more people and are visitable so community members can take ideas into the design of future structures. Schools are a great place to start, so kids can get tracking and adults have their hands free to do things like rebuilding homes. We create community and business nodes so that local people can begin revitalizing the place they live

84

during challenging times. I think we can do carefully thought-out urban acupuncture. To me, this is the way we can use our design skills in service of the planet and its people.

Currently a humanitarian architecture movement is growing. It may be small but it's got a lot of strength lately.

▶ A lot of the growth is driven by the integrity and excitement of students and young professionals entering the field. Practitioners are listening and learning from what has, and has not, worked; so the field is strengthened. For example, after the lessons learnt from the Tohoku tsunami, we're not going forward in the same way. Small sparkplug projects are really important, replicable quality instead of deployed quantity. Acupuncture interventions accelerating community members' innate abilities. Things like builder training and education are key practices. The devastation in Haiti stems from the poor quality of the concrete used previously. Substandard materials, together with lax building standards, resulted in the collapse of many buildings in Port-au-Prince. We work to develop replicable approaches that communities can take on, creating jobs and skills, adding depth to each community's 'toolbox', adding resilience.

So, the humanitarian architecture movement is growing. It's small but it's got a lot of bandwidth lately. Practitioners are listening and learning from what has, and has not, worked empirically. For example, after the Tohoku tsunami, we have learnt many lessons and we are not going to go forward in the same way now.

You have previously commented that 'Humanitarian design is not the new imperialism; it's the new compassion' [see www.nytimes.com/2010/08/02/arts/design/02iht-design2.html?_r=3&ref=alice_rawsthorn&]. Do you want to expand on this thought? ▶ There is plenty of room in the design field for those looking for more meaning in the work: designing elegant and solid work to benefit people who truly need it. Once you understand where we are in terms of the environment and basic human needs on the planet, it seems appropriate to work with communities on buildings that matter. These ideas lead towards community structures, like schools, and to collaborations with Indigenous communities, international partners, humanitarian designers, thinking in terms of resilient land use and design *with* deep community collaboration. I don't think there's anything imperialistic in any of this. The humanitarian design movement is making the related professions more relevant and inclusive and, yes, more compassionate.

What do you see as the core ethos of Architecture for Humanity, particularly in relationship to working with communities after disasters?

▶ Post-disaster we're looking to fund and create replicable 'acupuncture' projects that will help stabilize and regenerate communities. Always looking to pre-existing strengths and grassroots solutions and partners, we're focused on building a more sustainable future using the power of design. Through a global network of building professionals, Architecture for Humanity brings design, construction and development services to communities in need. One of our mantras is 'get it built'. In practice, this translates to how much high-quality work we can do with the funds we're able to raise. AFH generates significant resources, yet they still translate to the ability to make a handful of buildings after a given disaster – ten or more schools in Haiti, for example. The key is to choose the right projects with the right partners, so the buildings and programmes produced have amplified ripple effects. It's about creative financing, connecting with local teams with innate capacity

> I don't think it's our job to rebuild cities, but I think we can do carefully thought-out urban acupuncture. To me, this is the way we can use our design skills in service of the planet and its people.

and working together to make community-inspired architecture.

What's your specific role in the organization in terms of education? ▶ In addition to design/build work, working to connect international student design teams to real-world projects through educational outreach programmes. These university collaborations are all about leveraging emerging designers and faculty to assist on-the-ground Architecture for Humanity project teams. We're currently working on several built initiatives in the American West and connecting student teams with actual projects in collaboration with universities in Auckland, Barcelona, Oahu, Sydney and Tokyo. Often, students can add crucial assistance and value to projects, running down research and design avenues to support our lean HQ teams.

Is this like the post-disaster projects you have been doing with the Master of Emergency Architecture programme in Barcelona? I believe you were recently involved in student projects after the Rio floods in January 2011, where housing for sixty-one families is already under construction? ▶ In addition to multiple studios with design schools in Australia, New Zealand, Japan and the United States we've enjoyed an ongoing collaboration with the Sustainable Emergency Architecture programme in Barcelona for the past several years. Working with Masters candidates and faculty at UIC Barcelona, [ESARQ UIC (Escuela Tècnica Superior de Arquitectura de la Universitat Internacional de Catalunya) www.uic.es/esarq] we've been

connecting academic teams with design challenges ranging from self-help adobe housing requested by women in rural communities in Oaxaca, Mexico to post-flood community facilities for families whose homes were washed away in a rural Brazilian river valley. In each case, field trips allowed our team to participate in activities directly: gathering information, surveying sites, providing design/build responses, sharing knowledge and energy and informing and adding value to a range of rebuilding efforts.

I believe you also worked with students to build a fishermen's workplace or 'banya' in Japan? Can you tell me about that experience? ▶ Working with students and faculty from the Kyoto University of Art and Design, we researched and visited Shizugawa, Japan; a small coastal community completely levelled by the Tohoku earthquake and tsunami. Answering the call of a group of kelp farmers who joined together to rebuild a base for their continued livelihoods, our studio team helped AFH programme staff and community members to design and build a new workplace – called a *banya* in Japanese. Through interviewing and working alongside local ocean farmers, our group clarified 'client' needs and designed and built a response – furnishings, furniture, platforms for work and relaxation – to kit out the *banya* built by Architecture for Humanity that is now in use in the Tohoku zone.

Why do you think there has been such a rise in design not-for-profits in the last decade? For example, Architecture Sans Frontières (ASF) is now a network of more than fifty

not-for-profit design agencies working across Asia, Africa, Latin America and Europe. Except for groups like Rural Studio, there was nothing like this twenty years ago. ▶ Yes. There is a new wave. There are many reasons for it, but clearly a lot of us are increasingly seeking deep meaning through design practice. If you're a doctor you're hopefully able to heal people directly, but how do you do this as an architect? Humanitarian architecture is our profession's healing gesture: a growing frontier in architecture that is increasingly inclusive and focused on working with those who have historically not benefited from architectural collaboration. You don't give up anything by choosing this path. In humanitarian design the aesthetics, the materiality, the opportunity to make something useful, beautiful and lasting are all heightened, in fact. The challenge is greater and, arguably the need for beauty and solid design is also greater after events like Katrina, Christchurch, Port-au-Prince and Tohuku.

How do you think the design or the design problem-solving processes are different working with Native American communities compared to working with communities in Haiti or New Orleans after a disaster? Are they the same but different? What are your thoughts about that? ▶ We're always trying to work in a way that is native-to-place regardless of the community partner. The Native American work has brought this front and centre and, I believe, improved our ability to deliver culturally appropriate design for other communities with fewer traditional reference points. Indigenous knowledge and technology is a great place to access design inspiration, whether it's a post-disaster scenario or a community with severe architecture deficits. Being informed by what has worked in a given place over the long haul is a sound point of departure for a design team. This doesn't mean going back in time, but rather bringing useful thinking and place forms forward, together with non-gratuitous technology. In post-quake Haiti a lot of the best thinking stems from finding the best local architects and the exemplary vernacular buildings that have withstood earthquakes and other challenges. Understanding local knowledge through listening to long-term residents and gaining density-of-fact around what has worked previously in a given situation is crucial. The site and the people are always the most solid places for designers and community members to begin collaborating and are foundational to good community architecture and game-changing results on the ground. Even in the case of the Plastiki Expedition, we looked to long-term ocean residents for inspiration. The Plastiki cabin shell resists rogue waves with help from the geometries of ancient sources: horseshoe crabs and sea turtles. This strategy allows the building envelope to be made with local materials using skills of the people who are already residing nearby. Many problems have been created by shipping whole buildings. That's not how we should intervene. Asset-based process is the way: working with local people, materials and methods to achieve true replicability and resilience.

> ## Humanitarian architecture is our profession's healing gesture.

When I started working in Bosnia nearly two decades ago, there were a lot of engineers, doctors, lawyers, but architects weren't in the scene at all and that sort of got my mind ticking, you know – why? But perhaps it's shifted a bit since the Indian Ocean tsunami and now there are a lot more design professionals involved in somewhere like Haiti. Why is it, do you think, that architects haven't really been involved in this work and given that we all know that there are going to be more disasters, it's a strange kind of professional conundrum?

▸ Our generation has been the first wave that's come through that has really pushed community design and disaster-response design forward, standing on the shoulders of people like Samuel Mockbee, of course. There's always been a place for pro bono work in the legal profession as well as a mandate for doctors to do humanitarian work. Architecture came to the party a bit late. A lot of buildings are built without architects by owner-builders, design-builders or engineer-builders. Architects had lost some ground by 2001, and were largely servicing wealthy clients and corporations. There's nothing wrong with doing this work, yet lately we're finding ways and means to work with a wider range of clients. Some of the contributing factors are: new financing mechanisms, the rise of philanthropy, increasing climate chaos and the growing network within the humanitarian design movement enabling designers to form teams, to initiate funding campaigns and to make space in their portfolios for pro bono projects.

How is architecture in the post-disaster field different?

▸ These are projects that can't go sideways. These designs need to work. I dislike the word 'prototype' within humanitarian architecture; if you're going to build something in this space, make it right. Be your own guinea pig; test new ideas closer to home. Humanitarian design responses should be *less* experimental since we're typically working in more challenging environments with community members who cannot afford failure. Already things may not arrive on time and you can't just go down to the hardware store to pick up missing parts. These designs need to be solid. You can't experiment with a community unless you're confident that a given approach has the best chance of success and clearly relates to community-requested services.

How do we best equip or train young architects to get involved in the humanitarian field? I mean clearly now there are emerging postgraduate courses in this area, but what is the right way to train architects? Because it's not just, 'Hey I've finished my graduate degree, I'm ready to go and build some funky buildings in Haiti', which is a popular perception. ▶ There is plenty of work to do in our own communities, where we ourselves tend to have crucial local knowledge and connections. I suggest people start doing things close to home. Situations like New Orleans or post-Sandy New York and New Jersey are places to start for American designers. As for education: the Rural Studio started a design/build chain reaction and now many students are seeking programmes in both design/build and humanitarian architecture. UIC Barcelona, as we discussed, now has a Masters programme in Sustainable Emergency Architecture. As more schools begin to provide such options, field work and real-world collaborations will be more central to the design education process. Architecture has always necessarily been an apprenticeship field. It's important for young humanitarian designers to get a job in the field, and work with people who know what they're doing. It takes initiative and, as in all movements early on, you may have to design and/or fund the opportunity. Write your own ticket.

Nathaniel, why did you choose the *banya* project in Japan as an example of Architecture for Humanity's post-disaster work? ▶ Buildings account for approximately half of global greenhouse gas emissions. Architecture, then, is a dangerous occupation. Practitioners are quite literally given tools to harm the earth and humanity. To reverse this trend, we're engaging with communities to create culturally appropriate, healthy and resilient architecture sited within regenerative landscapes. One example is the ocean farmers' workplace, or *banya*, in post-tsunami Japan. Created by Architecture for Humanity in collaboration with long-time residents and students, this project provides a post-disaster centre to anchor sustainable kelp and oyster farming businesses while re-energizing a devastated community.

88

NATHANIEL CORUM

Shizugawa fishermen's workplace and warehouse
Shizugawa, Miyagi, Japan

△
Students collaborate with Shizugawa fishermen to design a workshop and warehouse to restore an industry in a tsunami-devastated community.

Project type
Community infrastructure

Architectural firm
Architecture for Humanity

Building fabrication
Silhouette Spice, Japan

Academic partner
Kyoto University of Art and Design

Design workshop facilitators
Daijiro Mizuno and Nathaniel Corum

Donors
Pact

End client
Fifteen Motohama fishermen

Location of project
Shizugawa, Minami-sariku-cho, Miyagi, Japan

Size
126 m²

Date completed
Ongoing

Cost
$108,000

NATHANIEL CORUM

Shizugawa fishermen's workplace and warehouse
Shizugawa, Miyagi, Japan

In Shizugawa, fifteen fishermen lost nearly everything in the Tohoku earthquake and tsunami (a few boats and some materials survived the quake and tsunami). Architecture for Humanity, in collaboration with long-time residents and students, designed and built a new workplace and warehouse (called a '*banya*' in Japanese). Although the fishermen previously operated independently, this project provides a post-disaster base of operations for a collective aquafarming business to re-energize the devastated community.

◁
A workplace and warehouse for the Shizugawa fishermen.

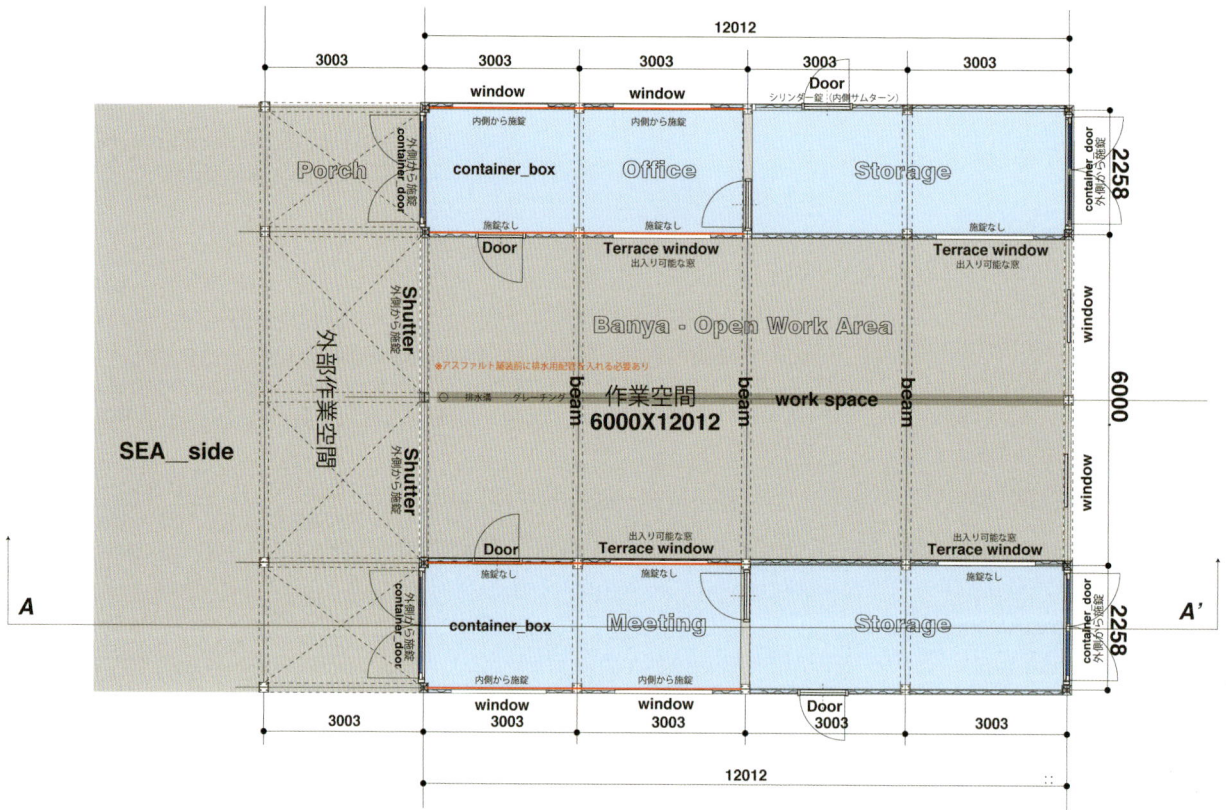

As-built plan of fishermen's workplace and warehouse.

Plan labels:

12012

3003 | 3003 | 3003 | 3003 | 3003

window | window | Door
シリンダー錠（内側サムターン）

内側から施錠 | 内側から施錠

container_box | Office | Storage

施錠なし | 施錠なし | 施錠なし

Door | Terrace window
出入り可能な窓 | Terrace window
出入り可能な窓

Porch

外側から施錠
container_door

2258

container_door
施錠から施錠

Shutter
外側から施錠

外部作業空間

SEA__side

Banya · Open Work Area

※アスファルト舗装前に排水用配管を入れる必要あり

排水溝　グレーチング

作業空間
6000X12012

beam | work space | beam | beam

6000

window

window

Shutter
外側から施錠

A

出入り可能な窓
Terrace window

Door | 出入り可能な窓
Terrace window

施錠なし | 施錠なし | 施錠なし

container_box | Meeting | Storage

2258

container_door
施錠から施錠

A'

内側から施錠 | 内側から施錠

window
3003 | window
3003 | Door
3003

3003 | 3003

12012

NATHANIEL
CORUM

David Perkes

is an architect and an Associate Professor in the College of Architecture, Art + Design, at Mississippi State University. He is the Founding Director of the Gulf Coast Community Design Studio, a professional outreach programme of the university. The studio was established soon after Hurricane Katrina to provide planning and architectural design support to Mississippi Gulf Coast communities and non-profit organizations. The design studio works in close partnership with the East Biloxi Coordination and Relief Center and has assisted in the renovation of hundreds of damaged homes and over fifty new house projects in East Biloxi. David has a Master of Environmental Design degree from Yale School of Architecture, a Master of Architecture degree from the University of Utah and a Bachelor of Science degree in Civil and Environmental Engineering from Utah State University. In 2004 David was awarded a Loeb Fellowship from the Harvard Graduate School of Design.

DAVID PERKES

DIRECTOR
GULF COAST COMMUNITY DESIGN STUDIO
MISSISSIPPI STATE UNIVERSITY
www.gccds.org

As an architect, if you have these sorts of skills they ought to show up in some way where they can make a difference.

|||||||||||||||||||||||||||||||||||||||

DAVID PERKES

GULF COAST COMMUNITY
DESIGN STUDIO
MISSISSIPPI STATE UNIVERSITY

David, how did your original architecture studies train you for the kind of work that you have been doing in Biloxi over the last three or four years?

▶ I don't think there was anything directly from school. However, in a very simple way it was very important in our post-disaster work to know how to run a practice, how to get building permits, how to do a set of drawings and how to manage new interns that need to be taught the skills not taught in school. My commitment to this work probably has more to do with wanting to put those kinds of skills to work than I may have explicitly been taught; it probably came as much from my very pragmatic upbringing.

I grew up on a dairy farm where work was just part of life. I grew up in a Mormon culture, a kind of pioneer culture, a pragmatic culture of getting things done. But also a culture that says that your beliefs ought to show up in your actions. As an architect, if you have these sorts of skills they ought to show up in some way where they can make a difference, where they can be beneficial.

So what was your journey from engineering to architecture school and then to what you're doing now with the Gulf Coast Community Design Studio?

▶ I got into architecture and then I started practising. I actually worked in Robert Venturi's office for four years in Philadelphia, and then started teaching at Temple University. I realized I enjoyed teaching and felt I could really make a difference through teaching. So I went back to school, and that is how I went to Yale for their Master of Environmental Design programme. I ended up in Jackson, Mississippi, for seven years and I got a Loeb Fellowship at Harvard University which was, for me, such a great gift.

Jim Stockard, the Director of the Loeb programme, said on the first day, 'We don't really expect anything of you while you're here; you can do whatever you want, but when you leave we expect you to go out and change the world.' Like here's the deal: we give you this year and expect that you pay it back after you get out. And that really made sense to me. I finished my Loeb Fellowship in 2004 and I was already looking around when Hurricane Katrina came. It was one of those times of my life – and I don't say this with any kind of pride because actually it was a terrifying feeling – I said, okay, something has to be done, and I was the person that should do it. I had all the tools in hand. I was already running a design centre in Jackson and there's only one school of architecture in the State of Mississippi. So I said to the Dean I really need to figure out how we can do something on the coast, something that will really make a difference. It was kind of like Jim Stockard in my mind saying 'Go out and change the world.' And this sense of duty? That's part of my deeper culture as well.

That way of thinking has shaped the whole making and running of the Design Studio. I have this very simple, pragmatic question that we ask ourselves, 'How can we be useful?' We're not saying 'What do we want to do here?' It's more like 'How can we be of help?' This has been an important way to bring the right people to the Studio. I think every organization has a certain kind of culture, an energizing set of values and I've been really fortunate that the people that work at the Design Studio seem to be in tune with those values.

The Gulf Coast Community Design Studio is a programme of the College of Architecture for Mississippi State University, but it doesn't function much like a university programme. It functions much more like a design practice. It's possible to really leverage and build upon and then, sometimes, actually push against the university to create a practice that can really address needs in a way that will make sense for the university. In the last four, five years we've always had around twelve people, all full-time employees. From the university's point of view, they see us the same way as other research centres. And we do have some research but, day-to-day, we are really a very active design studio where we do all the things that make up a practice.

The work environment is an interesting, open platform, where the case management, the coordination of volunteers by a non-profit organization and our Design Studio's work all occur

△
New house built in 2008 in Biloxi, Mississippi, as part of Gulf Coast Community Design Studio's reconstruction efforts following Hurricane Katrina.

> We ask ourselves, 'How can we be useful?' We're not saying, 'What do we want to do here?' It's more like, 'How can we be of help?'

in the same space. And this is another reason why we are unlikely heroes, because we're embedded in this other non-profit organization. This has been very good for us because the same people that we are doing work with, on their house designs, are going through other sorts of case management issues right here. It's also been very healthy for us because we are in the same work environment as people who are not architects and have very different values and language. We are learning every day about people's true needs – and to be humble about our skills in the face of these.

David, this public interest design movement that some are calling 'humanitarian architecture' – does the term resonate with you? ▶ It's such a good question. When I was trying to help the American Institute of Architects see needs-driven design as being different to client-driven design, they didn't like the title. 'All architecture is about need', they said. They felt the name 'needs-driven' was too broad.

And with the term 'public interest architecture', people often ask 'Isn't all architecture public?' But I reply, 'Yes, all architecture is public but not all architecture is in the public interest. Also, not everyone has the same

access to architecture and not everyone is treated the same way.' Whatever you call it, whether it's 'humanitarian' or 'needs-driven' or 'public interest' or 'community' architecture, if you believe in equity then it should show up not only in your process but also in the end result. Some of the questions that I ask myself are: what would equity look like in this project, where would it show up? If you believe in sustainability, what would it look like? How would you know if those values are actually showing up in the work? If we are interested in community involvement, what would it look like?

What are the roles for architects beyond those of the traditional kind of practices that were introduced to us in design school? ▶ Let me tell you about Bill Stallworth. When I first met him in Biloxi, he was running an *ad hoc* kind of operation out of a house where volunteers were coming to get work orders. He had one big map on the wall, and a bunch of post-it notes and said 'That's the map we use to split the volunteers into groups and work out where they should be working.'

I said 'Bill, we can make a map for you.' And he said 'Architects make maps?' And I said 'Sure.'

So we brought back a stack of grid maps that have been

an invaluable tool for years. This was just weeks after a new urbanist planning team came and purported to show the community what their community could look like with watercolour renderings of picturesque streets. As therapeutic as that was, for a lot of people it was like, 'No, you don't get it. We just need help.'

But maps? Now they were useful. Volunteers could take a map and find where they were supposed to be working. They could take the thing with them. There were no street signs; all the street signs were gone. Architects have these strong visualization and graphical skills, and they can produce good instruments for decision making. Time and time again that's what has come out. The kind of organizational skills of an architect that are really needed, a kind of structural, visual way of thinking that puts things in front of people in a way that often clarifies what the work is and how it needs to be done. The way of thinking that we take for granted in a building design is very helpful for a lot of other complicated systems that need to be organized to help people see how the pieces fit together.

There seems to be two broad models of housing reconstruction in the New Orleans region. One might be seen as a 'bottom-up' approach, working side-by-side with the local community collaborating on an appropriate design. The second seems to be based upon ideas from elsewhere with people trying to make them fit the site, regardless of context, budget and community. Is that an accurate description? ▶ I think so. However, there

96

△
Volunteers are involved in the construction of the Broussard Residence, working with the East Biloxi Coordination Relief and Redevelopment Agency.

little bit stifling, limiting, holding the whole thing back.

Did you ever have students bringing ideas to the housing that you were working on that were based on experimental prefabricated solutions? Perhaps, a yurt or shipping container conversion – all those kind of fantasies architecture schools seem to encourage? Did many of them cross your door when working on housing reconstruction in Biloxi? ▶ Oh yes. We actually got funding from the small business administration early on to look at alternative building systems and there was actually a lot of interest, even from the governor's office, to use alternative systems such as modular systems, the panel system – something other than just on-site construction. Some people in the state government saw Katrina as an economic development opportunity. There were also people who thought that if we have to build thousands of houses then we can't do it the way we've done it in the past.

We did a lot of research and engaged a lot of industry people. I had many meetings with various modular housing and panelized people. There were a lot of options and we were involved with a few of them. However, at the end of the day, none of them could compete cost-wise with just building on site as we had so much cheap or free labour because of all the volunteers. As a result, none of these more technical solutions ever made sense to us and the few that did were essentially subsidized by companies that wanted their products highlighted.

are a couple of places where they meet; for example, where some innovation that wouldn't have come from the bottom up is introduced to a project. However, the core of the idea still has its roots in the community. The projects in our work that I'm most pleased with do that, where we've brought in some innovation with either the building system or the way the design approaches the problem. Often these would not have happened if we had just worked with local assets. Asset-based design is important but you also have to bring in resources, something that's not already there as well. And I think it would be a good thing for all of us to understand more clearly how to do

that, because I think the bottom-up approach can be limiting if you're not trying to bring in new resources, if you're limited to what that community can do, and you're not bringing in new information or new skills or new materials and new sorts of expectations.

With Habitat for Humanity (HFH), there are some people who are more progressive and looking to bring things in, but there are others so limited in their thinking that they don't even want to make houses. There are some Habitat projects that are unnecessarily mean and stingy, partly because they say they do not want HFH houses to look extravagant. So sometimes grassroots can be a

What lessons have been learnt from your housing programme in Biloxi and are any of those lessons applicable to other post-disaster contexts? ▶ One of the really important lessons was to do everything you can so that the people in the house are part of the entire process. I actually don't use the word 'design' a lot because many people think it's some kind of extra. So I talk about decision making and planning. When we're talking with a family about their house I'd say that it's obvious they should be part of the decision about how or what they end up with. It shouldn't just be a choice between the colour of the walls or the laminates in the kitchen; they should have a real say in deciding how the floor plan of the house will be organized. It was vital that we learnt how to talk about design in a way that engages and empowers people.

Another lesson was that you can't always manifest long-term commitment to a place by just saying 'Here we are; this is our community too. We might not have been here when the hurricane happened but here we are now.' However, when people realized that we were not there just for a semester, they began to trust us.

And then the third lesson is to really work hard to build strong partnerships and then work hard to keep them and nurture them. It's those partner relationships that maintain a practice. You build strong partnerships based upon good, balanced relationships. We learnt to very deliberately take ourselves out of the role of being paid professionals because then when we're done with the work that relationship is ended. Instead we created partnerships that are going to evolve into future work as well.

And finally, what is the role of the university in this community rebuilding space? ▶ I've pushed the university system quite a bit even though our university isn't like most public universities. I mean all the universities that I know say teaching, research and service are the three missions, right? But here, we don't have a dominant teaching programme, but we are still working, realizing the university's mission. It's not easy to do that in most places because for too many university programmes teaching takes over and limits what the programme can do. Everything has to somehow fit into a timetable and, you know, you have to work with what students can and can't do.

We have a one-year Certificate in Public Design where at any time, three or four of the people in our studio are in this one-year Certificate both getting paid for work for three-quarters of the time and one-quarter of the time they are doing course credit. It's a small programme, but very, very popular.

We're not going to do this [the Biloxi housing rebuilding programme] as PR for the university, because if the community sees us doing that, rather than working for the good of the city, then they won't trust us.

David, why did you choose the Broussard Residence and the Bayou Auguste Neighborhood Wetland Park projects to illustrate the work you have been doing with the Gulf Coast Community Design Studio in Biloxi? ▶ The Broussard Residence combines many of the design issues of building on a site that is now part of a flood zone. The house design addresses the opportunity for an elevated house to create a well-used yard by making the space under the house part of the garden and by making the stair and upper porch take advantage of the gulf breeze and neighbouring live oak tree.

The Bayou Auguste Neighborhood Wetland Park shows how a community-based environmental restoration project can address the multiple role of urban water ways – natural habitat, storm water management, flood mitigation and neighbourhood park space. The project engaged the community to transform a degraded bayou into a neighbourhood wetland park and helped to increase the environmental stewardship of the community.

> Architecture is public but not everyone has the same access to architecture and not everyone is treated the same way.

DAVID
PERKES

DAVID PERKES

Broussard Residence
Biloxi, Mississippi, USA

△
Patricia Broussard moves into her new house following the devastation of Hurricane Katrina.

Project type
Permanent housing

Architectural firm
Gulf Coast Community Design Studio

Design team
David Perkes, Jason Pressgrove, Bryan Bell, Brad Guy, Sergio Palleroni, Vincent Baudoin

Donors
Katrina recovery funds from HUD, the house owner's own insurance funds and some FEMA funds

End client
Patricia Broussard

Location of project
East end of Biloxi Peninsula, Mississippi

Size
79 m²

Date completed
14 March 2008

Cost
$99,000

DAVID PERKES

Broussard Residence
Biloxi, Mississippi, USA

Broussard House is a design/build project completed in Biloxi, Mississippi, following Hurricane Katrina. Revised flood maps require the house to be approximately 4 metres above grade. The aim of the house design is to mitigate the dominant form of an elevated house. The placement of the stair in the centre of the house creates an outdoor space and separates the house's two main rooms. The house is LEED certified and well-suited for the climate, responding to the surrounding trees and gulf breezes.

◁
The Broussard Residence on the Biloxi Peninsula is built 4 metres above grade following Hurricane Katrina and the subsequent revision of local flood maps.

N

BEDROOM

BATH

UP

WINDOW
BOX

WINDOW
BOX

KITCHEN

LIVING

WINDOW
BOX

BREEZEWAY

GUEST BED

LAUNDRY

SOUTH PORCH

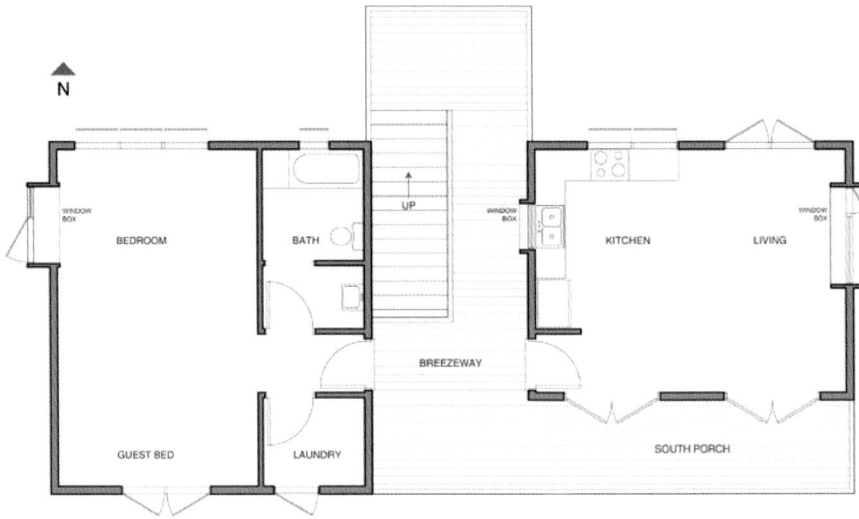

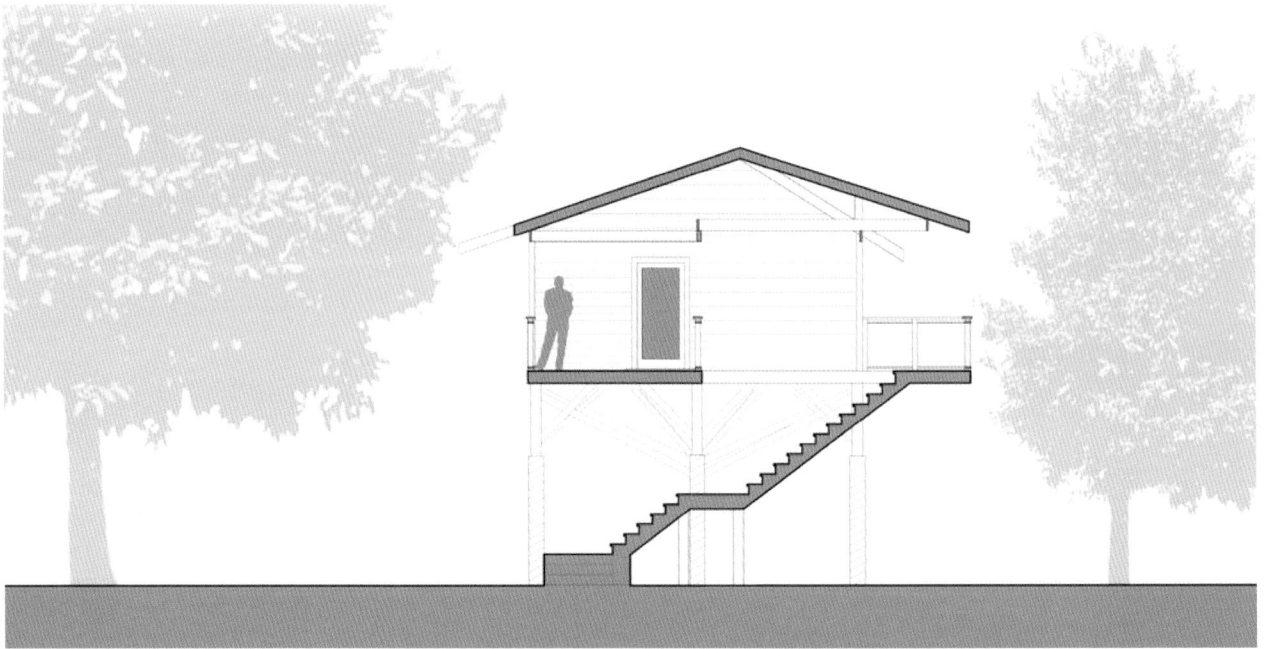

△
Plan and section.

DAVID
PERKES

DAVID PERKES

Bayou Auguste Neighborhood Wetland Park
Biloxi, Mississippi, USA

△
An 80-metre gabion wall delineates park and playground from natural landscape, provides public seating and allows storm water to filter through.

Project type
Ecological regeneration

Landscape architectural firm
Gulf Coast Community Design Studio

Design team
Gulf Coast Community Design Studio, Biloxi Housing Authority, Biloxi Public School District, City of Biloxi, Land Trust for the Mississippi Coastal Plain

Donors
National Fish and Wildlife Foundation, Southern Company, Fish America Foundation, Gulf of Mexico Foundation and project partner contributions

End client
East Biloxi community

Location of project
Back bay of Biloxi, Mississippi

Size
6,070 m²

Date completed
February 2012

Cost
$321,295

DAVID PERKES

Bayou Auguste Neighborhood Wetland Park
Biloxi, Mississippi, USA

Bayou Auguste Neighborhood Wetland Park transformed a degraded tidal stream into a landscape where nature and community come together. The urban bayou has been improved to serve three important functions: tidal habitat, storm water management and flood mitigation. The project also helped transform the surrounding East Biloxi neighbourhood that was impacted by Hurricane Katrina in 2005 and the Gulf of Mexico oil spill in 2010, and which has a long history of being undervalued. The restoration was accomplished with hundreds of volunteers, school children and city public-works employees, thus increasing environmental stewardship in the community.

◁
Completed Bayou Auguste Wetland Park.

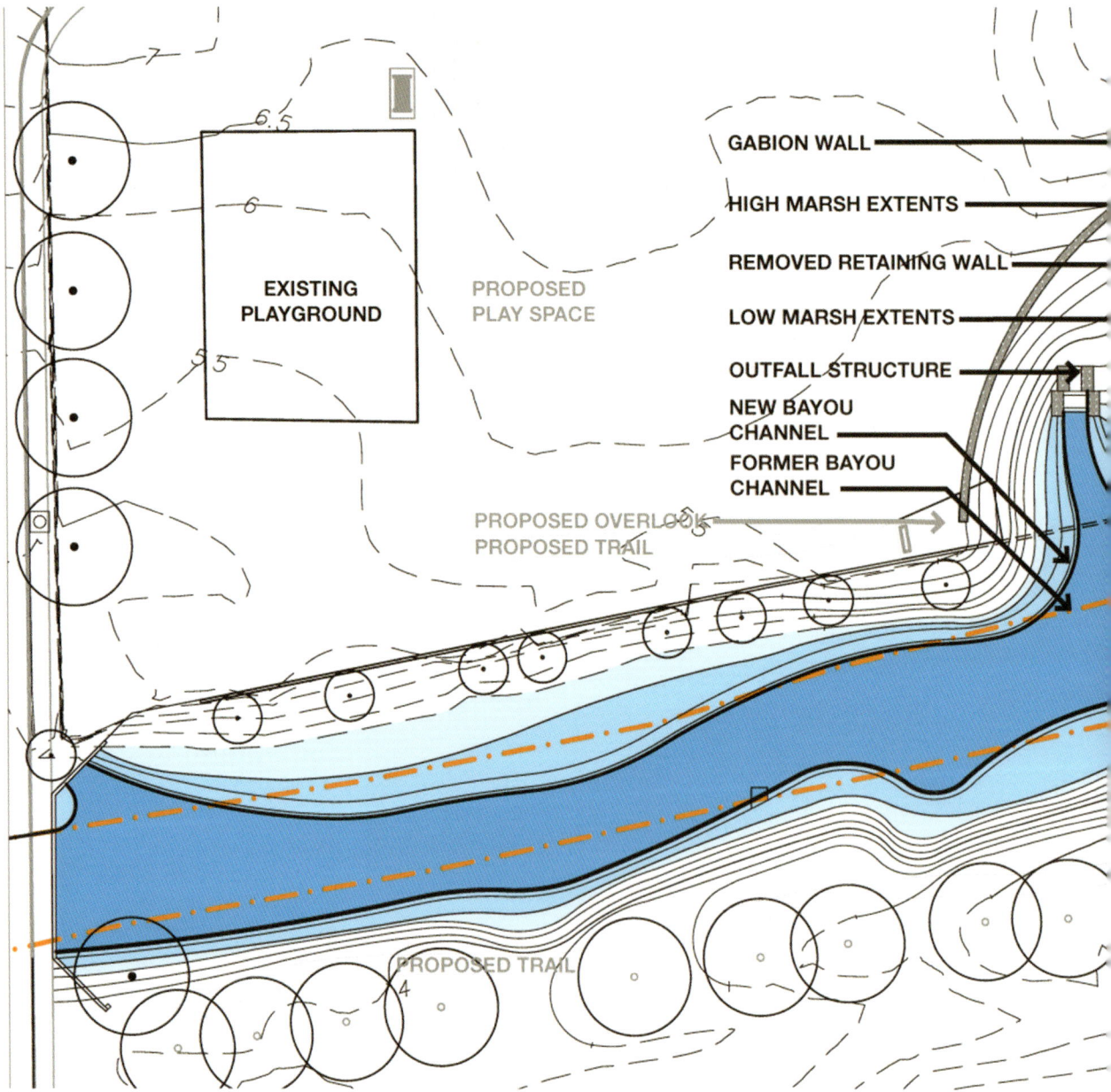

GABION WALL

HIGH MARSH EXTENTS

REMOVED RETAINING WALL

LOW MARSH EXTENTS

OUTFALL STRUCTURE

NEW BAYOU CHANNEL

FORMER BAYOU CHANNEL

EXISTING PLAYGROUND

PROPOSED PLAY SPACE

PROPOSED OVERLOOK
PROPOSED TRAIL

PROPOSED TRAIL

△
Site plan: the project plan shows the transformation from a straight channel to a stream with a meandering path. An 80-metre concrete retaining wall was demolished and over 2,300 m³ of soil removed. The streambank was regraded to create a new marsh flat.

DAVID
PERKES

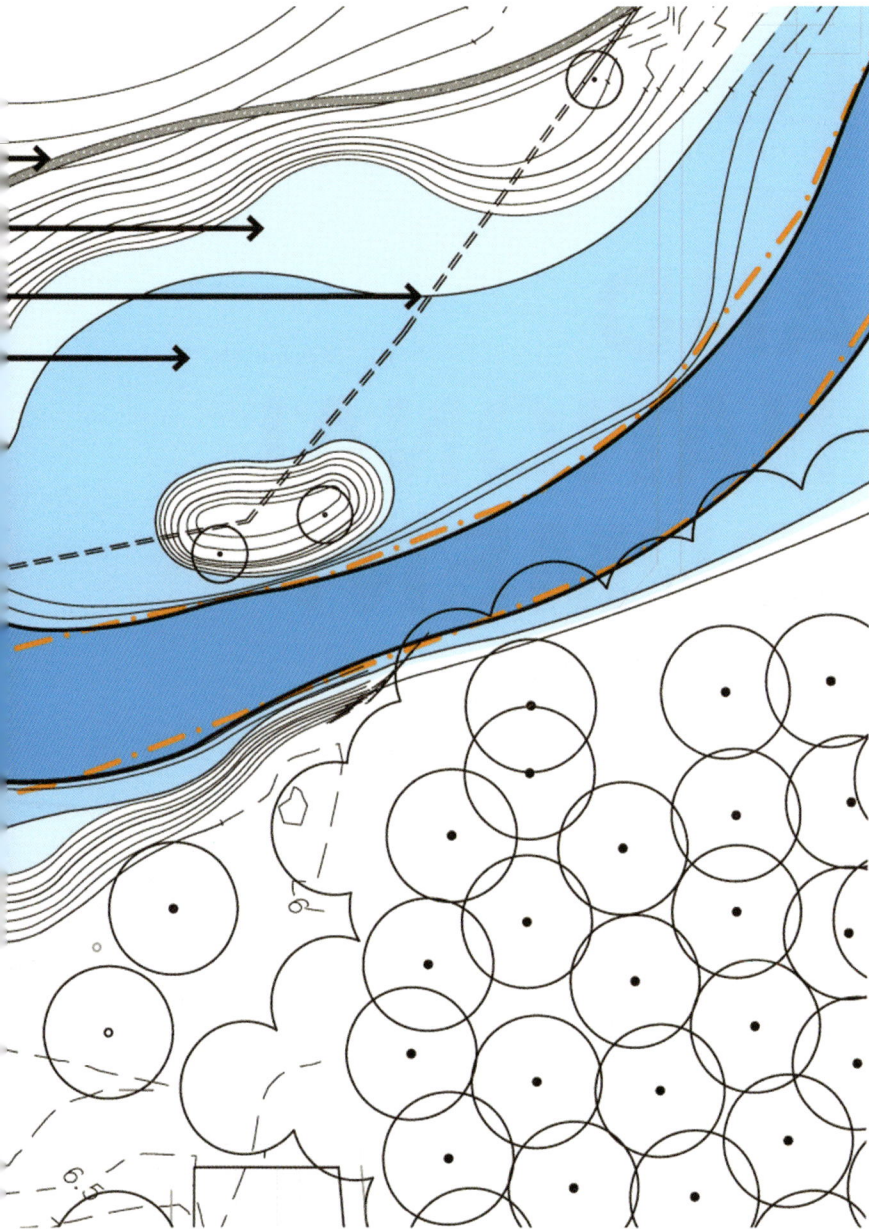

PART THREE

NGO- AND INTERNATIONAL DEVELOPMENT-BASED HUMANITARIAN ARCHITECTS

This section profiles architects working for NGOs and the international development sector. The rise of design not-for-profit groups, such as Architecture for Humanity and CASE, has greatly influenced the public recognition of the wider value of architects. The increasing presence of architects working for large international development agencies such as the Red Cross, UN-Habitat, Cordaid and World Vision International has also expanded the capacity for architects to meaningfully contribute their design, facilitation and technical skills to the complex task of rebuilding towns and communities after natural disaster.

Babister

If you look at the mission statement of most engineering institutes, you will see an emphasis on 'using engineering skills for the good of humanity'. The Royal Institute of British Architects' (RIBA) mission statement has no similar focus.

Cesal

I think it's unfortunate that the term architecture has become so washed out and so devoid of moral direction that we need to attach the word 'humanitarian' to it.

Moore

Architects have to be producers. In a sense we are one of the professions that deal with emergencies where a tangible outcome has to be the result.

Saunders

I would argue that it is not appropriate to send in twenty young architects from Lyon to Haiti or Guatemala, simply because they are keen and enthusiastic and they have time on their hands.

Shah

The 'emergency' syndrome – save money, do-it-yesterday, construct fast – catches up with all, the authorities, donors, intermediaries, contractors and even the communities.

Stephenson

If 'humanitarian' is interpreted as active compassion then isn't that a principle or objective for most architectural and planning practices?

Wachtmeister

Your solutions have to be developed under the enormous pressure of spending enormous amounts of money in a very short time.

LIZZIE BABISTER

HUMANITARIAN ADVISOR
CONFLICT, HUMANITARIAN AND SECURITY OPERATIONS TEAM
DEPARTMENT OF INTERNATIONAL DEVELOPMENT, UK

Lizzie Babister

is an architect now working as a Humanitarian Advisor with the Department for International Development in the United Kingdom. In a previous position with CARE UK, Lizzie led the emergency shelter and reconstruction programme for CARE International, which responded to a wide range of emergencies, including Cyclone Sidr in Bangladesh in 2007, Cyclone Nargis in Myanmar in 2008, the Padang earthquake in Indonesia in 2009, the Haiti earthquake in 2010 and the Pakistan floods in 2010.

> If you look at the mission statement of most engineering institutes, you will see an emphasis on 'using engineering skills for the good of mankind'. The Royal Institute of British Architects' (RIBA) mission statement has no similar focus.

|||||||||||||||||||||||||||||||||||||||

LIZZIE BABISTER

DEPARTMENT OF INTERNATIONAL DEVELOPMENT, UK

Note: Due to the nature of Lizzie Babister's current reconstruction policy work, no project is featured with this interview

Lizzie, tell me about your original studies in architecture and then what you did afterwards. Were you always interested in the humanitarian field? ▶ I originally thought about going to art school but I chose to study architecture, instead, because I wanted to do something practical. Then, along with a lot of other architects who were interested in this field, I realized that architecture was not just something practical but a profession that could also allow me to have a positive effect on society, to do something meaningful.

Was there something about your experiences at school or through your parents that encouraged you to think this way? ▶ My mother's side of the family was very influential because there are missionaries on that side. My mother and father also travelled around the world before they decided to have a family. My father is from India and my mother worked in quite a few countries, not in disasters or international development, but there was that link. They were role models for a career that seeks to have a positive effect on the world. I have a religious family so there is an element of faith in that choice as well.

Where did you study architecture and, then, did you work in commercial architecture? Or what was your career journey? ▶ I completed my whole architecture course at Cambridge University, including my professional qualification. I worked in my year out in London in a small architecture practice and, after my diploma, I worked in London again, and then in the small town of Leamington Spa. No one was really building very much in London at that time. So lots of young architects, like me, went to work outside of London where things were being built, in order to complete our qualifications and get experience.

What was your journey from there to working in the development field? ▶ It started when I was still at university. I did my undergraduate dissertation on homelessness in the UK, and when I came back to do my diploma, I was involved with the Shelter Centre in Geneva. My dissertation there was on emergency shelter.

What was the first project you worked on as a professional architect, in the field or moving out of traditional architecture practice? ▶ I had the opportunity at university to do voluntary work in Chile and also some research in the field in Macedonia, but the first time I was hired specifically in the development field was when Oxfam asked me to be their national shelter coordinator in Sri Lanka. I was actually working in a commercial practice just after my final qualifications and I was 'borrowed' by Oxfam on a secondment. My role in Sri Lanka was to visit all the Oxfam field offices to assist with planning the move from emergency shelter to the transitional phase. Oxfam had already started this but wanted me to provide support in thinking through the details.

Does it mean anything to you to be called a 'humanitarian architect' or is this term misleading? ▶ I guess the more projects I experience the less I am looking specifically for architects. Ten years ago I might have been more professionally 'chauvinistic' … is that the word? … and believed that architects have something unique to offer. However, I have found that a structural engineer is more useful to me. There are definitely some strong skills that architects have, but they don't always have all the skills that are required because there are lots of different roles in humanitarian shelter work.

If I was advising a young architect today, I would say, 'Make sure you've also got some really good, strong structural engineering skills. That will make you a lot more attractive to a humanitarian organization.' I would also tell her or him not to use the label 'architect' because

humanitarian organizations don't usually use that term. They are seeking comprehensive 'shelter professionals'.

The education of architects in the UK is very narrow. It is almost entirely focused on working in the UK and the developed world. I went through a process of being trained [as an architect] and all these skills were pointing to one thing, one identity, one role. I had to unpick all those skills again, have a look at the skills I had and add a few new ones and let a few lapse to create a new identity that would allow me to be useful in humanitarian work.

So what was it about being an architect that you had to drop? ▶ As a British-trained architect, I was taught that I was the generator of ideas. I was the designer. I was the leader of the design process. In humanitarian work you have to switch from being a lead designer to a lead facilitator because the best ideas will come from the communities where you are working.

Until recently, maybe it's been a decade, you rarely heard of architects working in the field after disasters. I met some architects when I was working in Bosnia in the early 1990s, but it was mostly lawyers, engineers, logisticians and so on. Why are we now hearing so much more of architects like you working in post-disaster and other development projects? ▶ If you look at the mission statement of most engineering institutes, you will see an emphasis on 'using engineering skills for the good of humanity'. The mission statement of the Royal Institute of British Architects (RIBA), like most others

△
Reconstruction post-tsunami in Sri Lanka.

in the Global North, has no similar focus. There is no official ethical leadership in the profession and so a humanitarian ethos is not filtering down through architectural education.

This is not stopping people being interested in this field, but it is stopping RIBA from recognizing the field as a valid calling for built-environment professionals. It stops them from providing the necessity for humanitarian design within the qualification process.

I also believe that the humanitarian sector does not have the capacity to recognize the benefits of employing more people with built-environment skills in the shelter sector, especially in their own agency headquarters. One of the goals I had when I moved into the humanitarian field was to address this weakness and help create more opportunities. We need more people from engineering, from architecture and from construction management.

How do you get a project actually going in a hugely traumatic environment, like after the Pakistan floods? How do you deal with that personally?
▶ Better than I used to.

In what way? ▶ I think technical people are protected, at least to a certain extent, because they can use the process of technical analysis to remain slightly removed from the traumatic aspects of it all. I once did a joint assessment with a health advisor who was so much closer to the details of the horrendous things people were going through.

With shelter I can go in and 50 per cent of my assessment can be done without talking to anyone because I am looking at the damage, looking at the materials and possible access problems, and then thinking about the scope of work that might be needed. I'm not saying you can do a whole assessment like that; but you are not engaging with people on the same emotional level and that can be a personal shield. I used to use that unconsciously until I realized

that I was being emotionally affected anyway, and I was not prepared for it. Generally, people can do about five missions before it all builds up and they have to deal with it. Unfortunately, there is still a huge lack of understanding of the need for staff counselling in the humanitarian sector where 'macho' attitudes are often still common.

So what is the range of tasks you have undertaken in the humanitarian field? ▶ I cover all aspects of emergencies. So the work I am doing can be anything from immediate emergency response in a sudden onset disaster to initiating a response in the middle of a chronic phase of a natural disaster or a conflict zone. I could be there at the beginning to facilitate response planning, supporting international fundraising once we know the reconstruction needs, or working with a design team. I could be helping the team recruit the right people, for example by writing the right job descriptions. I might be responding to requests for straight technical advice such as where to get equipment of the right standard. Many times I have been called on to assist with troubleshooting during implementation phases when problems arise. So, it could be at the beginning, middle or end of a project, such as doing some kind of assessment or evaluation. It really is the full range.

One area in which we are trying to do more work is enhancing the capacities of a country before an emergency happens. Every country needs a preparedness plan that says what it will do in an emergency. We are helping to facilitate this process and

I went through a process of being trained [as an architect] and all these skills were pointing to one thing, one identity and one role. I had to unpick all those skills again, have a look at the skills that I had and add a few new ones and let a few lapse to create a new identity that would allow me to be useful in humanitarian work.

LIZZIE
BABISTER

△
International Development Programme (UK)
camp following Pakistan floods.

reviewing plans with them. You know, asking questions such as who have you got in the country who can deal with this or are you going to be contacting us? Do you need us to help you to find people? Can you partner with parts of government or local NGOs or different international NGOs? What are the shelter issues in your country? More and more, we are trying to focus on capacity development so that when an emergency happens countries have the confidence and skills to respond, especially in the initial emergency stages when lives are at risk.

Are you often in the position where you put on your typical architect's hat and develop a shelter response in terms of an architectural design for a specific housing project? ▶ I wouldn't say I have done that very often. Every country has its own design and housing traditions and processes. So country offices tend to use me for design checks after they have a draft design and we can have a discussion back and forth, either remotely or in-country.

Graham Saunders from IFRC said in his interview for this book that in the shelter sector if it's not scalable then it's not relevant. Are there any examples you can give of this importance of scale? ▶ Oh, yes. For example, when I was working for CARE in Haiti, we built around 3,000 transitional shelters, but we also provided 17,000 reconstruction kits – all the tools and materials that families needed to strengthen the transitional shelters that they built themselves. However, it is not necessarily numbers that are important. What I think Graham meant was this: we need to be able to demonstrate an approach that is replicable by others, and especially replicable by the affected population themselves. If you can do that, then that's a really good thing.

How has your role shifted since the 2004 Indian Ocean tsunami? How have you seen the built-environment profession changing? ▶ I think the tsunami acted as a catalyst for design and shelter practices and organizations to emerge. It was an even bigger wake-up call for NGOs. For example, there were many agencies working in housing construction in Aceh. There was a lot of money involved too. But it was such a phenomenally complex environment to work in that there were major challenges we were unable to meet. The humanitarian community had to take a hard look at itself. Some of the organizations said they would never do construction again because they saw it as too much of a risk. Other organizations, such as CARE, decided to create new positions within the organization to handle construction better.

Within the professional institutions there does seem to be more engagement and more learning of what the humanitarian sector does so that built-environment professionals can know what skills to offer. There are certainly initiatives now that didn't exist before the tsunami, and there is definitely an improvement in how the private sector engages in this work.

New courses designed to educate built-environment professionals in post-disaster work are emerging in some countries. Are they equipping professionals in the design field? ▶ Every new course is a step in the right direction. We need more of them. However, universities tend not to understand the real need. So there is a gap in the training that's available because Masters courses tend to be very reflective rather than vocational. But you need the vocational skills and to have practised them before you have anything to reflect on! I'd rather have someone with a diploma from a vocational college. Then they can get experience in the field and, perhaps, after four or five missions, go and do an academic or other postgraduate course. We need courses that have compulsory elements of practice, not all desk study, reflection and theory too early in someone's career.

Are you still interested in mainstream architecture? Do you read architectural magazines? ▶ Yes. My husband is a commercial architect. I can't escape from it!

LIZZIE
BABISTER

ERIC CESAL

DIRECTOR
DISASTER RECONSTRUCTION
AND RESILIENCY STUDIO
ARCHITECTURE FOR HUMANITY
www.architectureforhumanity.org

Eric Cesal

is a designer, builder, analyst and writer. A native of Washington, DC, Eric completed his undergraduate studies at Brown University in Providence, Rhode Island, and has three degrees from Washington University in St Louis: a Masters in Architecture, a Masters in Construction Management and a Masters in Business Administration. Cesal began a career in humanitarian architecture as a volunteer on Katrina reconstruction, working on a community design programme in Biloxi and New Orleans. Cesal is currently the Director of the Disaster Reconstruction and Resiliency Studio at Architecture for Humanity, where he manages Architecture for Humanity's global portfolio for disaster response.

> Like a lot of young architects I came into the field with the belief that the architect had a role as a shaper of space, as a programmer of cities, and I harboured what perhaps later seemed like romantic ideas about what an architect did.

|||||||||||||||||||||||||||||||||||||||||||

ERIC CESAL
ARCHITECTURE FOR HUMANITY

Eric, how did your original architecture studies train you for the kind of work you are doing for Architecture for Humanity?

▶ I wouldn't say that it had direct relevance in the sense that some architecture programmes actually have studios and course work dedicated to humanitarian design. I would say that it had a direct relevance in as much as the training of a designer has specific relevance to many of the humanitarian problems that we're facing today.

So, you also call yourself a designer, builder, analyst and writer. You're kind of a modern renaissance man? ▶ I consider myself a generalist and I think I have understood for a while that these are the problems that I have wanted to interact with in the world and that they require a diversity of skills. I have made my living as a writer, as an activist, as a designer and as a builder. I consider all of these quality components of being an architect and communicating a design solution and making it manifest in the world.

Why did you feel you needed to do additional degrees after you took your first architecture degree? Was it because your original degree just wasn't equipping you for the kind of world that you saw out there? I mean, that's great that you did that additional study in business administration and construction management. It makes you an ideal candidate for all sorts of jobs, but it's an unusual path.

▶ In my earlier practising years between undergrad and graduate school, I was working in the private sector, mostly on educational and institutional projects. And like a lot of young architects I came into the field with the belief that the architect had a role as a shaper of space, as a programmer of cities, and I harboured what perhaps later seemed like romantic ideas about what an architect did. I was surprised at the extent to which other professions were crowding out the decision-making processes of an architect. By the time we sat down to a particular design and settlement, many of the important questions about the space had been answered, such as what the programme is going to be, what the siting is going to be, how large the building is going to be and how much work is actually required from a financial standpoint. And the architect's process would carry them through a series of decisions and result in a certain design product. And then, after that, several other professions in the form of contractors and construction managers would come in and add their influence.

Looking at the question historically, a century or so ago an architect was very much considered the owner's representative, the master builder, the person in charge of all the decisions that needed to be made. Now, it seems increasingly like other professions are chipping away at that authority.

I never really had any interest in being a construction manager or being in business, whatever that means, but I felt that gaining expertise in those fields would allow me to practise architecture in a different way and allow me to communicate with those other professions in a different way. So, I studied those other programmes in order to be able to defend our work in their language.

What was your path into the development/disaster field? Had you been working in the area before you joined Architecture for Humanity? ▶ My path was very serendipitous. I went back to school in 2004 to begin my Masters programmes. And about a year after that, Hurricane Katrina struck New Orleans and the Gulf Coast of Mississippi. By that time I had acquired a diversity of skills. I had been practising for almost six years. I had a certain amount of experience with my Master of Business Administration under my belt. And I felt like I could do something, like I could be of service somehow.

So I convinced my sister to drive me down to Biloxi, Mississippi, and I got involved with a couple of different organizations, one of which was Architecture for Humanity. By this point, it was about eight months after the storm, so the serious rebuilding was getting started.

And then you just continued – from disaster to disaster? ▶ From disaster to disaster to disaster. For me, you know, a disaster zone crystallizes a lot of issues that are present in design the world over and it really breaks down the practice of architecture into motives and principles. Intellectually it's challenging, because a lot of the support systems that we use as an architect are absent, the needs are more desperate, and the successes, I think, are more fulfilling.

You have mentioned that the role of architects after disaster is to formulate a 'development' rather than an 'emergency' plan and that humanity is much more important than architecture. Do you want to expand on that? What have you learnt from your experiences? ▶ First, there are no 'natural' disasters. There are natural events like earthquakes and hurricanes, which we can't necessarily predict or control, but we can control the extent to which those have an impact on the built environment.

Invariably, we see great disasters and great loss of life in places where the built environment has either not been taken care of or has not been built well in the first place. Which is why an earthquake in Haiti kills 250,000 people and the exact same magnitude

△
Proposal for new classrooms at Ecole La Dignité, Port-au-Prince, Haiti.

earthquake in Chile eight weeks later only has 100 casualties.

Second, this means that the core cause of any disaster is not the natural phenomena but poverty. People don't build poorly because they don't know any better. So, in any disaster or humanitarian situation, the long-term goal must always be long-term economic development. How do we use design as a tool, not only to rebuild this space but to rebuild, or build for the first time, communities and economies that can help themselves and protect themselves from disaster?

This term humanitarian architecture – other people dispute the term. Does this phrase have any relevance for you? ▸ You know, it actually bothers me quite a bit. I think it's unfortunate that the term architecture has become so washed out and so devoid of moral direction that we need to attach the word 'humanitarian' to it to let people know that that's what we're doing. You've never heard of a humanitarian doctor, you know?

You mentioned in your book, *Down detour road*, which you wrote in 2011, the idea that we need to be ten types of architects: the financial architect, the value architect, the risk architect, the pay architect, the idea architect, the knowing architect, the name architect, the citizen architect, the grain architect and the sober architect. But is that a theoretical construct? Can this multiplicity of capacities ever really be achieved? ▸ I don't think it's a Utopia. It would be extraordinary to see those capacities all in one person, but

I think as a profession we can leverage all those capacities towards a better future for architecture. I don't think that any one architect needs to necessarily do all those things, but I do think that as a profession we need to do all those things. We need those subjects to be part of the discourse in architecture.

I wrote that book as a reaction against the architecture that I grew up with, where the entire discourse seemed to be about form and tectonics and imagery and that sort of thing. And, you know, trying to raise a question about finance or about risk or even about citizen architecture within that discourse was very difficult. I don't think that architecture can be a successful profession if it continues to exclude considerations of our modern economy and financial system and practices.

How are you practising those kinds of values or ethics in the work you've been doing for Architecture for Humanity, most recently in Haiti and Japan? ▸ I still use the ten architects as an internal guidepost for how I practise and how I think about architecture. Take something like the 'value architect' – I have funders in much the same way that most architects have clients, and I'm thinking and considering how much value I can create for their funding dollar.

One of the decisions that we made when we went into Haiti was our choice of building systems. We had a lot of opportunities to interact with some very innovative building manufacturers that could deploy many, many buildings very quickly. But we made a

philosophical/ethical decision that we were going to invest our energies in teaching Haitians how to build more safely with the materials they already used and that they could get their hands on. Building and construction in Haiti is usually just concrete, and it's very possible to build that safely to seismic standards if you're building it right.

So, when we think about value against a choice like that, you realize that in the same way you might interact with an investor from Wall Street, you can interact with your funder. I can go back to my funder and say, 'Look, I didn't just give you a building for the dollar that you gave me. I did give you a building, but I also taught someone how to build. So, I gave someone a career. I left behind some knowledge. I left behind some techniques. I stimulated a local economy because now instead of buying prefabricated units that are built in Europe or in the United States, we're buying from local vendors, and we're buying concrete, we're buying bags of cement, we're buying concrete blocks to make these buildings.'

Are you now based in Japan or you've left Haiti? What's your situation? ▸ I've been transitioning a little bit, so I've been helping Architecture for Humanity build up our programme in Japan; we've had a programme here since the tsunami that is scaling up quite a bit. But I'm also doing some disaster-related work at headquarters. So, I am not really based anywhere at the moment. I still spend about 50 per cent of my time in Haiti and the other 50 per cent drifting between speaking engagements, Japan and San Francisco.

So when you are in Haiti, what is your day-to-day work? ▶ It changed rapidly over the years there. We started in March 2010 and our team was three people. Now the office is about forty. Earlier, we were doing vital rapid assessment work and now we have a full-service office where we can design, plan, provide technical advisory services, lots of training, etc.

So my own role has transitioned. I would usually get up around four and spend the first few hours of the morning sorting through emails and correspondence. Most of my current role is negotiating with partners and troubleshooting critical construction problems and things like that. Principally, what we've been trying to do over the last couple of years is to move the office to being an all-Haitian office. Managing that transition is a big part of what I do in terms of recruiting local talent and bringing in Haitians to the office. Currently, out of forty we only have about five non-Haitians left.

And then in Japan, are you actually doing Architecture for Humanity projects and trying to get projects off the ground? ▶ We've actually got a lot of projects off the ground and have about half a dozen in construction. We're opening an office in Ishinomaki, which is about an hour and a half north of Sendai. It was the hardest hit by the tsunami in terms of the losses to businesses and homes. The office will function much like our Haiti office. It will be a one-stop shop for survivors looking for reconstruction assistance, focusing primarily on small businesses, and we'll provide support both from the design and construction

△
Students pose at the completed building of Collège Mixte Le Bon Berger, Montrouis, on opening day, Haiti (photo: Gerry Reilly).

standpoint and in conjunction with our partners in small business assistance.

Have you come across many other design not-for-profits that work in a similar way to you in Japan? ▶ There are a few. Japan is, of course, very different to Haiti. It's a First World country. It's very developed. There is an extraordinary number of very talented architects here. So the challenges are different.

Architecture for Humanity always tries to position itself as filling gaps, right? We don't want to displace the work of local architects, and we don't want to try and do the government's job. We want to position ourselves in such a way that we're not interfering with whatever locals are trying to do.

Currently, our entire team here, with the exception of myself, is composed of Japanese nationals – architects, business people, etc.

Getting back to your background even before architecture, tell me about the professional lives of your parents and whether this influenced the area of work you're involved in today? ▶ I think it did, but I didn't really realize it until recently. My mother is an oil painter by profession. I grew up with a lot of art in the house. So, form and design provided serious nuggets of conversation. My father was an economist, and to be honest, I never really knew that much about what he did. But in point of fact, before he married my mother and had me and settled down, he did spend quite a bit of time abroad in the

I think it's unfortunate that the term architecture has become so washed out and so devoid of moral direction that we need to attach the word 'humanitarian' to it to let people know that that's what we're doing.

▽
Class in session in the new classrooms at Ecole La Dignité (photo: Architecture for Humanity).

ERIC
CESAL

foreign service. Back during the Cold War, economic development was considered tool number one against communist aggression. So, the US government invested a lot of effort helping countries in Central and South America develop economically, which was the bulk my father's career, advising foreign governments on economic and agricultural development.

So, there was a sense of a global world, a global responsibility that at least came through your father's professional career? ▶ Very much so.

Can we return to the rise of emergency architecture and the rise of design not-for-profits in the last ten years? When I was working in Bosnia and Beirut fifteen years ago, very few architects were working in the post-war sector. Then, something obviously changed with the 2004 tsunami. What are your views on that? ▶ What is most interesting is how humanitarian architecture has changed since the Global Financial Crisis. It prompted a re-examination of the purpose of the profession and forced people into asking larger questions. Why do we do this? Why do we spend so much time acquiring these skills?

Why do we put so much passion into our work? Is it worth it just to be in a magazine or to have an article written about you? Is it worth it just to have a very beautiful portfolio? Or is there some higher level of satisfaction that can be gained out of directing our architectural efforts elsewhere?

Before the recession, interest in humanitarian architecture was passing: 'This is something I'd like to go and do for a year while I take a break from my corporate job.' The conversation now is 'I want to have a career in humanitarian architecture and this is what I want to do with my architecture.'

△
Vision for Ecole La Dignité, Port-au-Prince, Haiti.

△
Classrooms nearing completion at Ecole La
Dignité, Port-au-Prince, Haiti (photo: Gerry Reilly).

Quoting from your book, *Down detour road*, you wrote that:

> Most architectural practice is similar to the practices of physicians and lawyers in that professionals work mainly with clients, wealthy individuals, corporations, institutions and governments who can afford to pay professional fees and who're receiving in exchange, highly customized responses to their specific need. This greatly limits the number and type of people served by the profession. Architects directly affect only 2 per cent to 5 per cent of all that gets built, which hardly makes a dent in the requirement that we, as licensed professionals, attend to the public's health, safety and welfare.

Bryan Bell talks a lot about this too, about creating new markets for architects where there weren't markets before because we were trained originally, in our design education, to just think that we would design a house or design a civic building and that was our role in the pyramid structure of becoming a great architect. But, in fact, there are many more roles that we can play for a much larger proportion of society. Is that what you were getting at in that quotation? ▶ I would like to get to a point in the profession of architecture where society recognizes the value, the contribution to public health and safety and welfare, which good design actually brings. I think that will create systems and support that will enable architecture to touch an overwhelming proportion of the population.

What if architecture also looked at its market as including the two billion people on Earth who have substandard housing, schools, health clinics, etc.? Now, not one of the two billion people actually has the assets themselves to pay even our fees, let alone a private sector architect's fees. But what we can do is make the argument to governments, to non-profits, to institutions, that good design is worth investing in.

In the same way that enlightened countries have a Medicare system that provides affordable health care for even those who can't pay what would otherwise be the market value of those services, I envision a future where the value of design is so recognized that it receives support from governments, from institutions, from communities, and allows access for those who can't pay the fees of an architect, allows them to enjoy the benefits of a good design.

On the more challenging and sometimes negative side, why do architects often assume that post-disaster design is a chance to experiment? I'm sure you've seen the range of shipping containers, funky prefabs and the idea that, like a vaccine, there is a 'universal' solution? ▶ I would point to the cultural training of architects and the mechanics of fame within our profession – that success lies in being able to create something new and innovative and noteworthy. Architects get recognized when they create something that no one has seen before or when they do it in a new way.

The media focuses us on superficial imagery. We can't experience a design necessarily in the same way we can experience health care. I can go to my doctor and receive medical treatment and if I get better I know that that person did a good job. The way that an American audience will experience Haiti is through imagery. They will not spend any time in that shelter. They will not get in close correspondence with whatever Haitian was lucky enough to win the Log Igloo sweepstakes. So the image is really the only way to experience and evaluate the architecture.

△
Built-in seating, Ecole La Dignité, Port-au-Prince, Haiti (photo: Gerry Reilly).

One of the things that I think that Architecture for Humanity tries to do is to not reinvent the wheel. I mean, let's innovate but let's not create solutions to problems that don't exist and let's not be arrogant enough to believe that something that works in one situation and in one in country will be that universal solution that works everywhere. I have received many offers of assistance from designers who continue to contemplate these universal solutions but I don't completely understand why. I think it stands at odds with history.

Underneath modernism was a thought that we could design universal solutions that would work everywhere and save the world, and it was definitely a failure. Good architecture is contextual. It makes sense for the people that are living there. It makes sense for the places that are there. Why is it hard to respect that? Is there an inherent prejudice that results from being educated as a First World designer and coming into an environment where things have fallen down?

I think where architects get tripped up is they don't appreciate what they can learn from other people. This first occurred to me in New Orleans. What I came to understand about New Orleans' architecture is that it's already fairly well designed. The prototypical New Orleans shotgun house was extremely well made, extremely well adapted to its environment, extremely sustainable, extremely affordable, extremely contextual. It made a lot of sense. A lot of the damage that resulted from Hurricane Katrina had nothing to do with the architecture. There were mistakes in planning; there were mistakes in infrastructure; there were levies that didn't work; there were communities that had been quarrying beneath sea level; and the natural barriers to storm surge

outside of New Orleans had been degraded.

If architects want to play a larger role in the world, they have to focus on solving problems that exist for people as opposed to solving problems that they think are interesting or that will gain them some measure of professional success.

You've got a whole chapter on risk in *Down detour road*. I only came to understood what a huge part risk plays over the last ten years doing not-for-profit projects for foundations or communities in need, and trying to anticipate the risk before we even started the project. But, again, I learnt nothing about that subject in my undergraduate degree or even in my Masters degree. What does risk mean to you? ▶ The crux of that chapter is really to understand the asymmetries and risks between the architect and the client. Architecture would say that they encourage students to take risks, but these aesthetic or design risks are of a fundamentally different kind from those that affect people's lives.

The whole financial crisis was about a group of people taking risks with other people's money. And we saw how that

I don't think that architecture can be a successful profession if it continues to exclude considerations of our modern economy and financial system and practices.

turned out. And this gets back to the mechanics of fame and notoriety in our profession. We get rewarded when we do risk-taking architecture, when we do something that the world has never seen before, when we do something that is visually shocking or striking, when we do something that may not even work functionally. We get rewarded by our own community of architects, right?

However, consider the many groundbreaking, award-winning architectural projects that leak, or that cause nightmares for the owners. It doesn't lessen our esteem for those architects who took risks and created those buildings. The point I was trying to make in that chapter is that an increasingly risk-averse society won't tolerate that kind of behaviour any more. Society will not tolerate that sort of risk-taking on someone else's behalf. It doesn't mean that we should shy away from progress or innovation, but we should be aware of the risks that other parties are taking and take our own risk in such a way that diminishes the risk level that they have to bear.

How, then, do we best equip or train young graduate architects who want to get involved in the humanitarian field? What would be your advice to them? ▶ Get out of the design studio! I don't mean to be glib but, seriously, get out of the studio. I think one of the most detrimental things about architectural education is the physical isolation of it. Having been through a number of different graduate programmes, it's what always stood out to me. In business school, people were intense, they worked hard. Same thing in construction management school, but they left the building. They would go and work in a coffee shop. Their friends were not sitting within ten feet of them.

I think humanitarian architecture, and indeed all architecture, is about the world. It is about human experience and how humans interact with space. And it is so unfortunate that we choose to begin an architect's training by isolating them. If a young person wants to get involved in humanitarian architecture, my advice is to take the summer off but don't spend it in some star-architect's office building models until three o'clock in the morning. Get a rail pass and go through India or, better yet, take a few years off and join the Peace Corps or do something useful like that.

That is interesting because the whole ethos of architectural education is the design studio. It's the way that you prove yourself. You do your work, make a display, and then you are critiqued – some would say 'torn down' – and then you get up and then you're torn down again. Or, at least that was my experience of undergraduate architecture school. And it does, on one hand, make you a bit tougher, but given that most of the studios are based on abstract problems, it does seem that a large component of this sort of pedagogy is framed around hypothetical projections. ▶ Business school, at least in the US, will not accept students who have less than five years' working experience. So, the students in a Master of Business Administration programme in the United States are usually in their late 20s, early 30s, late 30s, and only about half of them come from a business background. It was a wonderfully intellectually diverse place to be in. The conversations came from an architect like myself, a school teacher, a psychologist and an accountant. All these people would get together and have discussions about the same curriculum. There was a lot of exchange going on.

The personality of the design studio culture is that students are empty vessels that come into the studio and then get filled up with methods and ideas until they find their own design personality. Architectural studios bring people in from the outside world, devalue the experiences that they might bring, and then says, 'Okay, well, here's what architecture is really about. Here's what we're going to teach you.'

Architecture for Humanity always tries to position itself as filling gaps, right? We don't want to come in and displace the work of local architects, we don't want to try and do the government's job.

ERIC
CESAL

I think a better future for architecture is where students can come into the studio with experience, with agendas, with strong personalities of their own, and bring that into the conversation in the studio. For me a brighter future for architecture is what people can actually bring into the studio rather than what are they taking out of it.

How do you personally deal with being in places like Haiti or Japan, where there is such devastation and dysfunction? What do you do to just chill out or don't you need to chill out? Isn't it an unreal cycle that takes you from disaster to disaster and then you go back to the real world? ▶ Well, first, I take exception to the term 'real world'. I think what my career has taught me is that Haiti is much more real than the United States. But you're quite right. It takes its toll at a personal level. It is at times difficult. But what I have found true about disasters and disaster zones is that at the same time that you see the worst of the world, you also see the world at its best.

You see the best of humanity in everyday people who have the strength to carry on, who have the ambition to rebuild, who have the compassion and the humanity to be there for their neighbours and friends and complete strangers. As much as it takes out of me, it gives me more back. And it inspires me to see the sort of everyday heroism and compassion and endurance of some of these disaster survivors. It makes your own problems very small, you know? And it makes you feel really good about being a human being.

△
Interior view showing Ecole La Dignité's stone wall under construction (photo: Gerry Reilly).

Yes, I totally agree. I spent three years in Beirut and a couple of years off and on in Mostar and people were always saying, 'Oh, why are you living in these places? It must be so difficult, so tragic!' And I said, 'No, it's so empowering.' Because actually people are not down in the dumps. They're really happy to be alive, and all they've got is an amazing resilience, this human capital, left when everything material has been destroyed in their own city. ▶ Very much so.

And so, where to from here for you? You're in Japan and what's happening in the next year for you? ▶ I put a lot of personal focus on trying to make myself

useful and I want to continue to do so. In Haiti I'm still very useful and there's still a lot that I do there, but my role there is diminishing as is the role of every kind of foreign expert. You know, we're making a big push to transition the office to Haitian leadership as it should be.

The good thing about humanitarian architecture and, you know, it's nice and tragic at the same time, is that there's always more of the world out there that needs help and you could live a thousand lifetimes doing this and not run out of satisfying, necessary work to do. So, for me, personally, I'm going to continue to assist in Haiti and Japan and we're launching a domestic disaster initiative in partnership with the American Institute of Architects. So that will probably consume a lot of my attention, but I have no aspirations or intentions at this time to leave humanitarian architecture or doing anything much different from what I am doing now.

Why have you chosen the Ecole La Dignité project to highlight some of your wider views about working in the post-disaster field? ▶ I chose Ecole La Dignité as the project because it represents a commitment to using local materials and building local capacity through job training and skill training. The design and materials selection was atypical for that area – but not for the sake of architectural novelty. The design evolved around materials found within 1 kilometre of the site, and in response to a specific climate.

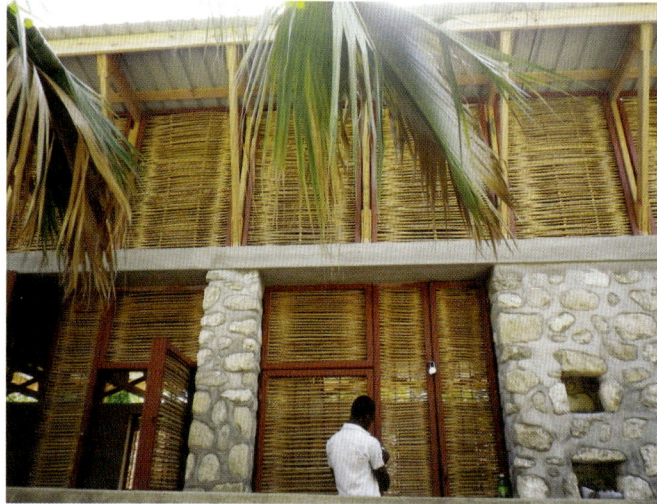

△
Traditional weaving on exterior facade (photo: Gerry Reilly).

I don't mean to be glib but, seriously, get out of the [design] studio! I think one of the most detrimental things about architectural education is the physical isolation of it. Architectural studios basically bring people in from the outside world, devalue the experiences that they might bring, and then say, 'Okay, well, here's what architecture is really about. Here's what we're going to teach you.'

ERIC CESAL

Ecole La Dignité
Port-au-Prince, Haiti

△
The extension of Ecole La Dignité on Haiti's Caribbean coast uses river stone, local bamboo and outdoor rooms to create a unique space for learning (photo: Tommy Stewart).

Project type
Education facility

Architectural firm
Architecture for Humanity

Design team
Haiti Rebuilding Center (Gerry Reilly, Ronan Burke, Amanda Márquez, Jean James Louis, Jessie Towell, Lisa Smyth, Natalie Desrosiers, Tamsin Ford)

Donors
Students Rebuild, Stiller Foundation and Pechakucha for Haiti

End client
300 Ecole La Dignité students and local community residents

Location of project
Cayes de Jacmel, Sud-Est, Haiti

Date completed
7 November 2011

Cost
$375/m²

Total cost
$75,000

ERIC CESAL

Ecole La Dignité
Port-au-Prince, Haiti

As part of the Haiti School Initiative, Architecture for Humanity built a two-classroom secondary-school extension for the only free private school in the Jacmel area. Ecole La Dignité supports eight localities from as far away as 3 km. The school currently has 300 students from grades one to eight, and is also used as a community centre, serving many different local groups. Responding to a need for students to have classroom variety and spatial delight, the Dignité extension creatively generates 'loosely programmed' space around the classrooms. Its features address problems of rebuilding in Haiti by including: abundant openings to generate low-tech airflow; hand-woven bamboo screens to let light and airflow through, while securing against unwanted visitors, burglars, bugs and rodents; resourceful alternatives to limited metal gusset plates for roof trusses, by using scraps of plywood and metal; stones from a local river worked into prominent architectural features; and natural foliage preserved to act as shade for outdoor spaces.

◁
Classrooms in use at Ecole La Dignité, Port-au-Prince, Haiti (photo: Architecture for Humanity).

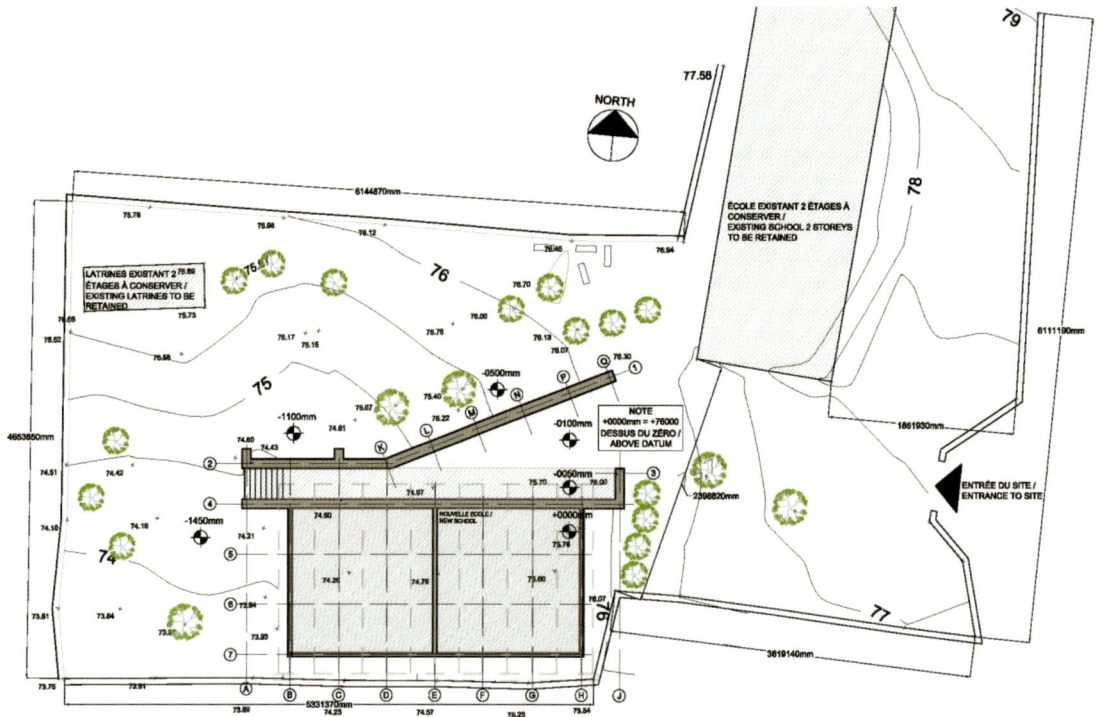

△
Site plan, Ecole La Dignité, Port-au-Prince, Haiti.

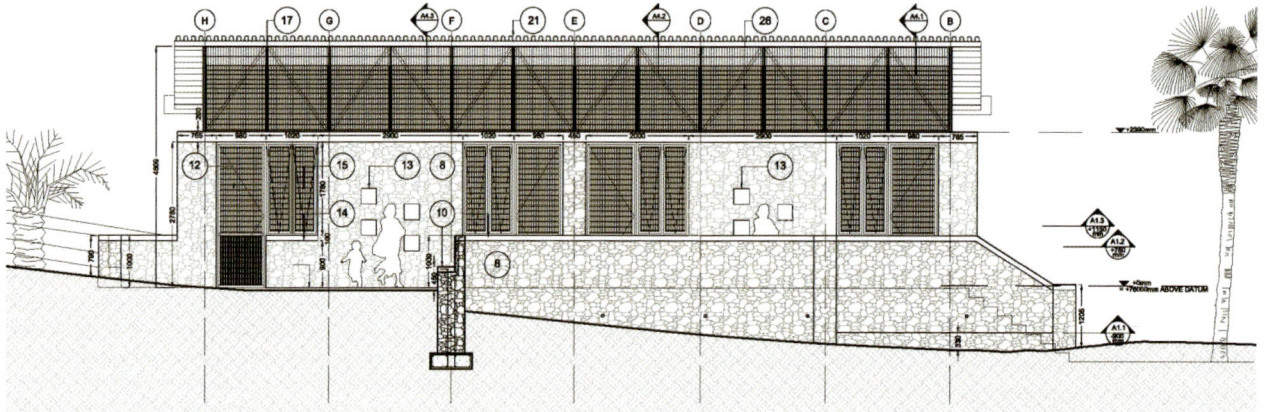

△
Section, Ecole La Dignité, Port-au-Prince, Haiti.

ERIC
CESAL

SANDRA D'URZO

SENIOR OFFICER
SHELTER AND SETTLEMENTS
INTERNATIONAL FEDERATION OF THE RED CROSS
AND RED CRESCENT SOCIETIES (IFRC)
www.ifrc.org, sandradurzo.org

Sandra D'Urzo

is an architect whose aim is to improve the living conditions of the most vulnerable. She began her career in the international office of Mecanoo in the Netherlands and has since worked with the NGO Architecture and Development, in Salvador, East Timor, the Philippines, Afghanistan and Palestine, and with Oxfam GB in post-tsunami housing reconstruction in Sri Lanka. Sandra D'Urzo is now a Senior Officer in the Shelter and Settlements Division at the International Federation of Red Cross and Red Crescent Societies (IFRC) in Geneva, where she is the focal person for shelter risk reduction and recovery and post-disaster operations and shelter programmes in the Americas.

As architects, what is our value add? Should we focus on technical expertise or strategic advice on risk reduction? What is the impact of our work?

||||||||||||||||||||||||||||||||||||||||||

SANDRA D'URZO

INTERNATIONAL FEDERATION OF THE RED CROSS AND RED CRES-CENT SOCIETIES (IFRC)

Sandra, please tell me about your journey in the development on disaster field before joining the IFRC. ▶ My architectural studies were in Rome. It's not a 'must' for an architecture student, but it was such a privilege to study architecture in Rome! I grew up in Brussels and, for me, going to Italy, and especially Rome, to study was inspirational, a dream come true.

Whether that equipped me for international work I don't know. I'm talking about the early 1990s, and heritage architecture was my passion. Architectural studies in Italy are quite conventional, focused more on the past than the future, but I don't regret it.

I think that I actually learnt a lot of things as a student that prepared me for international work. I learnt the self-determination and flexibility that you need to work in challenging environments. And its not being very internationally oriented gave me a hunger for new experiences.

At the end of my studies, I'm talking about 1995 or 1996, I went to an Aga Khan workshop in Istanbul where you and I first met. It was on post-conflict reconstruction and, after that, I did my thesis work on Mostar, the divided city in Bosnia. For more than four years, I had witnessed the terrible conflict that tore a country apart, just across the Adriatic Sea. So near and yet so far! It was somehow time for me to 'take action', and invest time in an architecture thesis that had real purpose and social meaning. It was that experience that led me to decide that international work was what I wanted to pursue.

I went to work as an intern for a year with Mecanoo in Holland. Mecanoo was doing a lot of social architecture, a lot of public work, a lot of interesting cross-sectoral work. It was an eye-opener to see that an architectural firm could actually be made up not only of architects and engineers, but also sociologists, economists, biologists and so on. So, when the task, for example, was to build a school, we worked with an educational psychologist and a paediatrician. It was very interesting to be in a big office

134

of over eighty people where there were only twenty or thirty architects. That was around 1999 or 2000.

I then went back to Rome to work for a private firm. I wanted to get my hands dirty, working 'on the ground' on building sites. This small firm was also building schools and convents in Central Africa and Tanzania. This work was quite new for me but, even then, I found it strange to be designing things in Rome to be built in a small village in Tanzania. I saw a big discrepancy between what we were doing and how I thought we should be designing and building.

It was sobering to have to challenge myself with such questions. It made me start to really think about the work I wanted to do even if it meant first finding out what I did not want to do. I knew very well by then that I didn't want to design kitchens in Paris or put the heads back on ancient monuments in Rome.

So I started to travel. I visited the project in Tanzania and then some projects in South America that I was aware of. When I came back I knew that I wanted to do socially engaged design work for the vulnerable.

At that point, the opportunity to work with the small French NGO, Architecture and Development, came up and I got a job as a Project Officer. My job was to hop from one emergency to another, recruit teams, work with local architects and set up joint programmes with bigger French NGOs. Architecture and Development was good because it not only did emergency relief after a disaster but worked with

other NGOs in longer-term reconstruction. It became evident to me that there was a real need for skills like ours in those disaster situations.

One project I worked on was to rebuild an orthopaedic centre and prosthesis workshop in the Philippines. It had literally been blown away by a typhoon. I did not have any experience with health facilities but the architect that I was working with was handicapped himself and was familiar with the centre because it had provided him with an artificial limb. I learnt so much from him and other people. They opened my mind and showed me how I could work out the real needs and workable solutions together, and then do the architectural design to make them happen.

Those years in the early 2000s were amazing because I was getting to know so many different sorts of emergency contexts. It

was the Philippines and then it was Salvador after the earthquake in 2001. Then, it was the Middle East and then Afghanistan where we were rebuilding a cinema in Kabul. I saw so many of these different contexts but was only spending three or four weeks at a time in each place and, no matter how hard I tried, it was never enough to properly understand what was needed. I wanted to stay longer in one place, perhaps starting in the immediate aftermath of a disaster, and set up a programme aimed at having a sustainable long-term impact and see whether people had really recovered or not.

The Indian Ocean tsunami shocked the world at the end of December 2004. It was a catalysing experience. I went from a very small, five-person NGO based inside a university to work with Oxfam as the national shelter advisor in Sri Lanka. It felt like I was growing up and now

△
A Cinema for Kabul, 2002–2003, with Architecture and Development (photo: Agostino Pacciani).

needed to learn to play in the big schoolyard, you know, with the big people. It was probably too big for me but it was an immense challenge. This was different from anything I had ever seen, the most major disaster I had experienced. I started two months after the tsunami in February 2005 and was supposed to stay six months. I ended up staying nearly three years.

First, we had to help house people in the aftermath of the tsunami. Many people had to be relocated away from the coast because of government policy to allow rebuilding only in safe zones. I was an advocate for Oxfam in making sure that the construction efforts would be equitable for the most vulnerable. I was going from coast to coast around Sri Lanka, one office to the other to make sure that we were implementing the transitional shelter programme properly: meeting the needs of the poorest, checking different technical aspects and helping decide what materials to use. We learnt about the differences in working in an urban context and in the rural east and between working in the Tamil north and the Sinhalese south.

We also had to try to make sure that our work was consistent with what all the NGOs, international agencies and the Sri Lankan government were doing. So, I set up a forum in Colombo for the many shelter experts and, every Monday evening from six to ten, after office hours, we would sit together and share our different approaches to deal with the huge task of rebuilding after the tsunami.

Sandra, through all these experiences in Asia, Africa and Bosnia, what were you thinking about the connections between architecture, development and social justice? ▶ Reducing inequalities by reducing vulnerability is the key for me. If people are more resilient to natural risks they will be able to live in safer environments, to invest in their livelihoods and improve their children's education: get out of the poverty cycle they are often caught in.

Right now in my shelter department team at the IFRC, we are using our background as architects and the training we've had and the field experience we've had to support national Red Cross and Red Crescent societies that are working directly with the most vulnerable communities. Of course, the word architecture doesn't come up on a daily basis. We're talking about 'sheltering' people – sheltering as a verb, not the noun 'shelter'. Sheltering is a process; it looks at designs, at the way people might use resources, at the way people could progressively build up from what they get just after the disaster to what they're able to build over time.

Thinking about shelter as a process does make us reflect a lot about what our contribution should be. Should it be technical, focusing on the way things can be built? Or should it be more strategic, focusing on issues of risk reduction, for instance? We have to connect with the research base, at least what research there is. What do we know about what might be working best in different post-disaster contexts and why? We're looking to learn about local

materials and Indigenous building practices, looking into energy efficiency and planning adaptable guidelines into the different options available.

And where does social justice come into this? ▶ When you mention social justice, this has everything to do with a more equitable approach to the issue of housing. We know that the post-disaster moment accelerates normal processes of building. If that goes in the wrong direction it can become very inequitable. We have a duty to make sure that there is more equitable access to those resources.

Think of people who never had access to a decent house before a disaster or who may have never had land of their own. What sort of reconstruction is best for them? For me, social justice is about equity.

What skills from your architecture training do you bring to the post-disaster work that you do now? ▶ Definitely not the design parts so much; but we know that the skill sets of architects are much wider than that. First of all, architecture helped my ability to listen and be flexible.

Disasters present as very complex scenarios but there are ways of unravelling the complexity. As architects, we are very good at connecting initiatives, making sure that the right synergies are made at the appropriate time. Connecting means putting people and knowledge together. At the IFRC, I coordinate 186 individual national societies, each working in their countries. I sometimes think I am a little like those old telephone switchboard operators, you know, who had to listen in carefully to what everyone was saying and then plugging people in to the right conversation.

Back to your personal background, Sandra, was there anything about your parents that inspired you to get involved in this kind of work? Did you grow up knowing what was happening in developing countries?

▶ Oh, yes. My parents were always very curious about other cultures. I grew up in Brussels, an international city, and went to an international school with children from all the nationalities of the European Union. But, as a school, it felt too narrow because people were all coming from an *elite* background.

My father was a pioneer of the EU. He was part of the dream of 'building up Europe'. And our house would always be very open to refugees, to people finding out about their status and whether they could stay or move on. My parents were always helping others out. My mother was an activist in Amnesty International. One eye-opener for me, when I was six or eight years old, was the Pinochet coup in Chile. The widow of one of the victims and her three children stayed at our house for six months. It was quite an experience! So, the love of sharing and being open to others, especially those who are less fortunate, is in my DNA.

Are you still in touch with the friends you studied with in Rome? What do they make of your work? ▶ They all set up their own private architectural firms. They've travelled, of course; but they think I'm kind of weird.

△
The IFRC assist a community in a flood-risk mitigation project (photo: Diego Alfaro, Netherlands Red Cross).

They think I am doing something which sounds very appealing, but they don't really understand exactly what I'm doing.

And why is it that it is only in the last decade or so that architects are working in the humanitarian and emergency fields? What do you make of that? Is it because the skills of architects weren't

recognized as being all that useful in the post-disaster space? ▶ I've been asking myself the same questions for years. Maybe, architecture is still associated with the elitist view that you only need architects for the rich and wealthy, for the top 1 per cent. What about the 99 per cent? There's such huge potential for more work in this direction. Think

△
Community members paint new infrastructure.

emergencies'. Today there's a flood in Colombia and, tomorrow, a very high tide in Peru; they need a response, and the provision of safer solutions.

For example, in Colombia we work with environmental specialists to raise risk awareness, with carpenters to elevate houses and infrastructure and with local municipalities to ensure that pilot projects can be replicated. Last year, our team in Port-au-Prince in Haiti needed urban planners. Two days later they needed legal advisors on land tenure issues. Then, two days after that, they needed an engineer who could do structural damage assessments. We can't even start the controlled demolition of damaged buildings, let alone build new ones, without constructional damage assessment. We had to find someone to process the rubble, in fact any kind of solid waste, to be able to recycle or reuse every available resource we have. There are so many different professions that we need to connect with in order to even get started with the programme.

about climate change and other urban risks, about slum upgrading, about post-disaster work, about retrofitting homes and schools! I still struggle to understand why there are not more design professionals involved in this field.

Universities, of both the North and the South, are not equipping us well enough to be able to say, 'Yes, I want to go into development. Architecture is needed even more by the needy than the rich.' It's still very conventional the way we're taught architecture for rich and wealthy clients and socialized into wanting to be one of the 'top ten' star architects.

The humanitarian and development sector is poorly understood, and probably not as appealing to architects. Yet, at a time when architectural firms are struggling to get business, there is a whole world out there that we could all contribute to. In India there are NGOs made of 200 architects working on housing alternatives for slum dwellers; and there are other Indian NGOs just as massive.

So there is certainly a huge potential and demand out there for architects working in an NGO and in humanitarian development.

When you're in the field after a disaster, what are the professions you are typically working with on shelter projects? Is it mostly engineers and logisticians? ▶ Quite a range of people, actually. It isn't always large-scale. The IFRC is the largest provider of humanitarian shelter solutions in the world, whether it's for small 'everyday' emergencies that never make the international news, or the ones that make the headlines worldwide. Much of our work is around the 'everyday

What's been your experience of architects working for small design not-for-profits in countries like Sri Lanka or Haiti? ▶ Apart from what I said before about mainstream architectural education, there

> Universities, of both the North and the South, are not equipping us well enough to be able to say 'Yes, I want to go into development. Architecture is needed even more by the needy than the rich.'

SANDRA
D'URZO

are design initiatives linked to universities. And the number of small-scale design-based NGOs is growing. What they are doing is very interesting. Some of it is very 'pilot', innovative and very small-scale. Often, they are doing prototype designs, especially looking at environmentally conscious aspects of construction. If they get their messages out, I think they can become an inspiration. If they are well thought through, any kind of initiative can be beneficial.

But, sometimes we do get cowboys or, at least, a cowboy approach. People flying in with very limited experience or professional qualified skills. We get people who are on vacation and think they could do some work and go home with nice stories to tell. Well, I don't see much of interest in them; they are not much of benefit to disaster-affected communities.

How would you advise new architects who want to get started in this field? ▶ First of all, I advise them to look at what is around them in their own country, in the South or the North. There are always small-scale organizations doing interesting social work that might engage an architect. So, my advice, first of all, is not to go international but to look domestically. For example, on the outskirts of Barcelona, there are really interesting initiatives with what some are calling the 'Fourth World'. They're providing homes for vulnerable urban communities, for migrants, for urban slum dwellers, for gypsies, for those communities that you might not even see in your daily life but who are really living just next door to you.

> I ask people not to apply to positions in Haiti or Pakistan as first visits. You would get hurt, shocked, disappointed... I think you should start humbly.

△
The IFRC assist in the construction of a new bridge using recycled materials.

I ask people not to apply to positions in Haiti or Pakistan as first visits. You would get hurt, shocked, disappointed. The risk is just too high because the complexities are too great. I think you should start humbly and say 'This is something that I really want to do but I recognize that I am not equipped to do it immediately.'

When people really want to work overseas, I tell them to look for opportunities in countries that are not conflict zones or where there are not particularly big emergencies. I suggest that they look to where there's long-term developmental work to be done; there are many interesting initiatives that 'make a difference'. It can be really beneficial working or volunteering with a bigger NGO. They need people to do specific research work, desktop and analytical work. That's another way. And then you can start not by going out in the field on your own, but in a team of people, starting to understand what it is all about and learn. That can help you decide if you might be suited in the emergency field.

So what is the one thing you have found is needed to work in the disaster field? ▶ I think you need to be competent. What is a competent architect? Someone who can make an outstanding design? No. It is simply a designer who can put aside a little bit of the ego and listen to others. Meaningful solutions don't come out of the head of the architect. They are the fruits of good collaboration between individuals.

Weren't you taught during your original architecture degree that there is a universal design solution to every human problem? They tried to teach me that. ▶ There is no universal solution to things. There are a lot of clever, creative people in universities. Many are researching prototype solutions but very, very few are ever tested in the field. We should be open to their innovation and research, but after a disaster is not the time to experiment on people.

Sandra, you've worked in some very traumatic zones. Do you become immune to these disasters? How do you deal with this as a human being? ▶ I don't think you ever become immune to disasters. I certainly hope I don't. I think it's very important to feel, to listen, to have your eyes wide open, to understand every new disaster for what it is, for what has happened. I think I have changed a lot as a human being after having kids. Being a mother, I think I am much more aware of the loss you can experience. Ten years ago I might not have had the kind of empathy I do now for a young mother who has lost a child. It becomes exponential, the understanding of what that loss really means. It's only something I can really see now.

How do you overcome these feelings? Basically to humbly go on with your own work. You have to empathize with the loss and grief, the conscious part and the unconscious part too. Then you have to try to put that aside, and make the best use of the resources you have and make everything you do an act of being in the 'here and now' and to do something meaningful, and with love.

Sandra, why did you choose the project in Choco' to illustrate some of your views about working in the humanitarian sector? ▶ It's a very special project. I have not been directly involved in implementing it but am monitoring it and visited it in October 2012.

The project encapsulates all that we do at the Red Cross – in this case helping to assist communities with improved flood-resistant designs.

The community is a very vulnerable one of about eighty families, living along the river banks of a huge tropical forest. The project is raising the houses and rebuilding dwellings on stilts about 2.5 metres above the river. There is also a 1 kilometre long footbridge made of recycled plastic bottles and an elevated school and environmental area.

It's a significant project not just in terms of shelter risk reduction but also for community resilience and environmental awareness. The design and improved building techniques and typologies are allowing the community to adapt to floods and, equally importantly, the people are now completely capable of replicating this 'model village'.

> We should be open to their innovation and research, but after a disaster is not the time to experiment on people.

SANDRA
D'URZO

SANDRA D'URZO

Choco' project
Department of Choco', Colombia

△
The Choco' community uses the new
bridge to avoid flood-prone areas (photo:
Diego Alfaro, Netherlands Red Cross).

Project type
Disaster risk reduction

Architectural firm
**Colombian Red Cross and
Netherlands Red Cross**

Design team
**Edwin Pinto Ladino, Javier
Gonzales, Jockny Martinez**

Donors
**DIPECHO, IFRC (Colombian Red
Cross, Netherlands Red Cross,
Norwegian Red Cross), Colombian
Disaster Management Unit**

End client
**Eighty households of San José de
la Calle, Department of Choco'**

Location of project
**San José de la Calle, Department
of Choco', Colombia**

Date completed
October 2012

Cost
**$3,000 per house (materials and
labour)**

SANDRA D'URZO

Choco' project
Department of Choco', Colombia

The Choco' community is a very vulnerable community of approximately eighty families along the river banks of a huge tropical forest area. The project consisted of elevating the houses and rebuilding dwellings on stilts (2.5 m), a 1 km long footbridge made of recycled plastic bottles and an elevated school and environmental atrium. It was a significant project in terms of shelter risk reduction, community resilience and environmental awareness. The design and improved building techniques and typologies allowed the community to resist floods. This 'model village' project can be replicated independently in other villages.

◁
Houses are elevated and rebuilt on stilts in a flood-prone area.

△

The Choco' project used community participation to improve the overall living conditions of eighty families who were struggling to survive following flooding. It supported a total of 5,527 people in surrounding villages with disaster risk reduction activities. Stilt construction was used to build eighty new houses and a 2.5 m high, 1.1 km long footbridge. Disaster preparedness activities, first aid, hygiene promotion and safe construction training were also provided. The project is now an example, both at regional and national level, of what can be done to support riverside communities to mitigate the effects of recurrent floods.

SANDRA
D'URZO

BRETT MOORE

SHELTER AND INFRASTRUCTURE ADVISOR
WORLD VISION INTERNATIONAL
www.wvi.org

Brett Moore

is an architect who works in the field of humanitarian aid and development. He has more than fifteen years' experience with the private sector, UN agencies and non-government organizations. Brett is now based in Australia with World Vision International as Shelter and Infrastructure Advisor. Brett's project experience covers several locations in Africa, the Middle East and Asia, both in the development contexts of housing, health, education and judicial infrastructure and in post-disaster and post-conflict humanitarian relief through emergency shelter and infrastructure planning, design and implementation. Most recently, he has been working on a transitional shelter programme for drought- and conflict-affected refugees in Somalia.

How can we, who are educated in a very Western design-oriented sense, contribute to the very big global needs around issues of poverty, urbanization and habitation?

|||||||||||||||||||||||||||||||||||||||

BRETT MOORE
WORLD VISION INTERNATIONAL

Brett, please tell me about your original architecture studies and whether or not you felt it prepared you at all for the kind of disaster work that you are involved in now? ▶ My original design studies, on the surface, didn't prepare me that well. It was also a factor of age and experience. When I studied architecture at the University of Melbourne in Australia, it was much more geared to working in corporate Victoria, particularly Melbourne. I think it takes some real soul searching for people to find their own path after that sort of socialization.

Was there any discussion of architects' involvement with communities in need or society at large in your degree? Were any of those issues raised in your degree? ▶ In the degree, the parts that were most pertinent were really looking at modernism and Bauhaus and the idea of architecture for, or architecture around, habitation – human issues. I don't think the degree gave us the tools to work closely in communities, but it did give us tools for inquiry. I also think some

of the electives I chose were very enlightening and it was good for me to have that balance during those academic years, looking at issues of state and culture and power and gender, especially around Third World development issues. That got me very interested in the plight of developing countries.

Tell me about your current work in the shelter field. And whether you use any skills from your original architecture degree? ▶ My title is Shelter and Infrastructure Advisor. Although my office is in Australia, I work for World Vision International; so I have a global role. I am now less engaged at the project management level than I have been in previous years. My role now is dealing with policy issues and process. I act as a facilitator of conversations around shelter and reconstruction issues in a multidisciplinary sense.

I am working in a dedicated global emergency response team of about thirty-two people. Each of us has a technical discipline to work within, and we are deployable post-emergency for up to three months for what World Vision refers to as a 'Category 3' emergency. These are the big emergencies, like Haiti, or a tsunami or the equivalent of a Pakistan flood. So we travel to such locations to assess the situation and design a response in an integrated fashion with other agencies, organizations and sectors.

I believe you worked in publishing after you finished your architecture degree? Did that inspire you to get into the development field?

▶ Studying architecture was an all-encompassing experience. The intensity of the course means that nearly all your friends are architects; your peers are architects; you're constantly thinking, living, breathing architecture – and one day I woke up and realized that there are a lot of other things out there that I might like, or I might be good at, but I'd never given myself a chance. Even though it was a sideways step out of architecture to work in publishing, it used some of the technical skills of architecture. You know … AutoCAD and some of our design and mapping skills, but also the idea of looking at architecture as a reflection of a culture and what architecture is historically. My publishing experience looked a lot at the architectural history of certain countries and the broad significance of that in tourism.

Would you say that you are now working in humanitarian architecture? Does this phrase mean anything to you? ▶ It might be if you are looking at the macro-level of things. We do architecture for

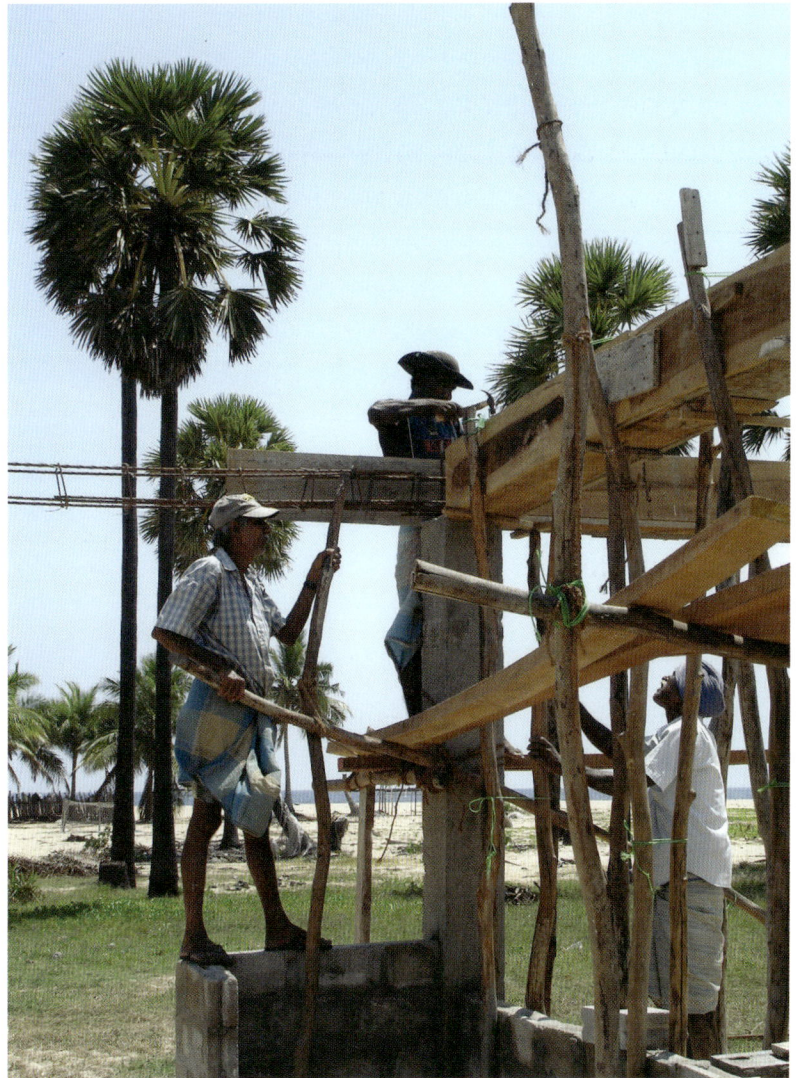

△
Construction of community infrastructure, including a fish market (shown here).

people-in-need in a very real sense, and not architecture as a field of high-design, which is how it is emphasized if you're within the Australian context. Our concern is to look out for the 99 per cent of people around the globe, specifically in developing countries, who would never be able to afford the services of

an architect in the Australian or high-design sense. What is their need for architecture, habitation and housing? How can we, who are educated in a very Western design-oriented sense, contribute to the very big global needs around issues of poverty, urbanization and habitation?

△
Potpathy (Sri Lanka) community reconstruction showing typical transitional shelters before permanent reconstruction phase.

Are you saying that there is an intersection of architecture with human rights and politics? ▶ I think that there is a necessary overlap for all of them. I think that some of the skills that architects have, not just in design, but of being a facilitator, an organizer, an analyser, these skills are very important in the emergency field. These are not skills that human rights lawyers and others who have had a humanitarian education necessarily have. Architects are one of the few professional groups that are educated in how

I think architects are one of the few professional groups that are educated in how to manage projects, to look at a problem and think of a succinct, rational solution with budget, materials, people involved, that also addresses a human rights issue.

to manage projects, to look at a problem and think of a succinct, rational solution with budget, materials, people involved, that also addresses a human rights issue – in this case, the right to safe and dignified shelter.

So, are you saying that shelter and housing is a human rights issue? ▶ Architecture in emergencies is very much about people's basic survival needs and you need to be highly accountable. You need to measure your impact and show results. It's about getting people shelter. It's life saving, and we have to be accountable to that as opposed to a design process in an abstract or affluent environment. We are not dealing with a computer; we are out in the field with materials, with people who need shelter, either because of a disaster or a war and displacements of various sorts. You have to produce something and it has to work and there's no other option.

That is a big responsibility. How has that played out in the field for you? ▶ In two ways. On the micro-level, architects have to be producers. In a sense we are one of the professions that deal with emergencies where a tangible outcome has to be the result. We have to produce something that is suitable for habitation. That's the micro-level output, but the macro-level is also important. This is where we are pulling back and looking at the political issues in a country, such as what groups do you work with? Do you work with the ethnic minorities? Do you work with the government? And what about the military? If you work *through* government, how do you work *with* the government? Do you partner with agencies?

△
The Potpathy community in Sri Lanka participate in road reconstruction efforts.

So we are dealing with these stakeholder issues at the national or regional level at the same time as producing a detailed product.

In this macro-context, I believe you've worked quite a bit on jails in the post-disaster context. Tell me about that. ▶ My first prison projects were with the United Nations Office for Project Services [UNOPS]. We were providing design services for the United Nations Development Programme [UNDP]. It was part of the law and justice sector strengthening projects that they do in many countries, particularly those they call 'fragile states'. My first experience on such a project was in what is now South Sudan. I was leading a design team on the hardware side of things, so we were designing and building prisons, police stations, court houses and police training colleges throughout South Sudan. I didn't know if I

wanted to be working on a prison project; I didn't even know if the UN should be funding prison projects. However, in the end, they ended up being great projects. In countries like South Sudan, which are desperately poor, even the health and education sectors are shockingly underfunded, let alone the prisons. Imagine what they're like – overcrowded, lacking water, sanitation and every other kind of facilities that we would see as the minimum requirement for human respect, let alone rehabilitation. So bringing these facilities up to a minimum humanitarian standard was a really worthwhile thing to do. And it was a life-changing experience for me to meet the incarcerated, hear their stories and see the conditions that so many people live in. I repeated these kinds of assessments and design projects in the Palestinian Territories, Sri Lanka, East Timor and Haiti.

Many people find they come to work such as this because of the influence of their parents. Was this the case for you? ▶ I grew up in a very small town called Yarram in rural Australia. My father was – and is – a dairy farmer and my mother's an art teacher. I always feel that she has been the creative influence on my life, and from my father we learnt about hard work and that we had a responsibility to put something back into the world. This was not just an ethical aspect, but also a respect for others and the hardship that others face.

The other influence in my life is my aunt, who is a nun. When I was young, she was constantly overseas working with the poorest of the poor. Unlike working with the UN or other organizations where there is a project lifespan, budget and an outcome, when you're working with faith communities there is no end. Her life was about accompanying people on a journey, and she would be with certain communities for years and years, bearing witness, serving and advocating. I think her experiences influenced my intellectual development and, even though I grew up in a small and isolated rural Victorian community, I had a curiosity about the world. I wanted to see it and I wanted to be part of it in a meaningful sense, to live and work and understand what life struggles were like for other people.

So you ended up working in Pakistan after major floods! ▶ Yes. The Pakistan floods were really, as they say, a 'slow-moving tsunami'. The extent of the damage was becoming more and more apparent on a day-by-day basis as more areas became inundated. My role there was damage assessment in the far north near to Peshawar, in a series of villages in an area called Charsaddah. I was looking at how to quantify the damage, get an appreciation of its extent and help prepare some ways for getting the community involved in the reconstruction process through rebuilding their own dwellings.

And you also have worked in northern Sri Lanka? ▶ This was one situation where I was personally not as prepared as I should have been. Maybe no one can be prepared to enter a conflict zone really, especially when none of us knew that it was about to happen.

I had gone there to help in post-tsunami reconstruction and then, after a couple of years, it was very clear that previous conflicts that hadn't really ended were emerging yet again. And that meant that our work stopped being post-disaster reconstruction and 'morphed' into emergency response. Certain towns and villages became battle zones. That meant large numbers of the population began moving and spontaneous refugee camps were being set up. We went from working in a development sense to working in an emergency sense without a clear transition and without adequate training and preparedness.

Why is it that there are not more architects like you? ▶ It could be as simple as not knowing humanitarian architecture exists and how to get into it. And from the other end, most international agencies and NGOs don't know the value of architects. Architects are probably poor at broadcasting or promoting their particular strengths. Many other professions, such as nursing and

△
Classes in a temporary school during the reconstruction period, post-tsunami (Sri Lanka).

medicine, have more obviously applicable skills for working in development or in an emergency than architects. However, a lot of people don't really know the full spectrum of things that architects can do and how they could be used in these situations.

This is changing now, isn't it? ▶ I think the Indian Ocean tsunami in 2004 was really important in the Australian context because it was essentially on our doorstep and the Australian government and individuals and organizations were major donors. Also, the tsunami reconstruction process involved a very definite and permanent reconstruction phase. This allowed the skills of the architect to be more overtly employed in contact with some of the major disasters that never get to the permanent reconstruction phase. For so many sad reasons, the international and national response to these disasters often ends up finishing after the emergency response or transitional housing stage.

What are the main characteristics of good practice in the shelter field and how do you effectively move between those emergency and transitional long-term recovery phases? ▶ The emergency shelter process isn't really architectural. The primary skill you need to have is good, clear communication with other individuals and agencies. You also need to be very … humble. No, that's not the right word. You have to be assertive about what needs to be done but cautious because you're dealing with chaos – and traditional ideas of project management or project planning often don't work. You

have to be highly intuitive and use your previous experience. You have to listen and work well with communities and be able to elicit answers and information from people who are often traumatized and unclear about what their shelter needs are. We have to be very careful about listening to that and asking the right questions at the right time in order to take action. Imposing an external solution will never work.

Different skills are involved in moving from emergency through to permanent reconstruction. Moving to a permanent reconstruction is inevitably more expensive because we're dealing with buildings of more complicated materials, construction, longevity, and you have to have a lot more professionals involved. So there's a wider stakeholder group. You're dealing more with local government and other agencies. When you're dealing with emergency response you have an understanding that the intervention you're doing will have a lifespan probably no longer than six months. Issues around land use, allocation, land ownership don't really need to be dealt with in the same way at that first phase. However, when you're doing permanent housing work, all the complex issues of land ownership need to be dealt with and that can take a long time and a lot of negotiation. Also, you need to develop a lot of understanding of things that we're not familiar with in the Western world, such as customary ownership and clan relationships.

Other people I have interviewed have told me that architecture students and even some experienced architects have

come to them with designs and plans for prefab housing, for example, in Haiti, Sri Lanka and New Orleans – and there's an almost modernist tendency to see architecture as about providing a universally applicable solution. What's been your experience in this regard? ▶ All my experience in the humanitarian sector has taught me that there is no 'one-size-fits-all' approach. This could be as simple as an economic imperative: what's cheap in one place won't be cheap in another. There is also a strong cultural imperative: what any individual or family feels comfortable with in one place certainly won't be the same in another. Architects the world over know this but, for some reason, if it's a disaster situation or an emergency response, we throw those rules away and say that we can still have a one-size-fits-all approach.

I'm not saying that this won't work in some certain circumstances. In some situations, it has to work. Like when you have to have the ability to fly in tents for people in those huge disasters where there are hundreds of thousands displaced. However, if you're looking at transitional shelter or something permanent, it has to be about local communities, local materials and local construction techniques.

The other important thing about shelter projects is that the provision of a shelter is only one of the products. You need wider community infrastructure, schools, shops, clinics and, yes, police stations and jails. There is an economic benefit in getting people involved in the construction of their own shelters and employed in rebuilding their local community. If you fly in a prefab solution, you are actually bypassing this very critical element – and you'll still have people who have no money and are unemployed. In many ways, and for many reasons, the employment and retraining aspects of providing shelter are just as important as the product is itself.

How do we best educate young architects who want to get involved in the emergency or humanitarian field? At what point of undergraduate design education could we begin to learn the necessary skills, given there are more and more disasters? ▸ With climate change, and through urbanization, people are being pushed to more and more marginal land. So the need for emergency response will increase. Architecture faculties are not dealing with these issues yet. It's being dealt with in project management and environmental engineering. These are the courses training people for shelter projects post-disaster and to make sure of good water supplies in developing countries.

I think that skills for post-disaster shelter work could be easily introduced into architecture. There are simple steps such as guest lectures. And design studios could get students thinking from their formative years about the housing needs of the poor around the world and about rural development issues and slum upgrading. Such studios would invite students to think about housing and infrastructure outside the discourses of high-design for the Western urban context.

> Most international agencies and NGOs don't know the value of architects. Architects are probably poor at broadcasting or promoting their particular strengths.

It is hard for some of our students to really comprehend what life is like in the Global South. What does it mean to be an urban slum dweller in Mumbai or in the kinds of peri-urban tracts that are exploding around cities like Manila and Jakarta? What does the lack of land ownership really mean in relation to producing shelter? And it means a lot, of course, but to really explore all that and how it might be manifested in design is a big project and a very interesting one. In the Western context we build for owners. We rarely build for people who don't own the land and don't own the house. However, we often have to do that in the emergency response context. So even the whole definition of the client and participation in decision making is very different from what they encounter here.

You have mentioned that 'the space architects can occupy in the aid world is limitless but comes at a cost'. What do you mean by that? ▸ In order for architects to be able to work in the development context they need to understand it in all its depth and ramifications. And to do that is more than just a three-week project. Ideally, we need a couple of years in a foreign context to get enough first-hand practical experience to be a good

practitioner. We need to go to an isolated area where there might be some insecurity and there will certainly be a lack of resources and maybe a fair bit of discomfort. We have to experience to really understand the people and the contexts that we want to design with.

Why did you choose the tsunami reconstruction programme in Sri Lanka to illustrate some of the principles you consider to be important in post-disaster design practice? ▸ I have chosen to profile a tsunami reconstruction programme in Sri Lanka as it was an integrated multi-sectoral programme including health, water and sanitation, education, livelihood, child protection, peace building and a range of community engagement and development activities. It is as close as I have come to 'complete' community reconstruction, requiring more than just design and construction knowledge, and appreciating how vitally and inextricably linked are other human needs to basic housing – a very humanitarian approach. I learnt how reconstructing houses can be a central action from which many other needs can be connected, operating in unison, to rebuild lives and communities.

BRETT MOORE

Tsunami reconstruction project
Potpathy, Jaffna District, Sri Lanka

△
151 Sri Lankan families are rehoused following the devastation of their community in the 2004 tsunami.

Project type
Permanent housing

Architectural firm
World Vision International with subconsultants providing specialist architectural and engineering design inputs

Design team
World Vision International in-house architects and engineers, Rudra engineering consultants (Jaffna)

Donors
World Vision International private donors, Disaster Emergency Committee (UK)

End client
151 individual Sri Lankan families

Location
Potpathy Village, Vadamarachchi East Ds Division, Jaffna District, Sri Lanka

Size
Each house approx. 46 m²

Date completed
July 2008

Cost
$60/m²

Overall cost
$2,800 per house. Size and allotment stipulated by the Sri Lankan government (Urban Development Authority)

BRETT MOORE

Tsunami reconstruction project
Potpathy, Jaffna District, Sri Lanka

As part of a post-tsunami permanent reconstruction programme, 151 houses were constructed in the northern Sri Lankan fishing village of Potpathy, in Jaffna District. These houses included individual houses that were constructed on private land, plus several small developments of fifteen–twenty grouped houses on government land that was later assigned to individual families who were granted individual ownership documents. Social infrastructure (schools, clinics, playgrounds and community halls) and civil works such as roads, drainage, and provision for power supply, were also included, as well as a toilet and water well for each family.

◁ The Potpathy community participate in reconstruction efforts, Sri Lanka.

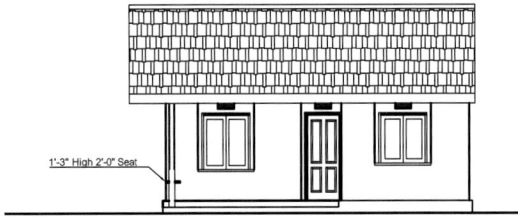

FRONT ELEVATION

1'-3" High 2'-0" Seat

◁
Front elevation, house plan and section through a house, Potpathy Housing Reconstruction Project, Sri Lanka.

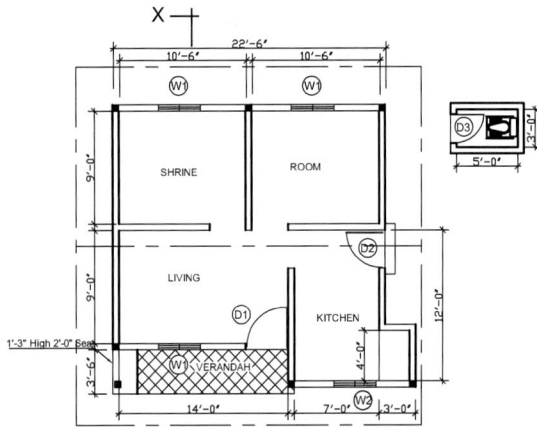

X

22'-6"
10'-6"   10'-6"

W1   W1

D3

5'-0"   3'-0"

9'-0"

SHRINE   ROOM

9'-0"

LIVING

D2

12'-0"

D1

KITCHEN

1'-3" High 2'-0" Seat

W1 VERANDAH

3'-6"

14'-0"   7'-0" W2 3'-0"

4'-0"

X FLOOR PLAN

TOTAL FLOOR AREA :- 507 sq. ft

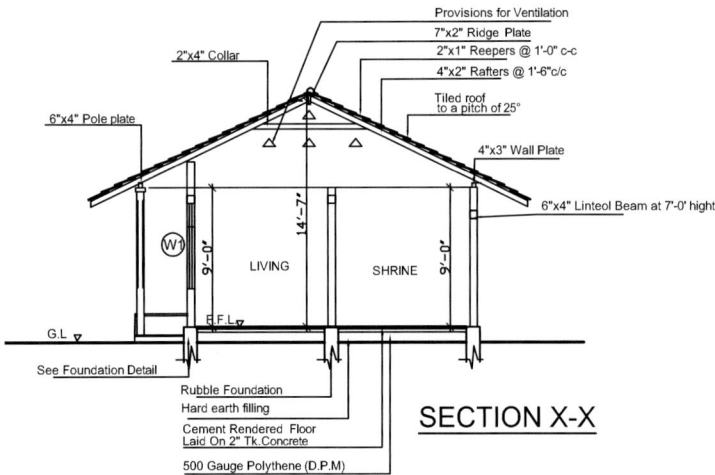

Provisions for Ventilation
7"x2" Ridge Plate
2"x4" Collar
2"x1" Reepers @ 1'-0" c-c
4"x2" Rafters @ 1'-6"c/c
Tiled roof
to a pitch of 25°
6"x4" Pole plate
4"x3" Wall Plate

6"x4" Linteol Beam at 7'-0" hight

W1

14'-7"

LIVING   SHRINE

9'-0"   9'-0"

G.L

B.F.L

See Foundation Detail

Rubble Foundation
Hard earth filling
Cement Rendered Floor
Laid On 2" Tk.Concrete
500 Gauge Polythene (D.P.M)

SECTION X-X

BRETT
MOORE

GRAHAM SAUNDERS

HEAD OF SHELTER AND SETTLEMENTS
**INTERNATIONAL FEDERATION OF RED
CROSS AND RED CRESCENT SOCIETIES
(IFRC)**
www.ifrc.org

Graham Saunders

is Head of Shelter and Settlements for the
IFRC (International Federation of Red Cross
and Red Crescent Societies) in Geneva. His
roles include supporting the IFRC in building
the shelter capacity of National Red Cross
and Red Crescent Societies, identifying and
promoting best practices within the sector,
assisting the emergency shelter interagency
coordination role of the IFRC in natural
disasters and promoting a broader shelter
network. Having studied at the Architectural
Association in London, Graham spent his early
professional career with Michael Hopkins and
Partners before going on to work with Roger
Zogolovitch and teach architecture at the
University of Cambridge. Graham has also
been the global technical advisor on shelter
and settlements for a leading NGO in the
United States, where he was actively involved
in post-disaster and post-conflict response
and reconstruction activities in Africa, Central
America, Central Asia, the Middle East and
South and South-East Asia.

Getting off the plane in Tirana, the fact that I was an architect was immediately recognized and I was able to sit down and do business ... They knew the range of skill sets and expertise and qualifications that come with being an architect.

|||||||||||||||||||||||||||||||||||

GRAHAM SAUNDERS
INTERNATIONAL FEDERATION OF THE RED CROSS AND RED CRESCENT SOCIETIES (IFRC)

How long have you been doing this shelter work Graham? Would you call it humanitarian architecture? ▶ I tend to use the term 'humanitarian shelter' because it brings in the two key elements. One is humanitarian action, an activity that is required to effectively fill in the gap when a national government can't respond or doesn't have the resources to respond, or when there are inherent weaknesses in the housing system.

The word 'shelter' is important because it places the focus squarely on shelter and settlement – although I have to say the word shelter still has problems. I mean, it's not a great word in English. I think in our business we all know what it means, but to anyone outside the business it's actually a strange term and I often give the example of my mother for whom the word 'shelter' means a bus shelter or similar. It doesn't mean home.

So what about your own transition into the shelter and humanitarian sector? ▶ That's an interesting question and I think it highlights some of the challenges we face in humanitarian shelter in terms of tapping into the built-environment professions that are out there. In my path, which was not too dissimilar from many, I qualified as an architect in the UK at Liverpool University and at the Architecture Association (AA). And of course, you know with that kind of background, particularly with the AA, the assumption was that I would have a high-flying career in bespoke architecture. In fact, that's very much where I went. I was very fortunate to get a job with Michael Hopkins. It was perhaps a little intimidating for me as a young architect, not only to be working from his house, this building I'd seen as a student architect, but my desk on that first morning was opposite his.

The whole focus was commercial architecture at Hopkins, very much one-off niche projects for major clients such as IBM, Financial Times, the Marylebone Cricket Club, Schlumberger, the Victoria and Albert Museum. They were high-tech, but very grounded in the simplicity and economy of design. In many ways, it was actually a very good education for what I currently do because he was incredibly down to earth. There had to be a solid reason for why you did anything. Why are you using a certain material? Can't you make it simpler? We had to find the most economical, efficient, productive solution.

As work experience alone it was fantastic. And I had that great opportunity to work on high-profile projects for several years, and then, for right or wrong, I thought. 'Well, that's great, but do I want to do this for another ten or fifteen years?' So I turned down the opportunity of associateship and went off and tried other things.

After Hopkins, a number of friends and I set up a practice and that was also terrific fun, a learning opportunity with a number of refurbishments of disused factory buildings in South London and Liverpool. And then we all fancied travelling and going our separate ways. I ended up in Africa looking at appropriate technology and materials and more low-tech solutions to housing and construction.

When I think of how I came to humanitarian shelter, I think it was similar to what happens to most people in the field. In early 1993 my phone rang and someone said to me 'Is that Graham Saunders?' I said, 'Yes', and they said, 'Do you know where Tirana is?' I said, 'Yes, it's the capital of Albania', and they said, 'Well, would you be interested in going there to do some housing?'

In short, following the overthrow of the totalitarian regime in Albania, the European Union had significant funding to support the emerging democracies in the region. One of the few humanitarian agencies then in Albania was working housing and needed an architect. It phoned around and somebody knew somebody who knew me. So I had a very interesting lunch, was introduced to the opportunity and six weeks later I was in Tirana, where I stayed for three years. It was a great sort of baptism!

It was initially to manage new construction. This was in a country where there had just been a revolution. Effectively there was no legislation, no building codes, no forms of contract, no nothing. Albania had gone from being a socialist, centralized economy to a free market one but, as yet, no replacement system had been established. I just brought in everything I knew. I brought in the UK standard form of building contract. I brought in the industry standard approach to construction costing and mechanisms for monitoring work on site. Getting off the plane in Tirana, the fact that I was an architect was immediately recognized and I was able to sit down and do business with contractors, with the ministries, with fellow built-environment professionals. They knew the range of skill sets and expertise and qualifications that come with being an architect.

You're not sitting down at a drawing board any more. What is it about our training and education as architects that enables you to do the work you do now? ▶ Architecture is one of those, I wouldn't say unique, disciplines; but one of those few disciplines that actually combines the need for a real management rigour, careful planning and organization with an understanding of science, materials, technology and engineering. Architecture requires spatial awareness and the art of design. But it also requires the ability to put stuff into practice, to problem-solve and work with people with different skills and expertise, to plan and schedule a series of activities that all need to interlink. I think it's a fantastic grounding in a way of going about business.

When I think about the way IFRC works, we are responding to disasters, which are uncertain events. Nevertheless, some disasters can be predicted and a range of preparedness activities and mitigation activities can be undertaken. That is a question of just being well disciplined, well organized. It's looking at resources. It's looking at who's doing what and where are the required capacities and expertise. It's looking at the range of likely activities and how these would be organized at global, regional and country level.

To be perfectly frank, I view all such activities as I would a typical design and construction project. Even though the output is not necessarily a building, it may be training, it may be the development of a set of guidelines, it may be a big regional sector event but, in essence, all such activities are the sum of many parts, often the combination of quite disparate components. That is very akin to the role of an architect, combining a range of issues, activities and contributors to deliver a product or solution over time with the required financial management and teamwork.

One thing that is quite distinct from working in mainstream architecture is perhaps the connection in your current work between the big issues of civil society and how they connect with architecture and social justice? ▶ My work in mainstream architecture and construction was very rewarding. I was fortunate to work on some fantastic high-profile buildings, and to work with some great people who gave me a great education in creative design, construction and project management. I look at those buildings I was involved with, even those in which I played a minor role, and I get a great sense of satisfaction just to hear other people talk about them. There is a sense of real pride in this for me. In mainstream architecture the process is important, but the focus is more on the end result and it is against the final product that one is judged. Is it a good building or not? The process is just a means to an end.

In humanitarian shelter it's almost the other way around. The product is important. Clearly, people affected by a disaster need to end up in a better position than they were immediately after a disaster. However, the process of achieving this goal is very important. This is because, as humanitarian actors, we are short-term players in the overall housing process in

a given context. This means that the resulting product or 'home', and its future iterations, should be determined by the people of the households themselves. As built-environment professionals we need to acknowledge and feel comfortable with being in a supporting role, an advisory role, and ensuring that 'ownership' of the process and the resulting product remains with the household or community.

We need to keep our fingerprints off the product as much as we can. Ironically, as an architect you are often aiming to make sure your fingerprints are very visible, to clearly have an impact through the design and construction and the resulting product. You want people to be aware of what you have contributed. The biggest challenge for built-environment professionals in humanitarian shelter is to ensure that built-environment concerns – from design and planning issues to material selection and building performance – are adequately addressed as part of a process led by the people of the household or community themselves. The process and the resulting product has to be theirs, *not* ours. That's the real mark of success.

A successful process brings in a much wider group of people than we are used to working with. You can't just talk to whoever is funding the reconstruction, but the wider members of the community who are going to be building it: the neighbours, the local construction specialists, whoever is responsible for demarcating access, the mayor, the village chief, and others who are typically involved in such local planning, design and construction activities. The process becomes so much more important.

I'm biased, of course, because I'm an architect and I work in shelter, but I do feel that the shelter or housing process is one of the primary vehicles for advancing cross-cutting issues such as the promotion of livelihoods, managing environmental concerns and addressing social and economic exclusion through inclusive consultation and project design and management.

Shelter or housing is the element that connects so many parts of people's lives, where and how you live informs your social networks, the wider settlement in which the home is located, the related public or communal spaces, and the links

> We need to keep our fingerprints off the product as much as we can. Ironically, as an architect you are often aiming to make sure your fingerprints are very visible, to clearly have an impact through the design and construction and the resulting product.

GRAHAM
SAUNDERS

with income-generating activities, opportunities for employment, and access to markets.

It's the whole sheltering process, which is so important, and it resonates around the words of John Turner that housing is a process and not a product, a verb and not a noun. This is the guiding principle in humanitarian shelter.

Why is it that architects have been largely absent from the emergency field until recently?

▶ That's a very big question and I don't think there's one answer. First, shelter itself, or housing after disaster, is really something that's not well understood by those outside the sector. Even those involved in mainstream architecture and construction do not fully grasp its complexity, uncertainty and lack of clear definition. Maybe, it is also viewed with a mixture of suspicion and a lack of understanding. It is also viewed with a degree of fear as it's seen as being potentially very expensive. It's linked to issues like land, tenure and property rights. It's very political. It's time consuming. It's doing something that could require considerable time before a tangible impact can be discerned.

For example, we have a problem with the decision makers in and around disasters. In many cases such decision makers are not sufficiently aware of shelter and housing issues, certainly not to the level that means we get the right things done. We see this time and time again. Haiti, following the 2010 earthquake, was a case in point. There was a lack of an appetite to take the bold, strategic decisions that were needed around housing, beyond

△
A carpenter pitching roof in self-help housing in Goma, Democratic Republic of Congo (photo: Steven Michel).

the urgency to address short-term shelter needs. It took almost a year before such key decision makers actually felt capable of putting together the sum of the parts and committing to the comprehensive, integrated strategies that could have been initiated within the first two or three weeks. But this was not unique to Haiti in 2010. This lack of understanding of the complexity, challenges and opportunities of and in the shelter sector is a common problem faced by the whole sector.

What are the recognition and reward systems in humanitarian shelter? I mean there's not a RIBA award for this kind of practice? ▶ No.

Should they have professional awards for this kind of work?

▶ A more important concern than the lack of an award for individual humanitarian shelter initiatives is the lack of a recognized professional career path in humanitarian shelter. Yes, you can obviously get qualifications in architecture and engineering, but beyond that there is no formal benchmarked professional career path. So there's not a huge incentive for individuals with an architectural background to get involved in humanitarian shelter.

It's very hand-to-mouth because the lack of recognition of the shelter sector means that there is a lack of permanent positions, whether in government departments, in donor institutions, or in humanitarian organizations. The reality for the

majority of individuals working in humanitarian shelter is that unless there is another disaster there are no or very limited employment opportunities. The lack of opportunities to obtain qualifications is a further impediment, not that qualification should be the ultimate goal. The only real reward out there for many such individuals is the fact that your position may be extended if you excel – and if there is new funding.

Getting back to your own background, your upbringing, was there anything there that might have sparked your interest in the humanitarian field? ▶   Neither of my parents had a professional background, although my father was an optical craftsman and ingrained in me an interest in how things are made and the skills, tools, time and application required. I was also certainly aware that the world wasn't necessarily an equal place, and that hardships could be experienced by family and friends as well as those in the headline news. My mother grew up in London during the Second World War, in the latter stages of which her home was bombed and she had to be dug out of the rubble. She was, effectively, an internally displaced person for the remainder of the war and, having lost everything, was dependent on relief assistance to provide her and her family with clothing and temporary shelter.

◁
The community erects timber frames for self-help housing, Goma, Democratic Republic of Congo (photo: Steven Michel).

> A more important concern than the lack of an award for individual humanitarian shelter initiatives is the lack of a recognized professional career path in humanitarian shelter.

What is your view on the rise of design not-for-profit agencies and the rise of humanitarian architecture which some see as a sort of neo-modernism, where the architect is going in to 'save the world'? ▶   I'm sceptical of the overall impact and benefit of what a design-oriented architect can bring to the disaster field *without* a prior grounding in the business of post-disaster housing and a recognition of the difference in roles, responsibilities and required skill sets from 'peace time' design and construction.

I have concerns when the focus of the conversation is solely on the product, unless there is equal or greater recognition that the end user must be fully involved. The net result has to be a home that is more resilient, more affordable, performs better than alternatives. It has to be clearly culturally acceptable and something that the household or individual concerned clearly feels is theirs and meets their requirements. In principle, this is the service a good architect should provide to all his or her clients. However, in the post-disaster context – where resources may be limited and the 'client' in question may have other competing needs such as securing food, addressing urgent health needs, and may have been

displaced from their original site, etc. – defining the required service is an enormous challenge for any architect. Unfortunately, many of the humanitarian initiatives that profile the role of architects tend to result in projects in which a clear architectural solution is the goal, often at the expense of functionality, cultural acceptance or the equitability of the response.

An individual who has a background as an architect can bring a range of experiences and skill sets to a humanitarian response initiative, from the ability to analyse a problem to an understanding of construction technologies and the practicalities of project management. However, promoting an architecturally interesting design solution as the most important deliverable – and invariably only for a select few fortunate recipients – can undermine the efforts of others to meet some of the needs of *all* those affected. I feel quite uncomfortable around the attention such initiatives are able to generate, the resources they attract and the limited scale of needs they meet.

Some people might think this is a harsh assessment but I feel comfortable making that comment because, for agencies such as the IFRC, scale is the issue in addressing the needs of the many. With National Red Cross or Red Crescent Societies in 187 countries, who are auxiliaries to their governments, the buck stops with IFRC and similar agencies. For example, a recent publication on an architecturally inspired shelter design had a two-page spread including glossy pictures and very well-written text, describing how seventy households had benefited from this shelter. My reaction was that this was great for the fortunate seventy households, but what about the other several thousand households who did *not* receive such shelters? These households could have benefited from more modest assistance in the form of materials, cash or technical assistance to the same monetary value as the architectural design time and more elaborate technology required to design and construct the fancy solution.

In medium-scale disasters, 20,000–30,000 households can require shelter assistance. In larger disasters this can increase by a factor of ten to 200,000–300,000 households. In Haiti, following the 2010 earthquake that devastated the capital Port-au-Prince and other regional centres, 1.6 million people needed immediate shelter assistance. By initially adopting a minimalist, equitable approach, *all* of these households received some form of protection from the elements within three months. Admittedly, the level of assistance was basic, and needed to be immediately complemented by support to enable families to start to construct something more durable. However, to have provided complete architectural solutions for only seventy of these households would have been an insult to the rest of the affected population.

Design solutions for meeting post-disaster shelter needs are important, but who is generating or supporting such solutions is equally as important. At present there is considerable interest from agencies in high-income, developed countries in dispatching architects and engineers to provide shelter design and technical assistance to low-income, hazard-prone countries. This is despite the fact that there are built-environment professionals with considerable experience of the hazards faced and the constraints and opportunities of available technologies and resources in these countries. For example, what would be the reaction of the Mayor of Lyon in France if, following some heavy flooding in Lyon and the surrounding area, twenty young architects were sent from Central America or neighbouring European countries because they don't have jobs at the moment but they have done their architectural training and they are enthusiastic? Would this assistance be welcomed? What would be the reaction of Lyon architects and, indeed, the regulatory authorities and affected households? I would argue that it is not appropriate to send twenty young architects from Lyon to Haiti or Guatemala simply because they are keen and enthusiastic and they have time on their hands.

You have mentioned to me that you receive at least five shelter propositions a week from many well-meaning builders and architects. Could you expand on why it is that architects assume that post-disaster design is a chance to experiment? ▶ We regularly receive shelter or technological concepts, invariably presented as *the* solution to solving the world's shelter problems. The investment in time, creativity and technical know-how is impressive, and it is inspiring that there is this significant level of interest, drive and enthusiasm. It is unfortunate that the majority are 'closed' or stand-alone solutions that lack any reference to or acknowledgement of existing shelter response solutions, technologies and processes.

Perhaps this can be attributed to the discourses of architecture which prioritize a finished solution – a building – as the goal, not the

The reality for the majority of individuals working in humanitarian shelter is that unless there is another disaster there are no or very limited employment opportunities.

process nor even a technological or material development that could be adapted and utilized by others as part of an open, flexible building process.

About a year ago we analysed the total expenditure on shelter across all major emergencies. This indicated that the average spend per affected household per shelter was $50. The implication of this is that sophisticated, cutting-edge or innovative shelter solutions are very welcome but, due to the limited financial assistance made available for shelter and the scale of the need, such shelter solutions should cost no more than $50. Although different disasters do result in different needs, and the resources available also vary significantly, there clearly is a 'reality gap' between the aspirations and solutions provided by the innovators and the possibilities at country level in a given emergency. The $2,000 solution is very desirable, but it will be the $50 version that is utilized at scale.

What are the two most critical parts of training the humanitarian architects of the future? ▶ First, people need to go into any such training with a professional background, that is a recognized qualification in architecture, engineering, planning or project management, or a vocational qualification in one of the main building trades. This should be complemented by appropriate practical experience, albeit recognizing that design and construction is a team activity and no one individual will have all the required expertise in all disciplines. This may be an obvious requirement but, in practice, over half of all those

> I would argue that it is not appropriate to send in twenty young architects from Lyon to Haiti or Guatemala simply because they are keen and enthusiastic and they have time on their hands.

working in humanitarian shelter are generalists without such a professional background. In addition, there needs to be an awareness and understanding that housing in the humanitarian context means unlearning some of the things that you had been taught or are deemed to be prerequisites. You are not in charge; you do not lead the process; you are not going to be the sole decision maker and, indeed, shouldn't be. It is the affected population, be it at household or community level, who should be in the driving seat.

Why is it that many leading architects, both academically but also practising in the humanitarian field, are originally from the UK? Is it something about your undergraduate training in architecture? ▶ A number of individuals who have been fortunate enough to have influential roles in humanitarian shelter over the past two decades have been UK-trained architects. It should also be acknowledged that the key publication in our sector, *Shelter after disaster*, was written in 1978 by Ian Davis who was, and has remained, a leading figure in the UK and who has continued to support fellow practitioners, both those with considerable practical experience

and those entering the field as students. The British government has also been an active supporter of the shelter sector, in particular focusing on technical expertise and promoting knowledge-sharing. It is also important to note that the role of the architect in the UK was that of the project developer and manager (although that role has been changing in recent years). Hence, a background as an architect lends itself very well to developing and managing humanitarian shelter programmes. Although the architectural training was not particularly oriented to design and construction in other countries, the fact that the UK hosts world-leading schools of architecture does attract interest from the wider world and a diversity of interest and expertise. Having graduated from the Architectural Association in London, as one of the minority from the UK, I can testify to the benefits of having such a 'global' architectural education.

How would you advise a young architect who wants to get involved in this industry? What are the most important steps that they need to take? ▶ First, get a good grounding in practical work experience in your country, both an understanding of design and theory of construction and, crucially, site experience. Don't assume that obtaining a degree in architecture means you are qualified to work in humanitarian shelter or, indeed, commercial architecture, in another country. What can you possibly contribute? I think it's disrespectful to your architectural counterparts in Bangladesh or Guatemala to assume that you have more to offer than they do. So get some experience of the practice of architecture and construction in your own country over three, four, five years so you have something to offer.

Second, and more challenging, is to get some practical experience on the ground. This is not easy as most employers require some initial experience, so how do you get that first job? Getting your feet on the ladder may require compromising your expectations, both in terms of the type of work and the financial benefits available. The lack of a recognized career path in humanitarian shelter is a major problem, and is exacerbated by the lack of recognized academic qualifications in this field. As a hiring manager, I have long complained of the lack of such formal learning and benchmarking in the humanitarian shelter sector. Thus, one of my important tasks today is helping to establish such opportunities through partnerships between academic institutions and leading humanitarian agencies to provide such professional qualifications. This should widen the opportunities for young architects and experienced professionals wishing to change careers to enter the humanitarian sector.

There still seems to be a chronic lack of built-environment professionals trained to work in the emergency field. ▶ Disaster trends indicate an increasing frequency and unpredictability in small- and medium-scale disasters, as well as a dramatic rise in hydro-meteorological disasters, that is cyclones, typhoons, floods and landslides. These disasters often do not warrant international assistance and, hence, have to be addressed by national or local governments with their own professional resources. This is a challenge for the built-environment professional institutes in these hazard-prone countries, both in terms of ensuring that their own training and professional structure is geared towards the need for this experience, and awareness-raising in their own countries of the role of such professionals. For larger-scale emergencies that do need international assistance, the challenge is that of maintaining the required capacity given the unpredictability of such events, or ensuring that such capacity can be mobilized when required.

Perhaps one of the few growth areas in architecture?
▶ Absolutely. Assuming that architects promote the wide range of skills and capabilities that make up the role of an architect, not just the provision of 'architecture'.

You mentioned previously that in the UK and Australia we need training for an architecture for 'fragile times'. That's an interesting concept, might you expand on that comment? ▶ When I 'crossed over' into humanitarian action in the early 1990s, it was understood that the work was primarily in hazard-prone or conflict-affected countries in the less developed regions of the world. However, the 1990s witnessed conflict and large-scale human displacement in Europe through the wars in the Balkans and the social and economic transformations with the collapse of the Soviet Union. Similarly, the earthquake in Kobe, Japan, and Hurricane Katrina in the USA, and the recent earthquake and tsunami in Japan, have highlighted that disasters can strike high-income countries that are relatively well prepared. The bush fires and flooding in Australia, although benefiting from well-resourced response services, have prompted major changes in the approach to planning, building and managing the natural and built environment.

> The $2000 [shelter] solution is very desirable, but it will be the $50 version that is utilized at scale.

▷ View of a Goma neighbourhood following volcano devastation, Democratic Republic of Congo (photo: Graham Saunders).

Globally, we are all now living in more fragile times – environmentally, economically and socially – and hence professions such as architecture that connect all of these key aspects of life have to reflect these changing times. This will impact on the job being asked of architects and hence should also be reflected in the training and the skill sets of the individuals coming into the profession. As architects we need to wake up and smarten up to what our business is and how we do it. The global environment in which we are living and working is becoming ever more perilous. We need to better understand our role, and the value we can contribute.

Why did you choose this housing project in Goma to accompany your interview?

▶ I've chosen the self-help housing in Goma, Democratic Republic of the Congo, because it was a self-help initiative whereby households determined their own shelter design using materials and tools provided, and informed by 'social animation' and awareness-raising on basic building principles.

GRAHAM SAUNDERS

Goma transitional self-help housing
Goma, Democratic Republic of Congo

△
Basic training in key construction
principles and common structural
designs was provided to the Goma
community, but households were
encouraged to develop their own design
with local technical assistance and to
add more durable external cladding,
flooring and finishes (photo: Steven
Michel).

Project type
**Transitional and permanent
housing**

Design and project management team
**Graham Saunders/Steven Michel
for CRS/Caritas Goma**

Donors
USAID

End client
**5,030 disaster-affected
households**

Location of project
**Goma, Democratic Republic of
Congo**

Size
126 m²

Date completed
September 2002

Cost
**$10/m² (labour and additional
materials provided by recipient
households)**

Total cost
$2.5 million

GRAHAM SAUNDERS

Goma transitional self-help housing
Goma, Democratic Republic of Congo

To enable 5,030 families displaced by the volcanic eruption to construct free-standing framed houses which could be subsequently relocated back to the site of their original homes, the Goma transitional shelter comprised a standardized kit of locally procured timber sections, roof sheeting, fixings and tools, and plastic sheeting for temporary enclosure. Basic training in key construction principles and common structural designs was provided, but households were encouraged to develop their own design with local technical assistance and to add more durable external cladding, flooring and finishes. The introduction of twinned small-section timber ('double chevrons') as an economical, lightweight primary structural element has become a feature of the local construction vocabulary.

◁
Another example of self-help housing in a Goma community, Democratic Republic of Congo (photo: Graham Saunders).

△
Example of transitional self-help housing
with banana-leaf facade in a Goma
community, Democratic Republic of Congo
(photo: Steven Michel).

GRAHAM
SAUNDERS

KIRTEE SHAH

HONORARY DIRECTOR
AHMEDABAD STUDY ACTION GROUP (ASAG)
www.propoor.org/ngos/?id=3109

Kirtee Shah

is a practising architect and the Honorary Director of the Ahmedabad Study Action Group (ASAG). ASAG is a non-government organization run by concerned professionals committed to using their skills for public causes, especially slum development, disaster rehabilitation, low-cost housing and policy advocacy. Kirtee has served on several expert committees and advisory groups for the Indian national and various state and local governments in the areas of housing, poverty and urbanization, as well as for UNICEF, UNDP, the World Bank, CIDA and others. He is one of the founders of the Ashoka Innovators for the Public, and was President of the Habitat International Coalition (HIC). He has also been actively engaged with the Asian Coalition for Housing Rights (ACHR) for over two decades. Kirtee is currently assisting the government of India's '50,000 houses' project for the war victims in the Northern and Eastern provinces of Sri Lanka.

Working and interacting with the villagers, living with them and solving problems together, taught us the first lessons in participatory design, consultative planning and multi-dimensional 'development'.

IIIIIIIIIIIIIIIIIIIIIIIIIIIIIIIIIIII

KIRTEE SHAH

AHMEDABAD STUDY ACTION GROUP (ASAG)

Kirtee, how did your original architecture studies prepare you for the disaster reconstruction and development work you are involved in now? ▶ I was born and brought up in a small village near Mehsana in Gujarat, a far eastern province in central India. I am truly a village boy in the sense that I had not even dialled a telephone until I was seventeen years old. My father died when he was only twenty-four years old and I was just eighteen months. We grew up in difficult circumstances in a small village with great financial hardships. This could have been a major handicap in terms of career development, but I am convinced that it has been a positive influence that shaped everything in my life later on.

During the latter part of my studies at the School of Architecture, Ahmedabad, now CEPT University, we started asking questions about the role of the architect in society. It took little to realize that architects then worked for the upper crust of society – the money-rich, cultural elites, those with political power and connections with high-end institutions. And, of course, totally confined to the big cities. The villages and small towns, and the lower-middle class, ordinary people – and their vernacular structures – were of no concern to architects. Someone told me at that time that 99 per cent of India did not exist for architects.

Not that those things have changed much now but, generally speaking, architecture then was an upper-class, elite concern. Architecture was a fashion statement for those who had arrived or were upwardly mobile. And, like many other aspects of Indian social and cultural life, architecture carried an overload of the colonial legacy also.

Without really knowing what it meant, and certainly not influenced by anyone or anything other than my personal background of growing up in a village upbringing in difficult circumstances which created an inner calling, I started feeling – and subsequently expressing – that I did not want to be *that* kind of architect practising *that* type of architecture. I wanted

174

to work in the villages for the non-rich. I wanted to serve not the conventional but the alternative client, the un-served client: the villager, the slum dweller, the poor, the marginalized. The Ahmedabad School of Architecture was a progressive and a liberal institute and saw the likes of Le Corbusier, Louis Kahn, Frank Lloyd Wright and their Indian disciples as gurus, but it did not equip its students to serve these alternative clients. It became clear that some kind of de-schooling, de-learning, re-learning and re-professionalization was essential.

That opportunity presented itself while I was in the final year of the School of Architecture. The event that changed my career, and possibly the course of my life, was heavy flooding from the Narmada River in South Gujarat, about 250 kilometres from Ahmedabad. A number of villages were partially damaged or completely destroyed and, as the luck would have it, I ended up leading a village reconstruction project.

The floods washed away the village of Mandva, 8 kilometres from the district town of Bharuch. An 83-acre site, 2 kilometres from the destroyed village and on a 5-metre hill, was earmarked by the state government to relocate and reconstruct the village. I initially volunteered to help a group of social work students build a demonstration house for the flood victims as part of their course, but along with a friend and a classmate, Jayant Shah, I spent 18 months in the village leading and guiding the reconstruction project, eventually dropping out of the School of Architecture.

The work in Mandva involved preparing the village master plan and designing small, low-cost houses for about 700 rupees each (US$13, at the current exchange rate). We managed the procurement of materials, trained and supervised locals and volunteers in construction supervision, managed the temporary camps for student volunteers and liaised with the state government for funds. It was a time for real learning and growing up.

That was the starting point of my career. We were young, not even out of professional school. We had never built a single house, not even a small room, but were in charge of the reconstruction of an entire village. We had never handled a single client. The first client we encountered was not an individual but a diverse group of 750 rural families, physically uprooted and financially ruined by the floods. Nothing could have prepared one better for the professional career or, for that matter, for life.

The learning was deep and fast. Working and interacting with the villagers, living with them and solving problems together, taught us the first lessons in participatory design, consultative planning and multi-dimensional 'development'. The village reconstruction experience helped us de-learn, re-learn and de-professionalize, and gave us the confidence to meet future professional challenges.

By the time I returned home to Ahmedabad, I had decided not to go back to the School of Architecture. I started looking for opportunities in the city to do something for the poor and the inadequately sheltered. While doing some exploratory work in the slums – with no money – I set up a group called the Ahmedabad Study Action Group (ASAG) with some like-minded individuals, including a professor from the School of Architecture, Dr Rasvihari Vakil (later Dean of CEPT), and the school teacher, Fr Ervity, who had taken us to Mandva village in the first place. ASAG was formally registered as a non-profit in 1971. Over forty years later, I still run ASAG as its Honorary Director. ASAG has done many projects and activities over these many years. Though focused on the poor, and working to help them improve their housing and living conditions, ASAG has refused to be called or seen as a charity or welfare organization. ASAG is in the business of 'development', facilitating creative problem-solving with people and communities in need.

While ASAG is not a charity, would you say it is in the business of 'humanitarian architecture'? ▶ Obviously, the phrase has different definitions and different cultural contexts, but there is definitely a tradition of humanitarian architecture in India. Even if one's focus is on the buildings, great monuments and the non-tangible dimensions of architecture, it cannot be denied that the architecture is for the 'people' and in their service – be that making of a functional house for a taxi driver, a monumental palace for a rich businessman, or a parliament building for a democracy. Architecture's connection with people cannot be questioned.

However, there is another dimension of humanitarian

> I have not seen foreign architects imposing their ideas and cultural biases or prejudices while working on post-disaster or other development projects. I have known them as humble, sensitive, willing to learn, concerned about the community's priorities and beliefs, and aware of their own short-comings and limitations as outsiders.

Kirtee, you were once interviewed by Sandra D'Urzo, who is also in this book. The question she asked you was, 'As an architect working in India how would you define the architectural profession and its commitments to society?' You replied to her, 'I have two identities – one as an NGO development worker and the other as an architect.' Please could you expand on this?

▶ For good or bad, I have been both a community architect and a mainstream architect in equal measure. I have worked in these two fields for over forty years. In both, the engagement has been long, intense and, I must say, very satisfying. It is important that the mainstream architects imbibe the spirit, orientation, attitude and concerns of the community architects. And it is equally important that the community architects learn to explore, even within the limits of their work environment, that search for beauty and aesthetics. The 'uplifting experience' of good design is fundamental to human existence and aspiration.

So, how would you say the role of architects has shifted globally since the Indian Ocean tsunami? For example, I was in Haiti in July and the place was full of architects trying to do good work, but there was also another element where they were trying to experiment with design solutions on traumatized communities. It's like the two faces of a coin: a very sincere one, and then people who see the rebuilding scene as more of an aesthetic and experimental platform. ▶ In India, individual professionals and groups were working on post-disaster

architecture: extending the architectural design services to the unreached – be that a rural farmer, the urban poor or the disaster victim. The challenge of serving the marginalized is a different design challenge to the commercial architect's traditional client. In fact, it takes far more skill to create small, utilitarian and functional designs with limited resources than it does to design a mansion with lots of money. And you are working in much more arduous conditions. The marginalized need the architect's design skills much more than the wealthy. They have very little to meet their needs and solve their problems. A caring, sensitive and creative mind, working with them, can go a long way in re-establishing their faith in the system and the justice of society.

Let me elaborate a bit more on extending architectural, planning, engineering and related services to the poor and marginalized. At ACHR, we have coined a term 'community architect'. The community architect is engaged with the 'housing poor' and

works for job satisfaction rather than money alone. The community architect respects tradition, culture, people's skills and knowledge, and practises participatory methods. The community architect respects climate and the environment and is committed to sustainable design, construction and development. The community architect does more with less, sees big in small and has clients who are not only individuals and groups, but a 'class'. The community architect dreams of changing the system; has a vision; values process and sees problem-solving as a way to build capacity and empower the people.

Humanitarian architecture is also a practice of architecture that recognizes, internalizes and responds imaginatively to wider global and societal challenges. Sensitive and creative responses to the environmental, resource and identity crises must translate into the practice of 'sustainable' architecture in the search for a more humane urban society.

reconstruction long before the Indian Ocean tsunami. My own work, as mentioned earlier, started with a village reconstruction project after the floods way back in the late 1960s.

Mainstream architects and other habitat professionals entering what you call the 'humanitarian architecture' field is a positive development. It helps both ways – the disaster victims getting fresh minds and fresh approaches to better solution making and, at the same time, mainstream architects getting a new feel for the lived reality of the pain and suffering of disasters, of the complexity of reconstruction and rehabilitation projects, of the need to work fast, to 'compromise' and accommodate, to be innovative and to think 'outside of the box'.

With the frequency and intensity of natural and man-made disasters striking the world, the scale of damage and destruction they cause, and the public and private investments being made in post-disaster recovery – housing, settlements, infrastructure and livelihoods – disaster reconstruction is no longer a small matter. It is an industry. But, it is only a few who are in this disaster business. Many more are needed.

I do not see any problem in architects seeking new designs even while working on post-disaster resettlement projects. Post-disaster reconstruction is also an opportunity. I call it 'reconstruction plus': ensuring more and better living spaces, environments and standards to communities than they had before the disaster. That needs new thinking, new ways of doing things, new approaches and new designs;

and, if an architect sees that as an opportunity to experiment and do something that might not work, it does not worry me much. My experience is that people know what is good for them, in most cases, and know what to accept and what to reject.

There is one more reason why I welcome the experimenting and the aesthetics of architects in the post-disaster reconstruction projects. The 'emergency' syndrome – save money, do-it-yesterday, construct fast – catches up with all, the authorities, donors, intermediaries, professionals, contractors and even the communities. The quality of design and the quality of construction are the first casualties. Unimaginative designs and poor-quality construction are the order of the day in many post-disaster projects. It is time the design and construction quality are given priority. A good design and good aesthetic could play as good a role in lifting the spirit, in motivating the people, in treating the trauma as any other effort and input. A good design can make them look to the future with hope. It is time post-disaster reconstruction improved in design and aesthetics. And the

young professionals have a role to play in that happening.

How would you advise young Indian architects who want to get involved in the humanitarian field? ▶ I would direct them to someone doing it to help them get some direct exposure. Nothing motivates one more than an opportunity to engage and find out for one's self. I would not want them to first know and taste the mainstream practice; 'idealism' has a way of dying and the capacity for risk-taking has a time limit. Humanitarian architecture now covers many interesting areas, such as heritage buildings, new forms of housing finance, participatory practice, advocacy for the poor, pro-people policies, new forms of interventions, and new roles for civil society in governance and development.

What have been your own experiences with foreign architects coming into India to work on development and post-disaster projects in your region? ▶ My experience has been extremely positive. For some who come to work with us, it has been a life-transforming experience. A planning student from Harvard,

> The 'emergency' syndrome – save money, do-it-yesterday, construct fast – catches up with all, the authorities, donors, intermediaries, professionals, contractors and even the communities. The quality of design and the quality of construction are the first causalities.

△
A slum dweller child's depiction of the flood scene and dream home, Ahmedabad, India.

USA, came to work with us in the 1980s, stayed eight years and started a new NGO. Two others came from South Africa in the 1990s to work for six months and stayed for over five years. They worked in tribal areas with the poor and, on returning home to South Africa, set up an NGO that became one of the pioneering NGOs in the settlements sector in South Africa.

I have not seen foreign architects imposing their ideas and cultural biases or prejudices while working on post-disaster or other development projects. I have

known them as humble, sensitive, willing to learn, concerned about the community's priorities and beliefs, and aware of their own short-comings and limitations as outsiders. I believe that the 'insensitive imposition' that we hear about is really a matter of perception and a hangover of the past. It is not to imply that there is no truth in it or that it does not happen. It largely depends on how the host organization and its team sees its work, the kind of orientation the guest professional goes through and their attitude to, and relationship with, the communities they work with.

In many countries, education is still largely focused on the celebrity architect, the pyramid model. That is, if you apprentice yourself to a master and work hard, one day you will get a great client and be widely published. The design media seems very focused on this Frank Gehry style of stardom. I'm interested in your response to that because many consider that this bias in much Western architectural education is resulting in a very narrow model of problem-solving. ▶ The situation we find here in India is no different than what you mention

178

Though the monumental architecture of the elite minority is not going away, the architecture of the majority is emerging. It was always there, though never seen that way. The non-designed 'ugly' part of the city, the functional and utilitarian buildings designed by the non-architects, have always been the overwhelming majority, in terms of numbers at least, over the designed masterpieces. The twin has co-existed for centuries and there is no reason why this will not continue.

Architecture as a subject, as an art form, as a *shashtra* [rules] is too big and ancient for me to comment on. But the architecture profession, as we perceive and practise it, certainly needs a rethink, a paradigm shift. We need it; and the people, our clients, deserve it.

Kirtee, I think you have a very unusual take on the architectural profession. And that's because you began this community work early on in your career, and it seems you are working as both a conventional architect but then you could also be working in a village, helping communities after disasters. So, I found that a lot of things you said at the Cooper Hewitt social impact design summit earlier this year in New York very interesting. How did you find that experience? ▶ Quite an experience.

Going all the way to New York for a day-long meeting was a decision by itself. Of the sixty to seventy participants, mostly American architects, teachers, academics, other design professionals and representatives of development and donor agencies, I was the only Indian. In fact, the only Asian.

in the West. It needs to be understood, however, the history of architecture is the history of monuments and monument makers. So, like it or not, there is no way of getting away from the masters and celebrity architecture. Even though the principle of 'form follows function' has been celebrated for generations, it is largely ignored. That is how you get to be a celebrity architect – if that is what you want to be. Sadly, I do not think it will change.

Our democracy, judiciary, governance, bureaucracy and education systems, despite many changes, continue to reflect their colonial origin and lineage. Though indigenization cannot be denied or ignored, the 'foreign' tag still has a premium and the foreign-trained architect still carries weight. Not much is local and indigenous in our architectural and planning education. An architect still looks westwards for ideas, inspiration, examples and masters, although Shanghai, Singapore, Dubai and even Bangkok are new destinations and image icons. There is nothing wrong in that but, what is necessary, is to be firmly rooted in one's local context and firmly anchored while looking around.

I learnt many things and I hope they did too. Like what the world needs to know about Asia and India. Our cities are dominated by informal systems, and managing that informality is a challenge to be faced. Much of the rural housing stock is people-produced – no real-estate market, no builders, no architects, no housing finance companies, no building by-laws or master plans. In its informality, the urban housing sector is only marginally different; the largest producers of urban houses are the slum dwellers. While India might be growing at 2 per cent per annum and cities on average at 3–3.5 per cent, the slums in big cities are growing at more than double that rate. This informal sector is vibrant.

In my presentation, I said that the Western model of urban development would not work in India. I also said that revamping architectural education to make architects socially responsible was no real answer as only a very tiny fraction of the buildings that get constructed in Indian cities are designed by formally trained architects. I also pointed out that improving living conditions in the urban slums in India required a paradigm shift in viewing them not so much as problems but as approaches to a solution. This is not exactly 'out-of-the-box' thinking, but it was a different voice for those in that meeting in New York.

Kirtee, why did you select the post-earthquake housing reconstruction in Gujarat, India, to illustrate your views on the humanitarian architecture field? ▶ The reconstruction work following the 2001 Gujarat earthquake is special for many reasons. With over 950 villages and six cities variously affected and over 400,000 houses to be repaired/retrofitted/reconstructed, the scale was massive, the challenge was daunting and the operative environment was imaginatively facilitative. I had multiple roles to play. One, as an NGO, our detailed submission and consistent follow-up made an impact. Two, as a member of the Advisory Committee of the Gujarat State Disaster Management Authority I had an opportunity to participate in policy making and progress monitoring. Three, our architectural firm was engaged in providing technical assistance, coordination, community engagement and project monitoring services in the construction of 10,000 houses in over 150 villages through fourteen NGO partners funded by KFW. Four, we also designed educational campuses in the Kutch area, the epicentre of the quake. And five, we set up and I chaired the Home Losers' Service Association of Ahmedabad, which organized the earthquake victims under the banner of HOLSAA to secure attention, assistance, services and entitlements for safe, cost-effective and speedy recovery. There was much to learn, give and contribute as a concerned citizen and a professional.

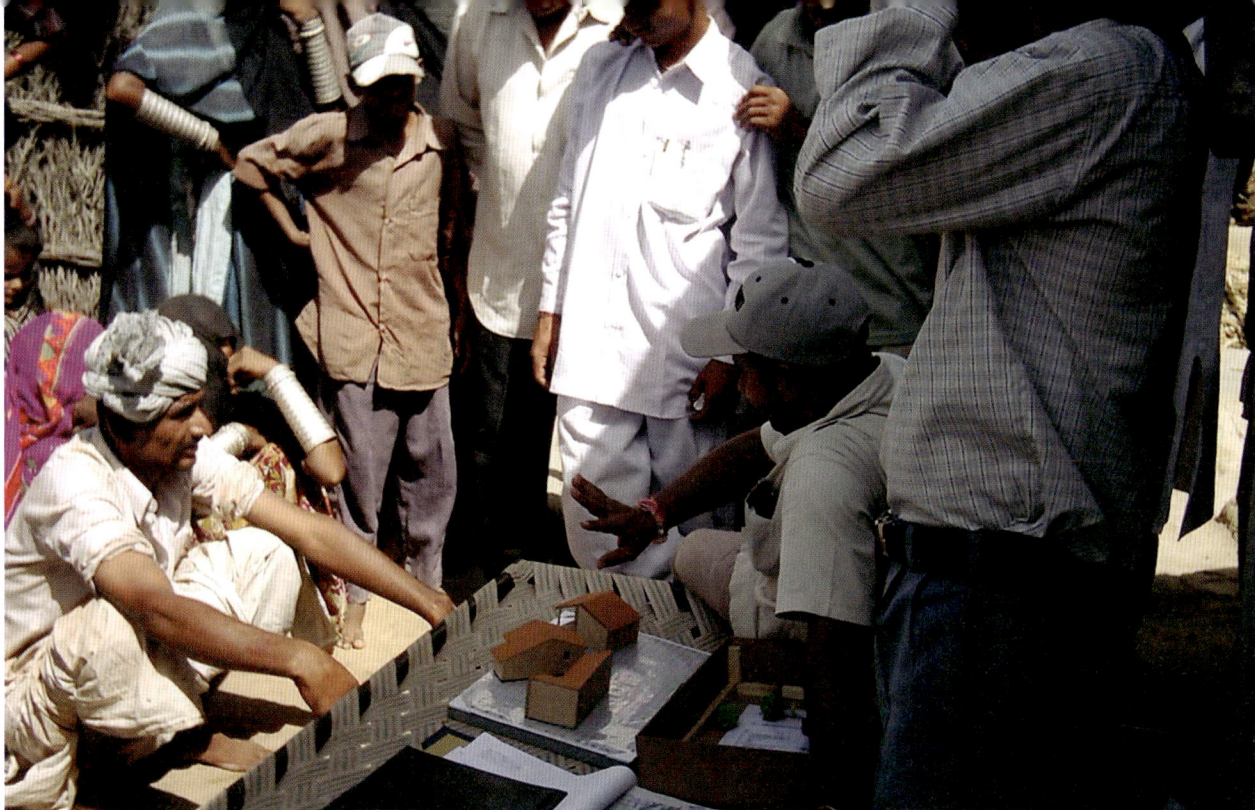

KIRTEE SHAH

Post-earthquake housing reconstruction
Gujarat, India

△
Community consultation using scaled
models for house designs in an
earthquake-affected village, Gujarat,
India.

Project type
**Temporary, transitional and
permanent housing**

Architectural firm
**KSA Design Planning Services Ltd,
Ahmedabad**

Design team
**Dr Nobert Wilhelm, Ar Kirtee Shah,
Ar Samir Shah, Mr Hauke Grages**

Donors
**KFW (Kreditanstalt for
Wrederaufbau)**

End client
**Thirteen implementing agencies
and owners of 10,106 houses**

Location of project
**156 villages of Kutch, Rajkot,
Patan and Surendranagar districts
of Gujarat, India**

Date completed
October 2005

Cost
$29/m²

KIRTEE SHAH

Post-earthquake housing reconstruction
Gujarat, India

The 10,000 houses programme in over 156 villages of the Kutch region of Gujarat was intended to rehabilitate the earthquake victims through community participatory processes, and has yielded good-quality houses, but also a sense of pride, belonging, togetherness and achievement among the community members. The project built communities while building houses, which is a key element of my design philosophy.

◁
Owner-driven housing reconstruction in Kutch, Gujarat.

△
A cluster of houses in an earthquake-
affected village in Kutch, Gujarat.

MAGGIE STEPHENSON

SENIOR TECHNICAL ADVISOR
UN-HABITAT
www.unhabitat.org

Maggie Stephenson

is currently the Senior Technical Advisor for Haiti at UN-Habitat. For the previous twenty years, in Europe, Asia and Africa, she has worked in architecture and planning education, urban government, housing and development, and post-disaster reconstruction for governments, the United Nations, non-profits and in the private sector. From 2005 to 2011 she worked with UN-Habitat and the National Disaster Management Authority in Pakistan, using people-centred approaches to help the millions of people affected by natural disaster and conflict.

> At university, we learnt the value of an architectural education to articulate alternative futures, to play the positive role of devising propositions.

||||||||||||||||||||||||||||||||||||

MAGGIE STEPHENSON
UN-HABITAT

Maggie, please tell me about your architectural studies, where you did them, and whether they had any influence on the kind of work you are doing now for UN-Habitat in Haiti? ▶ I started studying architecture in Dublin in 1984. I was really lucky that my five years in Dublin were at a time when the development of the city was being debated. The centre of the city had been run down over a number of decades and had reached a critical point where it might have become a de-populated transport interchange. The alternative was to revalue the past and look forward to a new Irish urban future.

It was an exciting time to be a student because lecturers in the School of Architecture were teaching us that architects ought to have something to say about what was happening. This was not simply as an academic process as critics and commentators. The school and its staff were also practical and engaged, working on concrete propositions and taking concrete action. As students we opposed inappropriate infrastructure projects and the demolition of historic buildings, and we worked together on proposals to regenerate the river and city quays as the major artery of the city. We learnt the importance of justifying and demonstrating opposition, but more importantly, at university we learnt the value of an architectural education of articulating alternative futures, to play the positive role of devising propositions.

Our design studios were not isolated or hypothetical. We were part of society, part of the body politic, engaged in dialogue with other artists and professionals such as journalists, economists and poets. We were part of a movement with local communities, with local businesses. We saw what can get done by people taking action. Working with other disciplines we heard different questions asked, different criteria applied to decision making, and we had to meet the challenge to address those different perspectives and not simply through a design-driven process. We grew up with design activism as part of our education of what an architect is and does.

△
House built in local 'dhajji', masonry-infilled timber frame construction regenerated from an almost lost tradition to over 110,000 houses post-earthquake in Pakistan. This house reuses the salvaged doors and windows.

University College Dublin had a very strong influence shaping a generation of architects in Ireland, but to the credit of the school, it was not a cookie-cutter system. For some, it was a foundation for excellent design work delivering high-quality buildings over the decades of the boom that followed and, for others, like me, it was a foundation in the possibility of public service, of activism.

I was extremely fortunate to get travelling scholarships to study housing and urban settlements from Sicily through North Africa to Southern Spain, and then to Aleppo, Syria. I had grown up on a farm in rural Ireland. These trips allowed me to have the time to experience a completely different world, not just different physically, but also different economies and different social structures.

In the mid 1990s, I went to East Africa, thanks to the Irish Department of Foreign Affairs' overseas technical assistance programme, to help set up the School of Architecture in Makerere University in Kampala. The role was not simply to teach design skills, but to understand the context and facilitate the creation of a corps of architects equipped to play strategic, transformative roles.

In the late 1990s I went back to study at the Development Planning Unit [DPU] at University College London, where I got a very useful grounding in the economies of cities, and in community-driven design and planning processes. I studied the history of housing policies and gained an appreciation that design is a minor part of the housing process. I already knew from UCD the importance of political engagement and working with other disciplines to achieve architectural and urban design objectives, but in the DPU I learnt about a global scale of urbanization and the importance for architects to work through the built environment towards development objectives – human, social and economic development objectives.

Did your views on the roles of the architect in society ever change during this time?
▶   I've always believed that architects should be useful. At one stage I thought I should be a doctor, because that's really useful! Maybe I feel life is short and the time is now; so there is only time to spend on things worth doing.

Why do you think you needed to be useful? Did you parents and upbringing have anything to do with that? ▶   My father is a farmer. He's useful in so far as he produces food, but it's not necessarily a public service ethic. Farming is a private sector: you grow it, you sell it or you eat it. But I learnt from my parents the idea of stewardship, that we inherit the land from those before us, that we will pass it on, and we need to take care and to add value with a very long-term perspective. I learnt the difference between information and knowledge or understanding, not necessarily formal knowledge, but manual skills, the ability to make things grow, to read the tides, tacit knowledge. From a very close-knit rural community and from my family, I would have to say that I learnt, not exactly public service, but community service in a low-key way; that we are responsible for each other in practical ways, to help whenever needed, without hesitation, without drama.

Maybe there is a satisfaction in time well spent when we do something useful, when we see results of benefit to others, especially when we solve a problem or make life better for people in bad conditions.

I think I would get frustrated spending all my time and energy building a perfect glass box out the back of one person's house. I don't think I am looking for gratitude for helping anyone or kudos for achieving more. I think it is more of an investment approach, that I want to see more return on the investment of time and energy.

Something fundamental to why I studied architecture in the first place, which was also reinforced at UCD, was the conviction that we can actually change or improve things. There are lots of things architects might want to change in the world, but building those glass boxes isn't one of them. I wanted to try a different way to be an architect.

One of my concerns with architects in most of Europe now is their diminishing relevance. The problem is not just usefulness; it's also relevance. What is the relevance of an architectural education? What is the value of it to society? How can we apply it? We don't have to do everything within the prevailing commercial and peer-validated model of architectural practice. We can create new roles for ourselves and make something wonderful possible.

That thought brings us to the term 'humanitarian architecture'. What do you make of it? Does it have any relevance? ▶   I don't really like the word 'humanitarian'.

Why is that? ▶   I don't really know what it means. What is 'humanitarian'?

> I think I would get frustrated spending all my time and energy building a perfect glass box out the back of one person's house.

If 'humanitarian' is interpreted as life-saving, then it probably better applies to medical professionals in all contexts, not only crises. Likewise fire fighters, police and others who work in frontline public services around the world. People working in disaster contexts are not heroes; they are doing a job just like thousands of others around the world in public service. If 'humanitarian' is interpreted as active compassion then isn't that a principle or objective for most architectural and planning practices, whereby we try to address a range of human needs: physical, social and emotional?

Yet I was speaking this morning to a construction engineer who said his experience with architects here in Haiti had been quite torturous. With a growing number of architects now working on – dare I say it, 'humanitarian projects' – why has his experience been so negative? ▶ I have found a key difference between engineers and architects over the last decade. Engineers see the building and how it is made, while architects are more likely to also see the people involved, how the building is used, though I don't think this simplification would explain a negative experience of working together as you describe.

I guess engineers may come from a problem-solving perspective, while architects may come from a propositional perspective, often creating new problems to solve, particularly when they are more focused on 'pushing boundaries' than meeting needs as simply and efficiently as possible.

Architects often have multiple agendas; they see it as an opportunity to innovate or to demonstrate their own personal position or theories. It's about authorship, the portfolio. It's a mixture of good intentions: trying to propose a better future using the vocabulary of architecture. And it's a lack of humility: not seeing that maybe no one wants or needs their designs as much as the architects themselves.

It goes back to the line: 'You're not the story.' People coming to work in crises, and not just architects, are sometimes playing out a role. The demand for what they're trying to do mostly comes from within themselves, and that tends to close them off from listening, learning and considering what the role of architecture as a public service might be.

Look at the impact of the proliferation of design magazines and their closed circle of peer review. Who comments on the role of architects? Other architects. Anyone else? Not really. So we're designing for each other. We have become our own legitimizing audience. The big questions about the relevance of architecture in a world in crisis or a world of rapid urbanization do not arise if we are only talking to each other.

Fifteen years ago, when I started in the post-conflict field, I was working alongside a lot of doctors, engineers, lawyers and logisticians, but not many architects. Yet, ten years later, probably beginning with the 2004 Indian Ocean tsunami and now Haiti, we are beginning to meet architects everywhere.
▶ No, not everywhere. The tsunami and Haiti were high-profile crises, which also attracted higher numbers of all types of international assistance. You will find more architects often in disasters where rebuilding appears to provide opportunities for architects. You're less likely to find them in normal development contexts.

Yes, there are a lot of places where we are not working where people need us or, at least our skills. But, what has been the shift that has brought so many architects to the disaster scene? Has there been a professionalization of the shelter sector? ▶ There is probably a number of factors within the architectural sector and within the disaster or shelter sector. Since the global economic downturn in 2008 or even earlier, many Western countries saw a decrease in the rate of construction and, therefore, in work for architects, particularly for young architects. It became difficult to get a job or even to get experience. Instead of starting new design firms or moving up the corporate ladder, young architects have had to look around and think about what they are going to do, and where and how.

At the same time the proliferation and professionalization of NGOs, particularly in crisis contexts, has meant there are increasing opportunities for architects to find work or experience in this field.

Unfortunately, I think many young architects assume they can lead design projects and that they already have significant skills. You're less likely to find architects assuming that they need to learn. It's also less likely that there are good support structures within organizations to facilitate mentoring and guidance to ensure that they learn what they need to learn.

△
As part of a self-help reconstruction programme, a mason's own house is built in confined masonry, Pakistan.

So, why do architects come to post-disaster environments like the country you are now living in, Haiti? And what can they do to be better prepared for work in a crisis zone?

▸ Perhaps, deciding to work in the 'humanitarian' sector is also driven by changes in architectural discourse over the last two decades. For example, the environmental and sustainability agendas. There has been a general shift in environmental consciousness and community activism in society in Western countries. Look at student work in architectural schools and you see the increase in the number of projects conceived in reference to recycling. Look at the number of post-disaster architectural projects focused on 'innovative' ways to reuse rubble. Continuing this example, architects see countries in the Global South as needing environmental transformation, and disasters are opportunities

to introduce that transformation. Architects often see pilot and model building projects as the means to demonstrate their approach.

What is the objective? We want the world to be more green, more sustainable. We want communities to have access to well-designed social spaces. We want people to have better housing and better lives.

However, we also need to understand issues at a political level. Why are so many millions of people living in terrible housing and in ugly and unsanitary cities? Do we want the world to be more fair? Do we want governments to be more competent, more accountable? Do we understand that the path to better housing may be a development path addressing equity, human rights and sustainable livelihoods? If our objective is to achieve a better

built environment, we will not do so only through architectural propositions. We may contribute to, or achieve, this objective better through other types of engagement: through broader analyses of context, through more complex and multi-factored diagnoses and propositions – through working for social, economic and political justice and sustainable development.

Are we equipped to read and engage with this kind of complexity, with weak institutional systems, with political fragility, with social strife? This is particularly difficult to do when you parachute into crisis situations and have to rapidly generate solutions.

I consider that I was very lucky to spend those years in Makerere University in Uganda. They allowed me to not only be embedded in an institution, but also to learn normal life, to learn how our students and staff live. My time in Uganda gave me the time to build deep understanding.

When young architects, engineers and planners ask for my advice, I recommend they try to find similar opportunities to this. Look for opportunities to learn, to be interns in municipalities, in government, in universities. They will learn not only about the interpretation of their own sector in a new context, but also the wider social, political and economic complexity. Most of all they will learn about systems – why they work, and why they don't.

I went back to Ireland at the start of the boom, and joined local government, Dublin City Council, where I learnt an enormous amount from my colleagues in different fields, with their own knowledge and experience. I learnt constraints and frustrations, to choose my battles, to build consensus, to think strategically, to harness the momentum of others. I learnt how government is a vital building block in making and managing cities. I learnt how cities are run, about tax revenue, how decisions are made, how plans may unravel, about private freedoms and public rules, about the public good.

> If 'humanitarian' is interpreted as active compassion then isn't that a principle or objective for most architectural and planning practices, whereby we try to address a range of human needs: physical, social and emotional?

When I understood more of how cities are made, I could see wider options for how architectural skills might play a part, and with our teams in the city council we developed a platform of opportunities for new and talented private sector architects to get a break, a chance to work in the public domain. In football terms, I was playing the role of the football manager. I was not the striker, but more like the talent spotter and strategist. All architects know that good architecture needs good clients. I had the golden opportunity of being the client – on behalf of the city – at a critical time, and I'm immensely proud of the quality of work done and the contribution we made to the regeneration of the city.

So early on, when you got involved in East Africa, were you working as an architect in the traditional sense of designing buildings and supervising construction? ▶ I started working in the School of Architecture, where the focus was educational, but we did also develop real projects with students. It's not always easy to deliver a project for a client and to deliver on pedagogical objectives, but we tried to strike a balance.

I also worked outside of the university as a traditional architect: designing and building schools, government buildings and houses. I really enjoyed learning how to use local technology to drive small projects. I have always really enjoyed making buildings. I really enjoy how things are made and used, whether a chair, a retaining wall or a building.

I thought I would always be a traditional architect. I love the design and drawing process. I love the construction process and site. I probably have less patience for the increasingly heavy paperwork involved, but when I stop travelling I will be happy to pick up a pencil or a mouse and draw again. I liked the idea of working quietly and practically. I was never a naturally sociable person or a good talker. I would never have expected, at age eighteen, that I would have spent most of my life in roles that involved so much talking.

So tell me how your roles have evolved in the different positions you have held in Afghanistan, Pakistan, to what you are doing here in Haiti. Are you employing the same set of skills? ▶ Sometimes my job is predominantly technical: materials testing, specification research

and development. I had to read more engineering texts during my time in Pakistan than I did in the twenty years beforehand because we were dealing with building codes and with a wide range of local technical questions. And I coordinated with the international networks for discussion and advice.

In Kabul I worked for the Aga Khan Trust for Culture, where the work was both very practical – working with masons, regenerating old skills – and very people-centred – working directly with communities in the old city to understand their lives and priorities.

At the moment with UN-Habitat in Haiti, I am primarily in an institutional support role – capacity development, policy and programming, strengthening national and municipal government systems. This is not just a theoretical, talking and writing role; it also involves the field work of understanding what's really happening on the ground, and capacity building by doing, working closely with government staff.

Architectural education brings the benefit of going beyond reading just the context to making

MAGGIE
STEPHENSON

positive propositions. We always have to put ourselves on the line, make the compromises and say, given the situation, here's what we think is possible. Sadly, I think architectural education and practice too often also develops a strong desire for authorship, for articulating and concretizing one's own vision, and this can contradict the need to listen openly and to facilitate the visions of others.

I guess something I learned from teaching in architecture school is that the goal is to get to the best version of each of a multiplicity of visions rather than to get multiple copies of my vision. The role of facilitating architecture students to learn and develop involves asking the right questions. Perhaps, that is the continuing core of what I do in all situations: asking useful questions, helping people find the space and skills to do something themselves. It may be engineers in our office, government officials or community leaders. This is probably the continuing thread in all my different roles. At least I have to keep that in the front of my mind and keep working towards helping people to understand, to discover, to gain confidence, to articulate, to decide, to organize, and to act.

Maybe it is the perspective of a farmer to think long-term about what can grow, to try to create the conditions for growth, and to know we have only a small role in the process.

So over that span of countries you have worked in, what do you see as being the main characteristics of a successful post-disaster shelter programme? ▶ First, you have to recognize that shelter or housing is a process, not a product. It is a process that was going on before the disaster and will continue in the future. The housing context has social, economic and political factors. We need to know the strengths and weaknesses of the housing process. We have to know where people want it to be in the longer term to know how to usefully intervene in the shorter term.

Second, and in reference and thanks to Ian Davis's *Shelter after disaster*, don't do anything for people that they can better do themselves. For me, this means most importantly letting people make their own decisions. Perhaps help them to have better information as the basis for those decisions, but it is vital that people have real choice and real responsibility.

Architects love designing houses. We love deciding what is possible with budgets, space, planning for future extension, imagining a life,

deciding on what shade of blue. Why would we want to take that away from others? Why would we not want to enable everyone to be architects themselves?

A good shelter programme should facilitate the range of choices, including less hardware-focused solutions (such as renting and staying with relatives), and accelerate and improve the long-term recovery or development of the housing sector by introducing elements such as hazard resistance, water management. A good shelter *programme*, as opposed to a *project*, must be concerned with coverage and equity. This is a question of our collective responsibility to fairness, and the obligation to avoid islands of often agency-driven, high-cost model projects in a sea of wider needs.

I guess I could talk about improving shelter programming for many hours but, in general, I would like to make a plea to architects involved in shelter and to agencies and donors to reconsider their objectives. Move away from indicators of outputs and counting visible standardized units, and measuring whether it was on time and on budget. We have to

> Architects may come from a propositional perspective, often creating new problems to solve, particularly when they are more focused on 'pushing boundaries' than meeting needs as simply and efficiently as possible.

> If our objective is to achieve a better built environment, we will not do so only through architectural propositions.

learn and to think instead about outcomes: optimizing the local economic impact, increasing skills and awareness, reducing risk.

Architectural practice is usually conceived in terms of outputs; we do not tend to look at the impact of our own work. But in shelter programming, and particularly in urban issues, we have to learn to understand and evaluate the outcomes and impacts of our interventions.

A lot of architects or designers see the post-disaster field as an opportunity to experiment. Here in Haiti, for example, an American company has brought a pre-built 'dome' solution, a polyurethane igloo. ▶ Especially since Katrina, too.

What do you think about that?
▶ Okay, I'll answer on a bit of a tangent. The World Conference on Earthquake Engineering happens every four years. Two thousand earthquake engineers came together to talk about earthquakes in Lisbon in 2012. Do you know what? There isn't one full-time earthquake engineer in Haiti!

This is back to the problem of lack of donor support to second technical expertise into government and institutions where they could best play a role. But it is also a symptom of the disconnection between the professional focus on innovation

and peer validation, and the need for the application of knowledge. It is not only a question for donors, but also a question for the professional technical community.

Is there a global engineering community or, in our case, a global architectural community? In an age of increased communication, of globalization, where is the technical community's interest in the issues of Haiti?

As regards experiments, there is a gap between the idea of research and development and the application. Are their lab experiments a waste of time and effort? Sadly, often yes, because they're not conceived or tested within a real context. They are conceived somewhere else and tested and proven in a lab. They are not tested in terms of affordability, let alone local acceptability, which are the real measures of whether it will ever be used.

This is why I say that housing reconstruction has to start from what was going on before any disaster, and understand people's own decision making. That's the authentic creative process; that's the design process. It's not a technical process on its own. It's not as simple as consulting people once you show them options. It's literally getting inside the lives of people who build or have to rebuild after a disaster.

From the excellent team of the National Society for Earthquake Technology in Nepal, I learnt how to train people about safe construction. We started by standing back, watching how locals work and then asking them why they do what they do, what they think about it.

We didn't start from anything we have to say. You listen to what people think about how they usually design and build. Do they think it is good or bad? Do they see any issues with it? Have they been thinking of how they might improve it in any way? What happened to the buildings they built themselves? What are the cost issues? Skill issues? What old skills have been lost? Do urban lives mean new materials, new building types?

Get inside their heads first. This is a very important part of how we might change how and what we design. I don't think we would ever end up with an igloo then, or a plastic dome. They come from an entirely different logic, and sometimes not only a technical logic, but also commercial and political logic.

I would have to say there are some invaluable people, like Svetlana Brzev in Vancouver and Marcial Blondet in Lima. They are highly technical engineers and academics, but they are also always focused on how best to respond to local needs in order to make a practical difference. They are helping us here in Haiti, from a distance, to address fundamental issues around the quality of concrete blocks. Amazingly, more than three years after the earthquake this is still a largely unaddressed question despite hundreds of millions of dollars of international assistance. This is what we need – not the new igloo, not magic solutions – but a recognition that improving concrete blocks can contribute to the improvement of millions of buildings. This would be a strategic investment of technical capacity in a context where, like other resources, such capacity is very limited.

One notable Australian architect became even more famous when he designed a 'future shack' for use in post-disaster contexts. When I asked him about the research he had done for this project, he said, 'I didn't need to research because architects can hypothesize people's shelter needs.' ▶ We can, but whether the outcome is good or not is another matter entirely.

His project generated a lot of press. It was exhibited at a famous modern art gallery in New York. But my point is not about the individual. It's about the tendency for architects to design, or believe in, a solution that is applicable to every culture, every climate and every kind of disaster. ▶ We have to think about whether these would be the kind of houses that people can live in.

Absolutely. Is the tendency to universal solutions just modernism reborn? ▶ I guess there are a number of influences. The universal solution to 'housing' can be seen as a design or technical approach, rather than considering, as I mentioned before, the idea of housing as a process. When you think this way, the solution might need to involve

designing housing finance tools, regulatory systems, etc. Funny how we actually know these are major drivers of housing design and decision making in our own countries but then, perhaps, we don't really embrace them as a field of intervention at home either.

Disasters seem to be questions in search of answers. I don't honestly think families are standing around thinking what will they build. For example, should they construct that plastic igloo or get one of those future shacks? Rather, it is donors, NGOs and government that think big, new answers are needed or that it's a good idea to assume responsibility for others. They are the ones who talk about bringing added value and go chasing pre-cooked solutions to help them to spend their funds. Actually, I think architects need to realize they are probably being duped into driving answers in search of a question.

There is also a 'designer shack' aesthetic: some good ventilation (which also lets in dust) and reuses disaster debris as recyclable materials. Modular meets extendable, diagrams for process, and you're good to go. It's a similar process to the use of words like 'sustainability' and 'resilience'; you can join the dots in design language too, but does it mean anything?

I would question the motivation and the ambition of proposing universal solutions. Is it about designing only on our own terms, as happens in many 'pilot' and 'model' projects? While there is a certain arrogance and detachment in the modernist search for universal solutions, there at least was a political ambition in

modernism – a search for reform and equity, values that have largely disappeared from mainstream architectural discourse.

Do we want to continue producing design-driven hypotheses about how the city could be, what housing may be, producing documents that probably only other architects can interpret? Or do we also want to roll up our sleeves and go inside the housing finance system, the municipalities, and have the discussions in real time, listening and learning, and being challenged to be accessible, to explain in understandable terms, to contribute strategically, to ask useful questions, to propose across multi-dimensions, to be relevant?

How do you train and empower architects to work in this way? There are some emerging courses, even degree programmes, in the UK and elsewhere in Europe. Are they moving in the right direction? ▶ Many courses teach about shelter, the international assistance landscape, the shelter cluster, community participation, and so on. This tends to equip people to be part of the machine of disaster response. I also think that it is unhelpful to have logistics-focused training as the basis for shelter response. It could even be problematic to have a new cadre of people, educated in generic international politics, operating in crises and making decisions in the shelter sector, but with no concept of housing processes. Architectural education takes five years; it takes time to develop an appreciation of built-environment issues. Courses in international politics and a textbook on development are not a replacement.

Part of the deficiency in disaster courses is the focus on shelter without a balancing focus on housing, land and urban development. I think we are playing a catch-up game with architects working in urban contexts, especially the rapidly growing informal cities in the South. We do not need urban design, not even urban planning as such, but courses in urban development processes, city economics and urban management.

Most development-based courses cover social development quite well, teaching important approaches in participation, needs assessment, monitoring and evaluation.

I think we might play a better role not only in developing countries but also at home if we were better equipped in dimensions which are often missing from architectural education, such as a strong grasp of governance, theoretically and practically. We also need to understand urban economies, the informal sectors, markets, services, livelihoods, land law and property rights. We particularly need to understand money as a key means to realize and drive agendas. These design tools are just as significant, no, more so, than the choice of building materials.

If we consider that technical people working in development will usually need to play key roles in training, mentoring, support, advocacy and capacity building, then it is imperative to also equip them with pedagogical understanding and skills. We all know how we best learnt ourselves. We can draw upon this key experience in our own lives to continue to actively learn ourselves, and to actively enable others to learn also.

Maggie, what project did you choose to explore your experiences in the humanitarian field for this book and why? ▶ I have chosen a post-earthquake reconstruction programme in Pakistan.

Many projects achieve results at pilot and small scale, but do not address the challenge of scaling up. In this programme scale was a design factor from the outset, everything was based on understanding the adoption and replication of improvements at scale.

This was about people and systems, understanding demand, motivation, preferences, priorities, incentives, concerns, aspirations, understanding communication channels, media, messages. These are critical lessons to address the challenges of scale in housing and cities in non-disaster situations also.

Do we want to continue producing design-driven hypotheses about how the city could be, what housing may be?

MAGGIE
STEPHENSON

MAGGIE STEPHENSON

Post-earthquake rural housing reconstruction programme
Pakistan

△
A family with their new home. Each house is different according to site, construction type and preferences, but over 90 per cent complied with the government standards.

Project type

Temporary, transitional and permanent housing

Programme design team

Government of Pakistan, Earthquake Reconstruction and Rehabilitation Authority, Nespak, UN-Habitat, NSET, PPAF, World Bank, SDC

Programme implementation team

Partners above, as well as state and provincial government, the Pakistan army and over fifty NGOs, technical and civil society partners

Donors

Government of Pakistan, World Bank, DFID, Islamic Development Bank, Asian Development Bank, KFW, SIDA, CIDA, SDC, USAID/ OFDA, AKDN

End client

630,000 affected families, 3.5 million people and federal, state and provincial government

Location of project

Pakistan

Size

126 m²

Date completed

December 2010

Cost

Various costs/m²

Donor funding

$1.6 billion + private funding estimated at $2 billion

MAGGIE STEPHENSON

Post-earthquake rural housing reconstruction programme
Pakistan

The programme was designed to enable people to take informed choices and responsibility for the reconstruction of their own homes, through financial and technical assistance. Technical options were to be affordable, achievable and appropriate, including the regeneration of local techniques and the improvement of conventional construction, and were promoted through design principles rather than fixed models. Equitable financial support for all ensured the lowest incomes could manage a basic home, and leveraged the better use of private funds by those with greater means. Sustainable and better housing rather than simply 'safer' housing criteria addressed natural resource management, environmental performance, diversity and cultural heritage.

◁
All members of the family took part in training and awareness activities, ensuring they could contribute to construction, site supervision or quality control effectively.

△
A UN-Habitat steel fixer on site at
critical stages to show correct details
for the first corner for the site mason to
copy during the housing reconstruction
programme in Pakistan.

ANNA WACHTMEISTER

URBAN PROGRAMME MANAGER
CORDAID
**(CATHOLIC ORGANISATION FOR RELIEF
AND REDEVELOPMENT AID)**
www.cordaid.org

Anna Wachtmeister

has worked for UN-Habitat, in the GTZ Participatory Urban Program, and at the Urban-Think Tank, among others. In Iraqi Kurdistan, she was involved with post-conflict urban revitalization for the ancient city of Erbil, including building the capacity of Iraqi professionals. Over the last two years, she has managed the processes of linking relief to development through Cordaid's integrated neighbourhood reconstruction programme, which is aimed at permanent housing solutions in Port-au-Prince, Haiti.

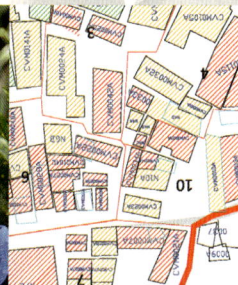

> I chose architecture because I thought it had a social conscience; that was my naivety. I thought I could make the world a better place, but when I arrived at university it was very much about other things.

||||||||||||||||||||||||||||||||||||||

ANNA WACHTMEISTER
CORDAID
(CATHOLIC ORGANISATION FOR
RELIEF AND REDEVELOPMENT AID)

Anna, it would be great to understand your background: where you have come from to where you are now professionally. ▶ I completed my undergraduate studies in architecture at the Welsh School of Architecture, and then I changed to Sheffield University for my Masters. Students in the UK need to choose what they want to study at university as early as the age of 16 if they are going to study the right prerequisite subjects for successful university admission. I chose architecture because I thought the profession had a social conscience; that was my naivety. I thought I could make the world a better place, but when I arrived at university it was very much about other things. I felt that culture of building, let alone the social impacts, and even political contexts were side-lined. I still think that way. On the other hand, the environmental impact of architecture was taught thoroughly at the Welsh School. Here, also, one of my favourite tutors advocated architects to act as agents on behalf of others and we were introduced to 'self-build' as a participatory technique.

That was a very good school because it was realistic, you know; you had to think about the fire escapes and how the materials came together. It prepared you to be able to build. But I was missing the social components. I secured a place at the University of Sheffield. There, I found that new conversations were taking place; for example about the impact of an architect's intervention – which might not always necessarily be a building – within a setting, within the city.

Between the Welsh School and Sheffield, I worked for Stefan Behnisch Architects for a year in Italy and Germany. I loved working there. It was international, and they had a design ethic, a social as well as an environmental consciousness. I also realized that there were many budding architects who made wonderful designs and had a much greater passion for designing landmark buildings than I. They would do anything to get into a design team for the latest museum. I didn't relate to this ambition that most of the other architects had to create an award-winning building.

I took another year out. I'd read that most buildings around the world were not designed by architects. I became totally fascinated about the non-engineered, the common vernacular, the people building their own homes. I felt that I, and architects and professionals in general, had a lot to learn from our built heritage and informal settlements. But if people are recognized for their contribution to the city, what was the role of the architect?

I began to rethink my profession. I didn't know about Nabeel Hamdi, or Architecture for Humanity, or anything about housing for the urban poor. They were not part of my undergraduate degree. While searching the internet, I found something called UN-Habitat. I successfully applied for an internship and spent seven months in Nairobi at the Sustainable Cities Program. I went home, completed my Masters at Sheffield, and that was what I wanted to do: to work with people in rapidly growing cities, wanted to participate in the debates on these phenomenal urbanization trends, focusing on improving the built environments of the marginalized. My best friend was living in Egypt at the time, so I just moved to Cairo and looked for a job. I ended up working at GTZ, the German international development agency,

in their Participatory Development Program in the slums of Cairo. I was there for a year and a half and, well, everything has just happened from there.

So to this field, humanitarian architecture. Some people say that it's a relevant term because every act of architecture should be humanitarian. What do you think? ▶ Humanitarian architecture in a post-disaster context makes me think of two professional cultures converging: humanitarian aid workers and architects. The humanitarian sector and the emergency response sector are people-centred but they work differently to architects. They also have different standards to architects. Humanitarian aid workers have to rapidly pinpoint a problem, zoom in, and relieve the suffering with any means possible while staying within international conventions such as SPHERE [www.sphereproject.org]. It has to be

the most efficient, target-focused operation. Humanitarians act. Architecture, on the other hand, is much more about the process. Architects know it will take time, that there will be changes along the way, and often we don't know the outcome at the beginning of the process. I also think that architects, in general, can be more developmental in their thinking. I think architects look at a situation in a broader way, from the materials that are being used in construction before the disaster to the cultural aspects or the systems that are already operating within the communities. This fascinates architects because they've been taught to take the context into consideration during decision making, while traditional humanitarian workers and donors would focus much more on fixing the need as rapidly as possible.

In Haiti, it was the first time I saw so many, particularly young, architects and other

▷
Community reconstruction underway in Villa Rosa, Port-au-Prince. In addition to housing reconstruction, paths were paved, surface water was channelled and a basketball court was revamped. All reconstruction was executed through community contracting instead of engaging contractors (photo: Ifte Ahmed).

built-environment professionals working as project managers and technical advisors in NGOs, creating this fascinating cross-professional culture.

So you have moved from slum upgrading, to working in the post-war environment, and are now working in the post-disaster and development contexts. What have been the fundamental differences between the development work and the post-conflict work and the kind of work you're doing in Haiti? Has it required a different set of skills? ▶ In Haiti, during the emergency period, we often used the expression 'to build the bridge while walking it'. You keep delivering while you strategize and make improvements to the programme. Your solutions have to be developed under the enormous pressure of spending enormous amounts of money in a very short time.

I don't exactly know why it needs to be like this. After a disaster, why do we have to rebuild everything in a couple of years, especially as cities, even individual buildings, take much longer to evolve. Yet, the post-disaster situation can involve large amounts of funding and international expertise and it puts urbanization on the agenda of the government. This should be taken advantage of.

But who is the client? There is a constant juggle between satisfying the donor and responding to your context. At Cordaid, the NGO I was working for in post-disaster Haiti, our funding was not fully tied to donor requirements and we had a certain freedom to pursue a more developmental approach to reconstruction using community-driven processes and going for permanent solutions with appropriate norms from the start.

What was your day-to-day work for Cordaid? ▶ Even though I was only 32 at the time, I was seen as one of the most experienced in the team; so I quickly became one of the managers. So in my first months in Haiti, I spend a large amount of my time recruiting. You don't think about it, but all these people have never worked together. Yet we had 150 colleagues we had to quickly gel to make a team.

The internationals were built-environment professionals; our local colleagues formed the community development team. The international effort was very much concerned with setting up systems to facilitate the work of our Haitian colleagues, who were working directly with the communities and our partners. One of the hardest things to explain to the team was that our mandate would soon end and, with that, our contracts. We were working ourselves out of a job. We tried to make sure that the foreigners would leave the team first once systems were in place. A Haitian colleague took over my job after six months. Sometimes, the internationals would become technical advisors to the Haitian managers. This also moved the process from construction-led to a much more community development-led process.

As part of the integrated approach, Cordaid encouraged partnerships between NGOs to benefit from each other's expertise and funding. As we teamed up, my time was also spent coordinating – how to coordinate urban planning while retrofitting latrines and homes and building the capacity of the community and local authorities? We had regular meetings and set up an important but complex data management system to help keep everything moving and integrated.

So, have you finished your work in Haiti now? ▶ The Cordaid emergency office has closed. After two and a half years we moved totally to a development mode. From managing *projects* in Port-au-Prince, I now manage *processes* from headquarters in The Hague. We still work with the same three neighbourhoods where we supported reconstruction. Even though the implementation of projects is left to local partners, such as authorities and landlords, Cordaid often still takes responsibility for the donors. At the moment we are hoping to create market-based solutions such as an affordable housing project based on real-estate development models instead of relief. This means getting Haitian banks to invest. The participatory process still has to be there.

> I didn't relate to this ambition that most of the other architects had to create an award-winning building.

Let's take a step back. Why were you originally interested in doing architecture? Was there something in your family background? ▶ My parents are very global in their outlook; they have always travelled and operate in a global network. My dad's a successful businessman who has travelled to quite unusual destinations. I move around the world with no difficulty. I have always belonged to a growing and, in my opinion, privileged global network of people who have chosen migration as a life and work style. I have never lived in my 'own' country, Sweden, and have recently married an Indian architect. So living among cultures other than my own is the norm for me. Why am I doing what I am doing? As I said before, I wanted to do something that has a positive impact. My strengths at school were mathematics, physics and art. So I assumed that was architecture. I don't think there is a more exciting reason than that. I do feel that I carry responsibilities and ambitions and a willingness and easiness to put myself out there. I also believe that the most destructive developments are results of human choices and that we can do better than we are doing at the moment.

When I was in Sri Lanka after the tsunami I saw many architects and contractors going in and experimenting with the latest prefab experiment. Have you seen much of this in your kind of work? ▶ We get approached by many who say 'We have a design for Haiti. Can I send you our brochure?' And I don't know why housing experiments such as igloos keep on arriving. I have no idea.

That's not the best way for architects to use their skills. I think architects are best at being a mediator between many different types of opinion, at understanding the importance of context and at listening, learning and responding to clients' needs. Architects are generally good at working with clients and the business community, as well as with finance, legal and other professionals. This means we can generally find locally appropriate solutions if we know our limitations.

A disaster interrupts development. 'Building back better' is understood by many as building sturdy houses that will withstand the next disaster. It doesn't seem to matter that the reconstruction does not build on local pre-disaster systems and cultures. Too often, the inexperienced see a disaster as creating a *tabula rasa*.

A noted civil servant of a relief-receiving government once said to me, 'It is the do-gooders that are the biggest threat.' This has stayed with me. Local systems made fragile by a disaster can easily be trampled by new arrivals fuelled by large amounts of money and the self-assured attitudes of the 'do-gooder'. All communities, even the ones living in the most precarious conditions clinched to a steep hillside, know what works for them.

Architects can support communities to become more equal partners by treating them as a true client. The tricky thing is that someone else is paying – the donor. Humanitarian organizations tend to choose contractor-led initiatives, mainly to meet construction standards, to quickly meet targets and to

△
Home-owners who participate in Cordaid's owner-driven housing construction project buy the materials themselves in Port-au-Prince, Haiti (photo: Cordaid/Jip Nelissen).

△
Reconstruction in Villa Rosa, Port-au-Prince. Cordaid built
capacity in the community, coordinating actors and funding.
Architecture for Humanity provided technical assistance
(photo: Ifte Ahmed).

satisfy procurement regulations. Notice how all these things are measurable? Architects can counter this by prioritizing more community-led approaches. They are trained to satisfy clients who are typically the end-users.

What was Cordaid's approach to reconstruction in Haiti?

▶ Cordaid's urban reconstruction programme sought to build upon the existing urban fabric and the community's ability to organize themselves towards a common goal. We tried to define our role as enablers and technical advisors to the communities. There is an enormous pressure to do and be more than this. But is this time pressure justified in the case of complex urban disasters? Would it not be smarter to slow down the process to ensure that the 'hosting' nation – not the NGO's targets – are central?

Mass destruction can be used as an opportunity as it might be the only time for a long time that there is room for the reorganization of land uses and the opportunity to introduce infrastructure. This takes some time but, just like in all cities, things are not built overnight.

There is a growing body of people from the built-environment profession involved in the post-disaster field, but maybe not enough to meet the demand. ▶ It's only really when I arrived in Haiti that I've reconnected with the international architectural world, even from the mainstream architecture world. Where I was in Kurdistan you couldn't even find it; if you

ANNA
WACHTMEISTER

Googled it you won't get anything. While in Haiti, every single architectural school seems to have had some discussion about how to rebuild Haiti. There seems to be a growing number of architects interested in this field.

But it is the Haitian and Kurdish professionals who should harbour the know-how! MIT, Berkeley, Brookes and two or three universities in Port-au-Prince – Kiskeya and l'Université d'Etat – set up the Haiti Center. There was a summer school for Haitian students together with international students. The idea was to take advantage of all the international expertise in the country at the moment, lectures, visits, internships, etc. I think the concept is very beautiful, a small step in the right direction. The World Bank funded it. If you think about building the next generation of disaster response team, the local architect, engineer, sociologist and others should not be forgotten.

So what would your advice be to young architects wanting to get involved in the work you are currently doing? I'm sure you get requests from outside: 'Look, I want to work in this post-disaster field.' What advice would you give them? ▶ I do see that more structured training paths can be taken. I don't know if it's useful to join an Architecture for Humanity chapter or another not-for-profit. I was never really part of that. I hear a lot of the people I met in Haiti came through the Shelter Center (Geneva) with Tom Corsellis.

I was never schooled in either development or reconstruction, but learnt on the job. I spent

years learning in the field; I made sure to work with world-class professionals around the world and the discourse opened up to me. I made sure that my experience has been varied; I have worked from many types of platforms; local private practice in Caracas, international NGOs, teaching at a knowledge institution, international expert consultancy …

I think one thing that's important is just to keep your gut instinct, so if you feel like this is something I want to be involved with, or this organization doesn't seem to do things exactly like I feel comfortable with, you need to use your own judgement because how else are you going to measure what's good or bad? Everyone thinks they're doing good.

And the other thing is not to be afraid, just go out there. For example, I just came back from Kurdistan, where I met a young Romanian architect who's just moved there because she knew there were things going on, and now she's finding very good job opportunities. I don't think the way to get the job is to sit in

London; you need to be in the place. I would also suggest going to the places which might not be getting much international attention. Maybe to work with local stakeholders, particularly the government, to get to know the 'receiving end' of humanitarian interventions?

So if you had gone straight from Sheffield University to Haiti and hadn't had that experience in between in development, would you have the right set of skills? Should people be doing a degree in development studies or joining some programme at the International Federation of Red Cross and Red Crescent Societies? Because there is a tendency within the architectural world to think that since we can design a teapot we can design a city. And clearly some of the skills that you've outlined that you have been using were never taught in your original design studies.
▶ Architects take on many different roles in humanitarian work. But in all positions, you will be communicating to an array of different people. Some don't even know what an architect is.

> Your solutions have to be developed under the enormous pressure of spending enormous amounts of money in a very short time.

When I was at architecture school some of us did what were called 'live projects'. I hear that the concept has really taken off in the UK now. Every year we spent time with different client groups, we even had budgets to manage. We worked, for example, with a multicultural community in Paris and a hospice. We worked with the director and the people staying in the hospice. When you walk into a room where someone is still alive who won't be alive on your next visit, and you're discussing what is important in the design of a hospice, you're a bit shaken. If there are opportunities to get exposure to the real world, you make sure that you get them.

Another thing, our final lectures at architecture school in Sheffield were on how to talk to the layman. So we were actually unlearning the jargon of architecture, so we could go out and talk to the non-architect about an aspect of the built environment; this is what was most important in my architectural education!

Anna, why have you chosen Cordaid's Urban Reconstruction Program to represent your larger views on the humanitarian sector? ▶ It illustrates the role NGOs take in the making of our cities. As international agencies take up not only the challenges of slum upgrading, but also complex urban emergencies, more architects are contracted by NGOs. A built-environment background is a necessity. This reconstruction project starts to recognize the self-determination and spirit of the community and local stakeholders. It starts to challenge the conventional model of reconstruction by balancing the immediate need to build back and the long-term ambitions and goals. It also starts to question the role of the NGO post-disaster, if NGOs should be building at all?

> Most of the designs should be home-grown. These people have ideas and they built houses before the emergency; it's not like they don't know how to, that they have no traditions.

ANNA WACHTMEISTER

Urban Reconstruction Program
Port-au-Prince, Haiti

△
Home-owners contract a local mason
to retrofit their damaged house (photo:
Cordaid/Jip Nelissen).

Project type
**Integrated neighbourhood
reconstruction**

Project partners
**The communities of St Marie, Villa
Rosa, Tisous and Nan Cocteau,
the mayor of Carrefour, the local
authorities of Turgeau, Cordaid,
Architecture for Humanity,
Architects De L'urgence,
UN-Habitat, IOM, Build Change,
IHDI, PANOS**

Donors
**Private donations of the Dutch
public, the government of the
Netherlands, UN-Habitat and
Trocaire**

End client
**80,000+ individuals living in four
neighbourhoods in Port-au-Prince
severely affected by the 2010
earthquake**

Location of project
**St Marie, Villa Rosa, Tisous and
Nan Cocteau in Port-au-Prince,
Haiti**

Date completed
2012

Cost
$13 million

ANNA WACHTMEISTER

Urban Reconstruction Program
Port-au-Prince, Haiti

Cordaid's Urban Reconstruction Program after the 12 January 2010 Haiti earthquake aimed to build upon the existing urban fabric and the community's ability to organize themselves – this is why I chose the project to illustrate my interview. The aim was to allow communities to improve their own neighbourhoods through community planning, community contracting and owner-driven construction, working in collaboration with the authorities with technical and financial assistance from international and Haitian partners. Its objective was to link the emergency response to rehabilitation, reconstruction and future development. We ensured, for instance, permanent solutions from the start, such as urban planning and building capacity of local stakeholders, and permanent incremental housing.

◁
A design service is offered by Cordaid and Build Change for home-owners of damaged and destroyed homes (photo: Cordaid/Jip Nelissen).

△
Site plan of Villa Rosa area: Cordaid undertook the first mapping and enumeration surveys of the area. The damage assessment (red, yellow, green) completed by the Minister of Public Works was also drawn onto the maps (photo: Architecture for Humanity).

ANNA
WACHTMEISTER

EPILOGUE

Bryan Bell
PUTTING THE PUBLIC IN DESIGN

Ian Davis
ARCHITECTURE AS SERVICE

Rory Hyde
SENDING OUT AN SOS

PUTTING THE PUBLIC IN DESIGN

BRYAN BELL

FOUNDER
DESIGN CORPS

CO-FOUNDER
SEED NETWORK, USA

In recent decades, designers have been responsible for using a great deal of resources to do very little. We now know this was neither affordable nor smart. The economic crisis that ended that era of waste was a wake-up call to the design professions. Design practice and purpose must change or continue to shrink, ceasing to be at all relevant and on a path to eventually dying out.

How can we reframe our role in the world? The answer is by addressing the real challenges of our time. Instead of doing little with a lot, we must do much more with much less. As natural and man-made disasters wreak destruction at an increasing rate, the world's resources are quickly decreasing at the same time.

Fortunately, the human mind is capable of the great creativity needed to address these challenges, and designers have the valuable skills needed to do it. The fifteen innovators described in the pages of this book show how a new generation, working with the impacted communities, shape responses that have highly

positive impacts. These are demonstrations of the highest and best use of the creative mind. While many people have said that every design idea has already been done, these pages show that the opposite is true – the best ideas have yet to come. The ideas presented in these pages are that part of the cumulative proof that is needed to demonstrate the relevant role of design for the world's future.

These innovators are not just designers of objects; they are designers of systems and processes. They inventively manage limited resources and help form effective collaborations. This is a leap in how creativity gains greater value in addressing issues in the world. This leap takes designers and their creative skill set to a new level of relevance. This higher level of involvement maximizes the contribution made by designers' talent throughout the process. In my own experience, I found I was able to contribute more as a designer by joining a non-profit organization, Rural Opportunities, in rural Pennsylvania, rather than the office of Steven Holl in New York. At Rural Opportunities, I became a part of the stream that provides affordable housing. I learnt how to create a project starting with the specific needs of the housing end-users and then to understand the system that could deliver the results. The highest use of my creativity was not designing elevations, for which I had been well taught. The highest use of my creativity was to envision solutions for the real challenges of our clients, either day-to-day or in times of crises.

It is clear that the current design professions are not meeting the needs of the world. Now, specialties have arisen from the field work of many who see this gap and are attempting to meet it. But these efforts need to reach stability and permanence. There is a great value to understanding their success so that this work can be replicated. We must also learn from failures so that they are not repeated.

The thesis of humanitarian architecture is that there are specific skill sets and areas of expertise for architects to respond to disasters. Esther Charlesworth points out that this is similar to other specialties such as humanitarian law. Humanitarian law is similar to humanitarian design in that it shares the specific mission to limit destructive effects and minimize human suffering.

As Charlesworth states, we need to shape this expertise based on best practices. And just as these professional specialties have evolved in this century, there is much evolution on the horizon in design. This is an exciting time when these professions

and specializations such as humanitarian design will mature and then go to scale to meet the need for them. This book examines this specialty.

First of all, we need to learn from each other. Right now, the predominant form of practice is isolated experimentation in the field. While many are succeeding in making positive impacts, this also has the potential to lead to many failures. We need to document successes and failures and draw transferable lessons from them.

The spirit of individual activism has led to many new ideas. However, it is wasteful of time and resources for us each to rediscover the best methods to use. For myself, it required ten years to find a means to learn how to professionally practise design in the public interest. Despite degrees from Princeton and Yale, and experiences in famous offices, I had little knowledge or practical skills to serve the public through my design abilities. What are the 'take-aways' of information that we each have to share?

Let me present two that are relevant to the subject of humanitarian architecture. One of them is about disaster preparedness and is a failure. The other is about disaster response and is a success. While both are anecdotal, the important transferable lesson is that open participation in a design process is critical.

Anecdote 1: Tohoku, Japan earthquake
One of the greatest disasters of the last decade was the 2011 earthquake in Tohoku, Japan,

which was both a natural disaster and a man-made failure. It led to 15,883 deaths and caused nuclear accidents, primarily the level-seven meltdowns at three reactors in the Fukushima Daiichi Nuclear Power Plant complex. While the natural disaster was bad enough, human errors and poor planning compounded the negative impact. Many of these human errors were known, but the top-down process of decision-making in Japan did not provide means for collaborative preparedness, even when the imminent impact was recognized. The lesson here is that preparedness needs to allow for a collaborative and open approach to assessment and recommending solutions.

Anecdote 2: Broadmoor neighbourhood
A positive example of disaster recovery is the Broadmoor neighbourhood of New Orleans, which is considered one rare success in the recovery after Katrina. Why was this neighbourhood successful where many others failed? There were steps taken immediately after the hurricane to organize an all-volunteer redevelopment planning effort. This allowed residents to meet to discuss and vote on components of the plan, and how differences over goals and priorities were mediated and resolved.

On 11 January 2006, residents of New Orleans' Broadmoor neighbourhood, which still bore the deep scars left by Hurricane Katrina, were shocked by the headlines in *The Times-Picayune*. The Urban Planning Committee of a mayoral commission charged with developing a reconstruction plan for the hurricane-ravaged

House constructed with the Gulf Coast Community Design Studio following Hurricane Katrina in Biloxi, Mississippi.

city had proposed giving hard-hit neighbourhoods like Broadmoor four months to prove that they were still viable and, hence, worth rebuilding. Worse still, the paper had printed a composite map, drawn from the committee's report, which showed six green dots indicating low-lying areas that could be turned into parks and 'greenspace'. One of those green dots covered Broadmoor. Incensed at what they viewed as a betrayal by their own city government, Broadmoor residents who had returned to salvage their flood-damaged homes began to consider how to save their neighbourhood from the bulldozers. Their efforts quickly coalesced around the Broadmoor Improvement Association – a venerable neighbourhood organization – and a determination to create their own plan for recovery. A core group of residents – many of whom had never met each other and none of whom had ever worked on a redevelopment plan – would take the lead in organizing the planning process for the still-scattered community (Scott, 2008).

One of these examples represents a successful process and the other does not. And a problem with both of these anecdotes is that they are anecdotes. They remain in the category of isolated examples with limited lessons despite the potential lessons to be learnt. And while story-telling has been an important method in public interest design over the last ten years, we need to move towards a more rigorous and systemic approach to successful processes and rigorous documentation of results.

What are the elements that make a project succeed in the public's interest? A multi-year effort to establish the core principles of the best practices have identified the following Social Economic Environmental Design (SEED) principles:

- Principle 1: advocate with those who have a limited voice in public life.
- Principle 2: build structures for inclusion that engage stakeholders and allow communities to make decisions.
- Principle 3: promote social equality through discourse that reflects a range of values and social identities.
- Principle 4: generate ideas that grow from place and build local capacity.
- Principle 5: design to help conserve resources and minimize waste (SEED, 2013)

A national survey of members of the American Institute of Architects confirmed that 97 per cent of respondents agreed that these principles together represent an ethical basis for the practice of public interest design.

But principles are not valuable unless they can be converted into practice and into actual projects. For this reason, a coalition called the SEED Network has established a standard process for design, documentation and evaluation, called the SEED Evaluator. The SEED Evaluator is a communication tool that allows communities to define goals for design projects and then measure the success in achieving these through a third-party review. Using the SEED Evaluator allows communities to develop their

leadership and decision-making from within while using a proven method and recognized standard of success, leading to SEED Certification.

The SEED Evaluator can assist individuals, groups, designers, communities, project planners and participants to achieve like-minded goals that are focused on the triple bottom line of social justice, economic development and environmental conservation. SEED responds to the critical questions of design in the public's interest:

- How does this project create positive change in the face of social, economic and environmental challenges? What does this success look like and how can it be measured?
- How does the design product answer the short- and long-term needs of a community that validates ethical and sustainable approaches to design through a triple-bottom-line approach?
- How can the design team directly engage the community and other vested parties in the total project process so that the outcome is driven by the community?

The SEED Evaluator provides guidelines for a design process that directs participatory design practices and tools to document the goals, process and results of a project.

Let's look at how a tool like the Evaluator could benefit the two anecdotal examples I have given here.

First of all, in disaster preparedness, SEED evaluation assures that a broad spectrum of the public is involved in planning, eliminating the top-down process that led to the human mistakes of Tohoku. The SEED Evaluator creates a platform for collaboration and consensus building. Completion of the three phases of the SEED Evaluator can lead to SEED Certification, which can add validity and needed 'proof' of a project's successes, from design concept through to implementation. Progress and challenges can be documented with evidence through each project phase. As a tool developed for architects, industrial designers, landscape architects, communication designers and urban designers, the SEED Evaluator provides guidance through a strategic matrix of questions that critique the social, environmental and economic viability of each phase of development. Because SEED believes in a bottom-up approach to problem-solving that truly activates community concerns, this process entails, and in effect requires, an inclusive and participatory process where many are able to contribute their ideas to the whole.

Second, the lesson from Broadmoor is that if communities are involved in planning before a disaster, then they are able to start from an advanced platform rather than building from zero after a disaster strikes. The Broadmoor Improvement Association had been active in visioning their neighbourhood before the storm. This enabled them to organize and pick up again quickly after the storm, which put them years ahead of other neighbourhoods in recovery, and helped them avoid becoming a 'green space' in someone else's plan.

To conclude, we must move from anecdotes towards systemic solutions. We must move from disparate individual efforts to collective action. We must provide the clear and meaningful professional standards of practice.

References

Scott, E. (2008). Case study of Broadmoor's community based recovery – 'Broadmoor lives': A New Orleans neighborhood's battle to recover from Hurricane Katrina (sequel). Kennedy School of Government, Harvard University. Available online at www.case. hks.harvard.edu/caseTitle. asp?caseNo=1894.1 (accessed 2 August 2013)

SEED Network (2013). Available online at www.publicinterestdesign.org/ tag/seed-network (accessed 2 August 2013)

Bryan Bell

founded Design Corps in 1991 with the mission 'to provide the benefits of architecture to those traditionally unserved by the profession'. In 1985 Bell worked as Project Director with Samuel Mockbee on three houses for rural families in Mississippi. Bell was selected for the ID Magazine Design 50 and Metropolitan Home Design 100. His effort to share ideas with the newest generation of architects led to a series of conferences hosted at universities, Structures for Inclusion, which are a forum for students and recent graduates to learn about grassroots efforts to make architecture more accessible. Selected presentations from these have been presented in two publications: *Good deeds, good design*, published by Princeton Architectural Press in 2003, and *Expanding design: Architecture as activism*, by Metropolis Press in 2008.

ARCHITECTURE AS SERVICE

IAN DAVIS

VISITING PROFESSOR IN
DISASTER RISK MANAGEMENT
**COPENHAGEN, KYOTO, LUND
AND OXFORD BROOKES
UNIVERSITIES**

A career in architecture engages with so many disciplines and aspects of life it is impossible not to enjoy it ... Successes and failures in architecture are part of the duality of being alive – happy and sad, good and bad, life and death. I am reminded that no amount of darkness can extinguish a candle's flame. That is why, for me, optimism always prevails.

(Ritchie, 2013)

I am often asked whether I get depressed visiting disaster sites, and then writing or lecturing about such experiences of acute need and devastation. I can only echo Ian Ritchie, since my optimism also prevails when witnessing the astonishing ability of disaster survivors (not *victims*) to cope. Amid the direst of circumstances, they devise shelter, rebuild their habitats and settlements, often learning in the process how to build safely and better (Davis, 2011a).

Initiation ...

My first decade in architectural practice, spent in the offices of prominent architects, was an excellent education into the anatomy of prestigious architecture as well as the nature of 'powerful architectural egos'. Erno Goldfinger (the inspiration for the James Bond villain) reminded his staff regularly of the immense privilege we all had to work for one of the last of the 'modern greats'. Later, in the early 1960s, I worked in Minoru Yamasaki's office in Detroit. As the architect of the World Trade Center's Twin Towers in New York City, Yamasaki had the world at his feet, with international clients pleading with him to design this or that skyscraper, airport or university.

As newly qualified, naive architects from many countries, we argued endlessly within these offices about the abstractions of architectural expression, declaring our allegiances to favoured members of the quartet of form-givers: Wright, Mies, Aalto or Corb. But I don't recall a single discussion concerning the needs of the elusive occupants of Goldfinger's concrete slabs or Yamasaki's shimmering skyscraper towers. It was a case of one-way traffic with clearly defined roles: over-confident designers *delivered*, while passive users or occupiers *accepted*, without contact with the designers of *their* living environments.

In sharp contrast to such design work for wealthy corporations, I used to visit a crowded upstairs room in Bloomsbury, London, on the way home from the Barbican design office. It was occupied by three people, comprising the entire staff of a fledgling Christian NGO – Tearfund (now, in 2013, it has developed into the fifth largest relief and development agency in the UK). Here, I was introduced to a world of acute need, far removed from architecture with a capital 'A'. I worked as a graphic designer, creating disaster relief posters and slide presentations that included the plight of those affected by the 1970 cyclone that devastated the Bangladesh coast, killing about 300,000 people.

Recommendation …

The next port of call on my journey from 'high design' to something very different occurred during a memorable interview in September 1972. I was applying to undertake a PhD on 'Shelter after Disaster' with Professor Otto Koenigsberger, a German architect and planner who had been Director of Housing to the government of India, before becoming head of the Development Planning Unit (DPU) at University College London (UCL). During this perplexing interview I was invited to forget about my architectural education,

reject the values and norms of these years working with the great, the good and the arrogant, and virtually start again from scratch (Koenigsberger, personal communication):

> My conditions in agreeing to supervise your research are as follows: you will agree to go to the next major disaster, wherever that is, and examine the way disaster survivors manage their shelter process, with your mouth firmly shut, ears and eyes wide open, and you will give me a firm promise not to design anything.

Vital seeds were contained in Otto's demanding conditions concerning the role, within disaster or development contexts, of a very different architect than anything in my past experience. Shelter could be regarded as a process, not just a physical enclosure. I learnt that it was *'sheltering'* that mattered, not just *'shelter'*, in a similar manner to Eisenhower's famous quote that 'it is *"planning"* that matters, the *"plan"* is unimportant'. I was asked to observe how survivors meet their own shelter needs, with a tantalizing question – just *who* is the decision maker of the shelters or dwellings: the trained professional or the untrained house owner/builder?

Maggie Stephenson reminded me that the idea of *choices* involves far more than design choices, since it concerns how to prioritize the use of money and resolving dilemmas about extended families subdividing or staying together [Stephenson, personal communication]. Such choices may not be about design criteria, but they will significantly affect the

outcome. There is wisdom in those well-known sayings:

> Don't experiment on people who have no choice.

> If people have very little, don't take away the last vestige of dignity, which is the right to choose.

Then there is the perennial question – does effective shelter and housing require a *supply-* or a *demand-*driven approach? Since professionally trained designers have no monopoly on designing or creating, what can we, as designers (or *facilitators*) usefully do to support the shelter and safe building and reconstruction needs of exceedingly poor, marginalized and vulnerable families? How can their latent design and construction skills and capacities be unlocked for the common good?

Stephenson expands on this issue:

> Not everyone designs or builds hospitals, but many people design houses, think about their design, have preferences, dreams, nightmares, probably even build, fix or improve their houses. It is a challenge not only to know what we can *add* to these processes, but *how* to add them and *how* to work with the people involved, deciding *what* the relationships would be.

Shortly after my interview in December 1972, Managua, the capital city of Nicaragua, was devastated in an earthquake. This became the setting for my introduction and education to disaster shelter and reconstruction needs.

During the subsequent forty years, my initial interest in shelter after disaster expanded rapidly into an ever-widening range of related concerns: safe building *before* disaster, disaster risk management, strategies to reduce risks, adaptation to climate change and reconstruction planning. Working in these varied spheres required travel to well over forty disaster situations in every continent except Antarctica, and these experiences evolved into courses and training manuals within many universities, UN or NGO offices. They also resulted in writing or editing various books – with my first book being *Shelter after disaster* (Davis, 1978).

Therefore, with this background, it has been a rich assignment to read some of the vivid contributions to this book, and reflect on the evolving roles of architects in disaster or development contexts, in such a dramatically different world from the early 1970s.

Along with many, I am not particularly attached to the titles 'humanitarian architect' or 'humanitarian architecture' any more than the equally misleading designation 'humanitarian disasters'. My reasoning is that *all* good architects and *all* good architecture, whether created for the meek or mighty, are by their very nature 'humanitarian' as they satisfy deep human needs and aspirations. And *all* architecture should be 'for humanity'. Thus, we still await an accurate descriptive name for architects working effectively in disaster contexts.

Motivation …

The only example of a currently well-known architect working continually in the humanitarian field is the Japanese architect Shigeru Ban. The interview with him reveals his passion to work in conditions of acute need:

> After working as an architect for a while I became disappointed in the way that the profession was working only for privileged people, rich people, corporations. And what we were doing was helping them represent their power and money with monumental architecture. Power and money are invisible; so they needed our buildings for show. I was a little bit disappointed that we, as architects, were not working for society.
>
> **(Shigeru Ban, p. 20)**

In 1995 I was invited to Kobe to review recovery plans following the earthquake. One of the most moving experiences was to visit the Paper Church that Ban had designed for Nagata Ward. While I was present a group of elderly Korean widows were attending a Japanese language class within the church. Here was an outstanding example of an architectural statement ideally suited to its context. This area was the worst affected section of Kobe and it resembled a war zone following both earthquake and fire devastation. In this setting, Ban's church, used for Christian worship as well as diverse community functions for the surviving community, was an oasis of calm, simplicity of expression and beauty, as well as being a centre of community activities of all shapes and sizes.

Ban has described his motivations in undertaking such work after repeated disasters (Pallasmaa *et al.* 2007: 101):

> Naturally I am conscious of my social responsibility as an architect but my involvement in humanitarian work is not because of a feeling of obligation. It is a natural response to help someone in distress; responsibility is not just about a sense of duty.

Ban's poetic work has always intrigued me, since he clearly uses his innovative architectural design skills, working with disaster survivors more as clients or consumers rather than design or construction participants or even the 'architects'. The interview in this publication provides rich insights into his unique role in designing structures in many disaster contexts, always sensitive to local cultures, based on strong links with local architects, and always seeking low-cost, sustainable solutions.

Integration…

> we have retreated to the more simple things we think we can better control – things like designing decorative buildings and the idea that every problem must have a building as a solution.
>
> **(Paul Pholeros, p. 56)**

The philosophy that inspires the development work that Paul Pholeros leads among the Indigenous people of South Australia in the organization he co-founded, 'Healthabitat', echoes the experiences of post-disaster interventions by sensitive architects. His holistic approach, with the integration of social, public health, economic and ethical dimensions into a design brief and working relationships with users, is a model for any architect working in a context of deprivation. Thus, Pholeros highlights in his interview the need for 'social' reconstruction as well as 'physical' reconstruction.

Currently I am co-authoring a book on reconstruction with David Alexander (Alexander and Davis, forthcoming) and we have developed a pair of models to describe our essential message in graphic terms. Model 1, 'Progress with recovery', describes the stages of recovery and the critical need for 'development recovery'

that goes well beyond replacing the vulnerable status quo that gave rise to the disaster.

Model 2, 'Recovery sectors', picks up on Pholeros' holistic approach that began when he had a progressive architectural education at the University of Sydney in the 1970s, with

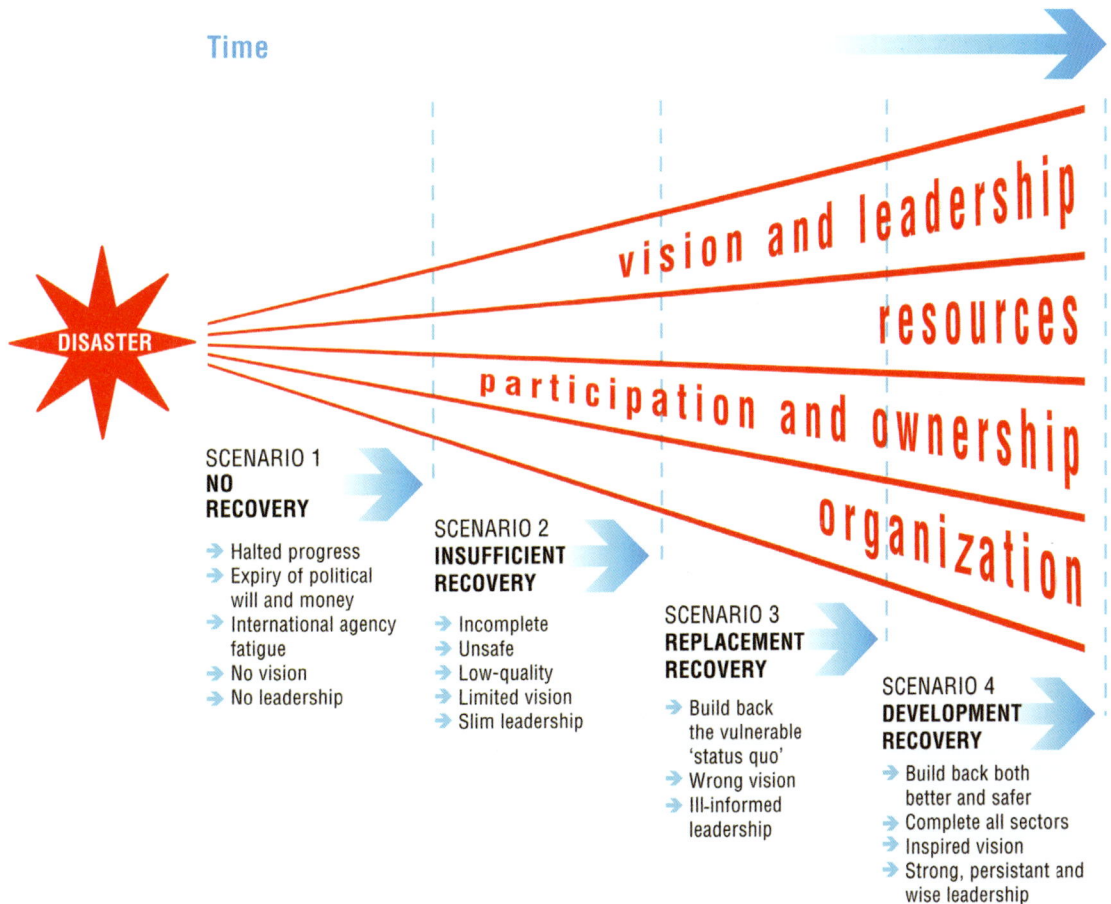

Time

DISASTER

vision and leadership

resources

participation and ownership

organization

SCENARIO 1
NO RECOVERY

→ Halted progress
→ Expiry of political will and money
→ International agency fatigue
→ No vision
→ No leadership

SCENARIO 2
INSUFFICIENT RECOVERY

→ Incomplete
→ Unsafe
→ Low-quality
→ Limited vision
→ Slim leadership

SCENARIO 3
REPLACEMENT RECOVERY

→ Build back the vulnerable 'status quo'
→ Wrong vision
→ Ill-informed leadership

SCENARIO 4
DEVELOPMENT RECOVERY

→ Build back both better and safer
→ Complete all sectors
→ Inspired vision
→ Strong, persistant and wise leadership

△
Progress with recovery.

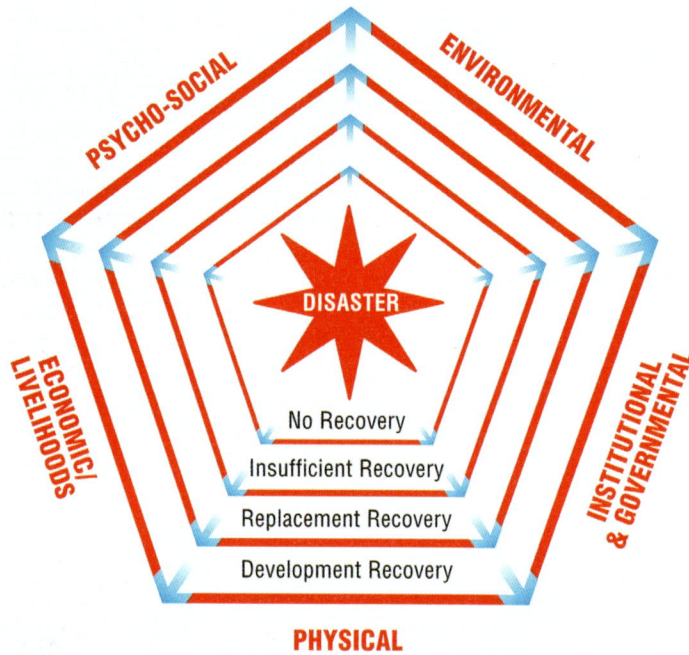

PSYCHO-SOCIAL
ENVIRONMENTAL
ECONOMIC/LIVELIHOODS
INSTITUTIONAL & GOVERNMENTAL
PHYSICAL

DISASTER

No Recovery
Insufficient Recovery
Replacement Recovery
Development Recovery

△
Progress with recovery.

wide integration of the social and ecological in his studies. This model considers recovery as a pentagon comprising five integrated recovery elements. An effective reconstruction programme can meet all these needs in a joined-up manner. Physical building can assist the psycho-social recovery of participating survivors, create livelihoods and boost the local economy, and the materials being selected for shelter can of course support environmental recovery. The entire recovery process may start by assisting the local government to get back on its feet.

Communication …

Patama Roonrakwit undertook postgraduate studies at Oxford Brookes University, where I teach occasionally, so she may even have listened to one of my lectures in the mid 1990s. But I wish I had listened to her at that time, since she must already have had a clear and infectious vision of 'architecture as service'. Her interview reveals a passion to work *with* people, to enable them to play crucial roles in the creation of responsive living environments. She writes:

I use the discipline of architecture as a tool to communicate with people … Unfortunately, poor people

often find it difficult to believe in themselves, and so wait for someone to lead. Instead, I use architectural design thinking to encourage them to be more confident.
(Patama Roonrakwit, pp. 68–69)

Patama's experiences are a vivid reminder of the many programmes I have seen or helped design, dating from the Guatemala earthquake reconstruction of 1976, where local builders and craftsmen and -women rapidly grew in confidence as they were trained in safe building. Gradually, the leaders of these programmes were able to 'pull back' as self-confidence grew in the trained builders from their rapidly developing building skills – a case of effective two-way communication.

Inspiration ...

When I was working briefly with UN-Habitat in Haiti in 2011 following the earthquake (Davis, 2011b), and visiting the reconstruction projects following Katrina in 2012, I had the pleasure of meeting a host of deeply committed architects working on diverse recovery projects. So it has been intriguing to read about Eric Cesal's experiences in working in both reconstruction situations in his interview in this book, and in his own inspiring book, *Down detour road* (Cesal, 2010, pp. 185–8):

> Like one million of my fellow Americans, I saw Hurricane Katrina as a call to arms ... this was one event that was hard to turn away from.

Later, Eric Cesal travelled to work on reconstruction projects in the blistering heat of Biloxi and, despite the hardships, his heart was light, having reached a vital stage in his architectural journey:

> I felt I was getting in touch with architecture at its purest, most honest level. I was exploring architecture as shelter, as community, and as activism. I felt I finally understood what architecture is supposed to be about. I understood what a house was – it was safety, it was security, it was peace, health care, and the mark of just society.

His reflections on the experience are a touching inspiration for anyone aspiring to use their architectural skills as service (Cesal, 2010):

> I worked with men and women who would likely never be on the cover of the *New York Times*. Men and women who did not aspire to make a statement, or a 'weird metal thing ... that doesn't look like a house.' Men and women who merely desired to use their skills to answer that basic human call for service. At night, falling asleep ... I would wonder whether service had any place in architecture – and whether architecture had any future without service.
>
> (pp. 185–188)

My work in Haiti following the earthquake was with an Irish architect, Maggie Stephenson, a member of the UN-Habitat team in Haiti. Before this experience, she had worked in user-build housing reconstruction programmes in Sri Lanka and Pakistan. So I asked for her thoughts on Eric Cesal's night-time question and the title of this contribution, 'Architecture as service'. She replied that, while recognizing that architects are comfortable with the notion of service to individuals or communities, she believes there is no recognition yet of the added value of working in *public* service with its high potential and critical importance at every level of government and within technical spheres. Despite the multiple systems failures following the Haiti earthquake, architects failed to engage with the varied systems, which included access to credit, quality control of building materials, tenure problems, etc., and in lieu of accepting such challenges (Stephenson, personal communication):

they preferred to go directly to work with the communities because they enjoy that better, because the systems are too complex, or it would take too much time, or they don't have the necessary tools.

Perhaps this withdrawal also relates to the complexity and difficulty of engagement in politics, power and institutions. However, building accountability is as much an 'act of service' as working with your sleeves rolled up side-by-side with people in a community.

Then, getting into her stride, she took a well-aimed swipe at the political apathy of today's architectural profession:

> I also wonder about the collective architecture community, do we have joined-up things to say? Or are we mostly looking for projects and authorship? Do we have something to say about housing and justice, about public space and interaction, about culture and memory?

She queried the sharp contrast between the attitudes of architects currently working in disaster contexts with earlier times when the modern movement was being formulated – a time when:

> architects were highly political, and mobilized themselves to have something to say about housing and cities. Where is that platform now in an era of information and communication?

I conclude with a photograph of Haiti that was taken nine days after the earthquake. The image speaks for itself, as it defines the complex agenda for concerned

IAN
DAVIS

Canapé Vert, Port-au-Prince, Haiti,
19 January 2010 (photo: Alain Grimard).

architects. They may even follow the sequence of my journey in this text, as they may seek to initiate, recommend, motivate, integrate, communicate and inspire the process of creating safe, secure and well-built shelters and public buildings.

So, I thank Esther and her colleagues, and all those who have been interviewed for this book, *Humanitarian Architecture*, in providing such a rich gallery of inspiring examples of 'architecture as service'.

References

Alexander, D. and Davis, I. (forthcoming). *Recovery after disaster: Providing shelter and rebuilding communities*. London: Routledge.

Cesal, E.J. (2010). *Down detour road*. Cambridge, MA and London: MIT Press.

Davis, I. (1978). *Shelter after disaster*. Oxford: Oxford Polytechnic Press.

Davis, I. (2011a). What have we learned from 40 years' experience of Disaster Shelter? *Environmental Hazards, 10*(3–4), 193–212

Davis, I. (2011b). What is the vision for sheltering and housing in Haiti? *Summary Observations of Reconstruction Progress following the Haiti Earthquake of January 12th 2010*, Port au Prince: UN-Habitat.

Pallasmaa, J., Sato, T. and Ban, S. (2007). *Alvar Aalto: Through the eyes of Shigeru Ban*. London: Black Dog Publishing.

Ritchie, I. (2013). *Being: An Architect*. London: Royal Academy Publications.

Ian Davis,

a British architect, has specialized in shelter, reconstruction and disaster risk reduction since 1972. His book *Shelter after disaster* (1978) is a seminal text in the fields of disaster relief and development. Currently Ian is Visiting Professor in Disaster Risk Management in Copenhagen, Kyoto, Lund, and Oxford Brookes Universities.

|||||||||||||||||||||||||||||||||

SENDING OUT AN SOS

RORY HYDE

DESIGNER, RESEARCHER,
BROADCASTER AND CURATOR
AUSTRALIA

If you think about architecture as a methodology – independent of the outcome, as agnostic from its product – you would see that architecture has a deep culture of synthesis informed by civic values ... If you have that capacity, that's the most valuable capacity of this time in history.
Bruce Mau (Hyde, 2012)

I like this line, it's nice to be told that you have the 'most valuable capacity of this time in history', particularly by an outsider. It makes me optimistic about architecture, and gives hope that we can reclaim some public relevance going forward. But abstracting the methodology of architecture from its product is not as easy as it sounds.

Over the past half century, and probably longer, the profession of architecture has steadily retreated from its civic obligations. We've retreated to the relative safety of the avant garde, creating fanciful images of architectural speculation for the entertainment of our peers. We've retreated into icons, producing formal novelty in the service of marketing agendas

and our own celebrity ambitions. And above all, we've retreated into commerce, where architecture is reduced to a service industry, fulfilling the market demands of property speculation and real estate.

In the good times, when the phone was ringing and money was coming through the door, we scarcely noticed what we'd lost. More troublingly, this *professional* service industry of architecture came to be mistaken for the *discipline* of architecture itself. It had built a fortress of self-justified legitimacy – fortified by an insular culture of institutes, accreditation, contracts and awards – and anything beyond these walls was 'not really architecture'.[1] But architecture has always been more than that, it's an inherently pluralist and diverse discipline, with sub-streams of activity in policy, activism, history, civics, strategy, community, ecology and more, all running in parallel. Indeed, we apparently have a 'deep culture of synthesis informed by civic values', if only we knew it ourselves ...

Nathaniel Corum's team building a straw bale house (photo: Skip Baumhower).

With the bursting of the economic bubble, and the associated collapse of the real estate and construction sectors, this fortress of professional architecture instead became a kind of *prison*. The narrow definition of architecture that it once defended – as the source of singular edifices of rarefied detail and aesthetics – came to represent decadence and irrelevance in the eyes of the public. In the years since, the profession has been forced to expand its boundaries, searching for these 'other ways of doing architecture' (Awan *et al.*, 2011) that had been so marginalized and dismissed. One of these ways is *humanitarian architecture*.

Presented in this way, it's easy to be cynical, to think that the recent bubbling of activity in the humanitarian field is mere opportunism; that architecture's ethical pendulum is simply swinging back again, as it has done many times before. But there are two key reasons to believe that this time is different. The first is the crisis of employment. As Paul Nakazawa argues, graduates can no longer depend on a job, as 'the foreseeable future only requires about half of the pre-recession workforce in architecture' (Nakazawa, 2011). This fundamental restructuring will require the profession to seek out new terrains, and not just as a hobby. This first internal 'crisis' seems trivial in light of the second: the savage effects of climate change. As Charlesworth cites in the introduction to this volume, 42 million people were displaced by natural disasters in 2011, more than by wars and armed conflicts. This is an unfathomable challenge with immense spatial

consequences, and one that architects urgently need to address.

But don't confuse this plea with some sort of a moral obligation to the developing world, this is simply survival. Natural disasters do not discriminate between your world and 'theirs'. Even the rich world is vulnerable in as yet unknown ways, as recent crises in Japan, the USA and Australia demonstrate. It is up to us to build environments which are resilient. We claim to be experts in problem-solving, lateral thinking, collaboration, operating at multiple scales, over long time spans, with technical skills and practical vision. Can we reconfigure our practice sufficiently in order to apply this capacity outside the safety of our professional fortress?

The fifteen interviews in this book suggest that we can. Together, they present a picture of incredibly generous, selfless and inspiring work for the other 90 per cent, demonstrating beyond doubt the urgent value and relevance of architects in humanitarian crises. The architects featured here have been instrumental in reconstruction and development efforts following the Indian Ocean tsunami in 2004, Hurricane Katrina in New Orleans in 2005, the flooding in Pakistan in 2010, the 2010 earthquake in Haiti, the 2011 earthquake and tsunami in Japan, the 2011 earthquake in New Zealand, as well as various other 'slow-motion' human catastrophes, such as those in Palestine and North-Western Australia.

The contributions made to the countless thousands of people over the past decade is surely confirmation enough of the positive

role architects can play in the aftermath of a natural disaster. And yet, running at odds with these encouraging examples, is a recurring theme throughout this book: that architects are *not* prepared for the humanitarian sector, that we remain in thrall to the image, and hold unrealistic views of what is required to work in a condition of crisis. Charlesworth refers to 'design cowboys', who fly in and fly out as if on a vacation, hoping to leave a mark. Lizzie Babister is suspect of architects' capacities in the humanitarian sector, claiming 'a structural engineer is more useful to me'. And none of those interviewed reflect upon their architectural training as adequate preparation for the work they do today.

At the core of these doubts is the conception and perception of the architect as a mere *aesthete*. Both Graham Saunders and Paul Pholeros claim to be sent five shelter designs a week from architects, all presumably eager to helicopter-in to save the victims of the latest disaster. These 'Future Shacks' – to borrow the title of one particularly misguided example (designed by Melbourne-based architect Sean Godsell in 2001, the 'Future Shack' is a converted shipping container intended as relief housing which is highly aestheticized, elegantly detailed, exhibited internationally, yet remains undeployed in a post-crisis situation) – are indeed symptomatic of the naive delusion that is pervasive among architects: that *form* and *design* can solve all the world's problems. Now, of course architecture is form and design, in its built manifestation it is inherently both of these things. But that was never meant to be the main point. What is architecture if

RORY
HYDE

not a *medium for conveying social effects*? Form and design are merely the means of embedding these social effects into the built environment, in order that they may continue to manifest over time. While mainstream architecture is distracted by its own images, humanitarian architecture offers an alternative example of an architecture that repositions form and design as secondary to the production of these social effects.

It is this shift in priorities that is critical, and what is at stake is our *relevance*. As Maggie Stephenson asks:

> **Do we want to continue producing design-driven hypotheses about how the city could be, what housing may be, producing documents that probably only other architects can interpret? Or do we also want to roll up our sleeves and go inside the housing finance system, the municipalities, and have the discussions in real time, listening and learning, and being challenged to be accessible, to explain it in understandable terms, to contribute strategically, to ask useful questions, to propose across multi-dimensions, to be relevant?**

As the profession of architecture flounders in search of relevance and purpose, this is a question that we ought to take note of. Here, 'relevance' is not to be confused with mere functionalism or dull problem-solving instrumentality, but to consider spatial design as one tool within a larger strategy, one that is culturally engaged, and informed by a broad set of social, economic, political and material criteria, and to be motivated by making

a difference, rather than making money.

But why shouldn't a humanitarian architect make money? It's a cruel injustice of this world that those who ostensibly do the most 'good' for society – nurses, teachers, police, etc. – are so poorly compensated. Add 'humanitarian architect' to this list. Time and again in these interviews, we hear of this work being undermined by faltering economic and political will. Despite the critical importance of this type of work, it remains an immensely difficult mode of practice to sustain.

One example: for Paul Pholeros' group Healthabitat to be awarded UN-Habitat's World Habitat Award in 2011, and in the same year have their Australian government funding slashed, is barely comprehensible.[2] Similarly, Graham Saunders describes the working situation as 'very hand-to-mouth', due to a lack of recognition of the shelter sector, concluding that 'unless there is another disaster there are no or very limited employment opportunities'. Fortunately for Saunders – and unfortunately for others – if there's one thing the past decade has shown us, it is that there's no shortage of disasters. And so the question remains, how can we legitimize this work to the point where it can function as a sustainable practice?

This lack of legitimacy is stranger still when we consider the sheer number of people this work is reaching. Lizzie Babister, as part of her work with CARE in Haiti, describes building 3,000 transitional shelters, as well as providing 17,000 reconstruction kits. How many architects can

claim to reach even a fraction of these figures in their entire careers? It's statistics like these which make the questions of legitimacy seem like nothing more than petty exclusion on the part of the mainstream profession. But even these numbers don't come close to fulfilling the total need, thereby only highlighting the true scope of the global challenge of humanitarian architecture. Hsieh Ying Chun articulates this point more poetically: 'Like a black hole, [post-disaster reconstruction] is an area untouched by modern architecture.' Considering the scope of the task ahead, how can we give these practitioners and others like them the necessary backing, support and financial confidence to continue their work?

Charlesworth proposes a bifurcation of the profession, a fork in the road, to create sub-categories of greater specialism in humanitarian fields, such as how the legal and medical professions are structured currently. Yes, we will need people specifically trained to operate in this space and respond to its unique challenges, but there is a danger in further distancing this work from the mainstream architectural profession. Instead of autonomy, what's needed is integration. Discussing the appropriateness of the title of this field, Michael Murphy argues that 'if we bifurcate "humanitarian architecture" from "architecture" we fail to demand of architecture its responsibility to the public.' In other words, all architecture ought to be humanitarian, and to create an internal division may only further excuse architecture as a whole from its obligations to social relevance and the inclusion of a broader spectrum of society.

Shigeru Ban is one of the few architects featured here who manage to straddle this divide, producing both high-profile capital 'A' architecture through his commercial practice, as well as designing shelters for aid agencies in the wake of natural disasters in Japan, Rwanda, New Zealand, Haiti and Sri Lanka. It is this parallel approach that makes it viable; as Ban explains, 'You have to have a proper job otherwise you cannot continue.'

And yet, the transfer of skill and resources is still one-directional, with Ban's commercial practice sustaining the humanitarian work. This relationship of dependency is precarious, especially as the margins of the commercial architecture practice are increasingly eroded. What is needed is a new culture, a critical mass, a discourse to further humanitarian architecture's legitimacy, supported by education, media, theory, strategies, networks, alliances and dependable funding beyond the reach of party politics. We need a compelling counter-narrative to what Eric Cesal describes as the 'mechanics of fame', the awards, the magazine profiles and the respect from peers which are granted to architects who are in the pursuit of novelty. There is evidence of this happening. New courses are emerging – for instance, Architects without Frontiers recently established a course offering 'pathways to the humanitarian sector for built environment professionals' (www.architectswithoutfrontiers.com.au/site/training.html) and Oxford Brookes University's School of Architecture is offering a degree in 'Humanitarian Action and Conflict' (www.google.com.au/#q=oxford+brookes+humanitarian+action+and+conflict). Informed discussion is occurring in the media, such as the discussion of the appropriate way to rebuild the Christchurch Cathedral, critically damaged by an earthquake in 2011, which has gone beyond practical issues of engineering to focus on architectural concerns of memory, identity and urban renewal (*The Age*, 2013). And even the spreading of ideas through highly visible platforms such as TED (Sinclair, 2006).[3]

But above all, mainstream architectural practice *needs* to be involved with the humanitarian movement, because of what it can stand to learn from it. The principles embodied in humanitarian architecture – the *human* part – are the very same principles that mainstream architecture has neglected. These principles are universal for making good architecture, no matter the context or client. By drawing these practices closer together – to create architecture that is social, equitable, diverse and *human* – we can do more than merely save the profession, we may even help some actual humans too.

Notes

1 E. Charlesworth, personal communication. This critique was levelled at Esther Charlesworth by a colleague from the architecture department at RMIT University. It echoes a similar statement made in this volume by Patama Roonrakwit, who was told, 'Are you crazy? You're not an architect, you're a social worker.'

2 World Habitat Award: www.healthabitat.com/events-page/world-habitat-award-winner-2011

3 Cameron Sinclair of AFH was awarded the 2006 TED Prize. His online talk has been viewed more than half a million times.

References

Awan, N., Schneider, T. and Till, J. (2011). *Spatial agency: Other ways of doing architecture*. Routledge.

Hyde, R. (2012). *Future practice: Conversations from the edge of architecture*, Routledge.

Nakazawa, P. (2011). 'Embrace the change', *Architect*, January. Available online at www.architectmagazine.com/business/embrace-the-change-move-your-practice-forward.aspx (accessed 7 February 2014).

Sinclair, C. (2006). Cameron Sinclair: My wish: A call for open-source architecture. Available online at www.ted.com/talks/cameron_sinclair_on_open_source_architecture.html (accessed 7 February 2014).

The Age (2013, 6 April). Critics slam 'bizarre' choices for Christchurch cathedral. Available online at www.theage.com.au/world/critics-slam-bizarre-choices-for-christchurch-cathedral-20130405-2hcd1.html (accessed 7 February 2014).

Rory Hyde

is the author of *Future practice: Conversations from the edge of architecture* (Routledge, 2012). He studied architecture at RMIT University in Melbourne, where he also completed a PhD on emerging models of practice enabled by new technologies. He is contributing editor of *Architecture Australia*, editorial advisor to *Volume* magazine and co-host of *The Architects*, a weekly radio show on architecture, which was presented in the Australian pavilion at the 2012 Venice Architecture Biennale.

HUMANITARIAN AGENCIES AND PEOPLE

Ahmedabad Study Action Group (ASAG) is an Indian voluntary non-government organization that seeks to use the skills of professionals to promote public causes associated with re/settlement planning, slum upgrading, housing and rural development. Established in 1968, ASAG is involved in advocacy, resource mobilization, participatory design, planning, construction and community organization. ASAG has designed and built 10,000 low-cost houses in more than sixty settlements in urban, rural and tribal areas of Gujarat since its inception. www.propoor.org/ngos/?id=3109

Asian Coalition for Housing Rights (ACHR) is a Bangkok-based regional network for community organizations, non-government organizations and professionals involved in urban poverty and slum upgrading in Asian cities. Founded in 1987, ACHR enables shared learning of community organization, inclusive finance and links with city governments and international institutions. It provides support through professional exchanges and grants and loans from the Asian Coalition for Community Action fund. ACHR is a sister network of Slum Dwellers International. www.achr.net

Architects without Frontiers (AWF) was established in 1999 by architects and planners Esther Charlesworth, Garry Ormston and Beau Beza. AWF's mission is to improve the living conditions of vulnerable communities in the Asia-Pacific region, with a focus on sustainable design outcomes in the health and education sectors. Since its inception, AWF has provided over fifty design proposals and delivered thirty-four built projects to vulnerable communities in twelve countries, including schools, hospitals, orphanages and cultural centres. www.architectswithoutfrontiers.com.au

Architecture and Developpement (A&D) is a French non-government organization involved in post-disaster and development projects to improve the lives of vulnerable and marginalized people. Founded in Paris in 1997, A&D provides assistance across project phases, from project conception through to delivery and evaluation. Their services include, for example: needs assessments, project feasibility studies and evaluations, technical expertise and the design and implementation of housing, education and cultural projects. www.archidev.org

Architecture for Humanity (AFH)

is a US-based not-for-profit design services firm. Founded in 1999, AFH provides international design, construction and development services in communities where there is acute need, by drawing from a network of more than 50,000 professionals who volunteer time and expertise. Through meaningful local infrastructure projects for a diverse range of clients, AFH directly assists approximately 100,000 people per year, in addition to the more than 60,000 people who are impacted by AFH advocacy, training and outreach programmes. www.architectureforhumanity.org

Architecture Sans Frontières (ASF)

is an international network of architecture organizations concerned with the equitable, social, cultural and environmental commitment of architecture, construction, urbanism and the conservation of historical heritages to human development. The network supports organizations to achieve fair and sustainable development projects, including through knowledge sharing; opening dialogues and establishing strong relationships with and within less affluent countries; by fostering the socially responsible role of built-environment professionals; and through support for participatory processes and approaches. www.asfint.org

Bryan Bell is the founder of Design Corps, a US-based architecture practice that targets those who are traditionally excluded from the services of the profession. Bell has received high accolades for his Design Corps' summer design/build internship programme, which teaches young designers interested in the social application of architecture about critical community organization skills. Bell's efforts culminated in a series of university conferences entitled *Structures for inclusion* and in the publication of two books: *Good deeds, good design: Community service through architecture* (2003) and *Expanding design: Architecture as activism* (2008). www.bryanbell.org *Also see: Design Corps*

John Cary is a Research Fellow in the College of Design at the University of Minnesota whose work focuses on expanding the public interest design field. Among his many achievements, Cary founded publicInterestdesign. org in 2011; curated 'Public interest design: Products, places, processes' as one of the first guest curators in residence at the Autodesk Gallery in San Francisco (on display/touring over five years until 2017); and is founding chair of the first annual Public Interest Design Week (March 2013). Cary is also author of *The power of pro bono* (2010), a strategic advisor to the new $1,000,000 TED Prize, co-lead of The City 2.0 and the 2012 TED Prize. Cary consults with a broad range of urban stakeholders, building on seven years' experience as Executive Director of Public Architecture (San Francisco) and brief leadership of Next American City (now Next City).

Cary's accomplishments in public interest design are internationally recognized, most recently with the Social/Economic/Environmental Design (SEED) Award for Excellence in Leadership (2013). www.johncary.us *Also see: publicinterestdesign.org*

Centre for Development and Emergency Practice (CENDEP)

is a multidisciplinary centre at Oxford Brookes University, England, focused on disaster risk reduction and response, chronic poverty, building urban resilience, conflict transformation, refugee studies and torture prevention. Established in 1985, CENDEP draws together aid workers, academics, professionals and practitioners in practice-oriented learning for shelter after disasters through partnerships with organizations such as International Federation of Red Cross, CARE, UN agencies and Save the Children. CENDEP's Emeritus Professor Ian Davis is widely regarded as the founder of the subject of shelter after disaster based on his seminal work *Shelter after disaster* (1978). www.architecture.brookes.ac.uk/ research/cendep *See also: Shelter after disaster; Nabeel Hamdi*

The Clinton Foundation

(William J. Clinton Foundation) is an American non-government organization that seeks to improve world health, strengthen economies and protect the environment through partnerships that leverage the expertise, resources and passion of businesses, governments, non-government organizations and private citizens. Established in 2001 by former American president Bill Clinton, the Clinton

Foundation responds to local needs around the globe, with a focus on economic inequality, climate change, global health, childhood obesity and on producing measurable results. The foundation comprises a series of initiatives, including the Clinton Foundation in Haiti, which has raised $32 million in relief funds for projects aimed to restore Haiti's communities through sustainable development, education and capacity building. www.clintonfoundation.org

Community Architects for Shelter and Environment (CASE)

is a Bangkok-based non-government organization that works with communities in informal settlements to improve their shelter and living environments. Founded in 1997 by Patama Roonrakwit, CASE draws together a group of architects committed to participatory design. CASE projects involve the community at every stage, from site mapping through to construction. www.casestudio.info

Cooper-Hewitt Design and Social Impact Summit

brought together a broad range of leading practitioners and educators to explore the gaps in, challenges for and strategies to advance the field of socially responsible design. The day-long summit, held in 2012, sought to bring together innovators in socially responsible design, as well as supportive public and private funders. The summit was organized by Cooper-Hewitt, the Lemelson Foundation and the National Endowment for the Arts (NEA), with support from the Surdna Foundation. A white paper entitled *Design and social impact: A cross-sectoral agenda for design education, research and practice* (2012) written by Julie Lasky for Cooper-Hewitt, NEA and the Lemelson Foundation reports on the day's discussions (available online). www.cooperhewitt.org/conversations/2012/02/21/social-impact-design-summit; www.cooperhewitt.org/publications/design-social-impact

Cordaid (Catholic Organisation for Relief and Development Aid)

is a Dutch civil society organization focused on supporting vulnerable people suffering the consequences of poverty, exclusion and injustice in vulnerable regions and areas of conflict. Although only founded in 2000, its mission dates back to pioneering humanitarian work during the First World War. Cordaid is one of the largest development organizations in Holland, with 200 staff at its headquarters in The Hague and ten field offices abroad with a further 300 staff. The organization is supported by a network of 890 partner organizations (including national and local authorities and private sector representatives) in twenty-eight countries. Cordaid's major contribution is to human security, which enables local opportunities to be created so as to build flourishing communities. www.cordaid.org/en

The Cuny Center

is a non-profit research and educational institute that studies and develops practical solutions to address the needs of societies affected by disasters and complex emergencies. The Center was founded as the Intertect Institute in 1987 by Fred Cuny and later became the Center for the Study of Societies in Crisis. In 2000 the name was changed to The Cuny Center to honour its founder, who disappeared in Chechnya in 1995. www.cunycenter.org

Design Corps

is a US-based architecture practice that targets those who are traditionally excluded from the services of the profession. Founded by Bryan Bell in 1991, Design Corps successfully involves people in the decisions that shape their lives, including those relating to the built environment. The Community Service Program, which has been running for over ten years, draws on the skills of recent graduates of architecture and planning to provide technical assistance to communities in need. www.designcorps.org
Also see: Bryan Bell

Development Planning Unit, University College London

is a leading postgraduate teaching and research unit that assists in building the capacity of national governments, local authorities, NGOs, aid agencies and businesses in achieving socially just and sustainable development in the developing world. DPU is located within The Bartlett, University College London's global faculty for the built environment. www.bartlett.ucl.ac.uk/dpu

DFID (Department for International Development)

is a British ministerial department leading the UK government's action on world poverty. Established in 1997, DFID runs long-term programmes to address the underlying causes of poverty and respond to humanitarian emergencies. These efforts are sustained by a staff of approximately 2,700, who operate from DFID's London headquarters and from the field. DFID also provides funding assistance to organizations with parallel missions. www.gov.uk/government/organisations/department-for-international-development

Down detour road: An architect in search of practice (2010) by Eric Cesal (MIT Press) has been described as an essential roadmap to the present architectural scene and its challenges in an era of financial meltdown. www.mitpress.mit.edu/books/down-detour-road

Emergency Architects have, since 2001, been bringing together architects, engineers and town planners to use their professional expertise to bring appropriate and lasting help to all the victims of natural, technological and human catastrophes, without distinction of nationality, sex or religion. www.archi-urgent.com

Emergency Architecture Australia (EAA) is a not-for-profit, non-sectarian, professional organization with registered charity status and affiliations with partner organizations in France and Canada. EAA seeks to mobilize construction professionals to bring assistance to those in need due to natural disaster, climate change or armed conflict, with a focus on building capacity and skills to rebuild in a way that mitigates risks from future disasters. EAA sends experienced architects and other built-environment specialists into the field with the aim of working alongside governments, agencies and communities to rebuild in a sustainable way. EAA's process emphasizes early construction of permanent rather than temporary structures, use of local materials and skills, building capacity at all levels in the process, but most importantly at the community level, giving women and others a voice and the tools to rebuild their lives. www.archi-urgent.com

Engineers Without Borders Australia (EWB) is a member-based not-for-profit organization with ten years' experience in creating systemic change through humanitarian engineering. EWB does this by: working in partnership to address a lack of access to basic human needs such as clean water, sanitation and hygiene, energy, basic infrastructure, waste systems, information communication technology and engineering education; educating and training Australian students, engineers and the wider community on issues including sustainable development, appropriate technology, poverty and the power of humanitarian engineering; and leading a movement of like-minded people with strong values and a passion for humanitarian engineering within Australia and overseas. www.ewb.org.au

GHESKIO (Haitian Group for the Study of Kaposi's Sarcoma and Opportunistic Infections) is a non-government health organization in Port-au-Prince, Haiti. Established in 1982 in partnership with the Haitian Ministry for Health, GHESKIO was the first organization in the world committed to the fight against HIV/AIDS. Following the 2010 earthquake, GHESKIO provides humanitarian assistance and emergency care to disaster victims, as well as ongoing life-saving support to people with HIV/AIDS. www.gheskio.org

Gulf Coast Community Design Studio (GCCDS) is a professional service and outreach programme of Mississippi State University's College of Architecture, Art and Design. Established in Biloxi, Mississippi, after Hurricane Katrina in 2005, GCCDS provides architectural design services, landscape and planning assistance, educational opportunities and research to organizations and communities along the Mississippi Gulf Coast. GCCDS works together with local organizations, communities, government, not-for-profit organizations, universities, developers and other partners across all three Mississippi coastal counties. www.gccds.org

Habitat for Humanity is a global NGO and Christian housing ministry. Founded in 1976 by the late Millard Fuller, Habitat for Humanity seeks to eliminate substandard or poverty housing. Habitat for Humanity works in partnership with families in need to build, rehabilitate and repair simple, decent, affordable homes in sustainable communities. With support from home-owner families, volunteers, donors and partner organizations in more than twenty countries across the Asia-Pacific region, Habitat for Humanity has built or improved more than 500,000 homes worldwide, providing safe and affordable shelter for more than 2.5 million people (as of September 2011). www.habitat.org

Haiti Center is a unique partnership of public, civil society and academic institutions to facilitate the integration of Haitian universities into the reconstruction processes following the devastation of the 2010

earthquake. Developed within the Massachusetts Institute of Technology (MIT) following the earthquake, the Haiti Center is a platform for university collaboration to provide a forum for students and academics to develop expertise on disaster risk mitigation and reconstruction, and to interact with government and reconstruction practitioners. The Haiti Center is one of the initiatives selected by the Haiti Structural Assessment Program, which receives funding from a Global Facility for Disaster Reduction and Recovery grant. Among the numerous participating institutions for the Haiti Center are: the World Bank, MIT, United Nations Office for Project Services, the International Organization of Migration, Oxfam America, Build Change and Cordaid.

Nabeel Hamdi is Emeritus Professor of Housing and Urban Development at the Centre for Development and Emergency Practice, Oxford Brookes University, and Teaching Fellow at the Development Planning Unit, University College London. Hamdi received the UN-Habitat Scroll of Honour for his work on community action planning. Hamdi consults on participatory action planning and slum-upgrading for major international development agencies and non-government organizations. Hamdi is widely published in this field, including *Small change* (2004) and *The placemaker's guide to building community: Tools for community planning* (2010). Other achievements at CENDEP include founding the Masters course in Development Practice, and centre co-directorship (1991–2004).

See also: Centre for Development and Emergency Practice

International Federation of Red Cross and Red Crescent Societies (IFRC) is the world's largest humanitarian organization. Founded in 1919, the Swiss-based organization carries out relief operations to support victims of disaster and development work to enhance the capacities of its member National Societies. IFRC's primary focus is humanitarian values, disaster response, disaster preparedness and health and community care. IFRC comprises 187 Red Cross and Red Crescent National Societies, a secretariat based in Geneva, and more than sixty delegations located across the globe. www.ifrc.org

InterTect: *See The Cuny Center.*

Make It Right is a not-for-profit organization that builds healthy, energy-efficient, well-designed homes and buildings for people in need in New Orleans, Kansas City and Newark in the USA. Founded in 2007 by Brad Pitt, Make It Right works with communities across the country to achieve change in the way buildings are designed and built by positioning the community as a leader in defining and designing their environments. Make It Right projects meet the highest standards of green building: they are LEED Platinum certified and inspired by a cradle-to-cradle philosophy. Make It Right have built approximately ninety homes in the region since Hurricane Katrina in 2005. www.makeitright.org

MASS Design Group is an American not-for-profit that seeks to use architecture to improve health and empower communities. Founded in Boston by Michael Murphy, Alan Ricks and David

Saladik in 2007, MASS Design focuses on innovative design in resource-limited settings. MASS Design Group, from their offices in Boston and Kigali, Rwanda, plans, implements and advocates for designs and innovations that produce better health outcomes for communities around the world. MASS has also established capacity building and research programmes to reposition the role of design in international aid. www.massdesigngroup.org

Master of International Cooperation: Sustainable Emergency Architecture is a unique degree programme of the ESARQ School of Architecture at the Universitat Internacional de Catalunya, Barcelona. This Masters programme seeks to prepare architects to develop and rebuild communities impacted by rapid urbanization, poverty, conflict and natural disaster through its joint focus on international cooperation, sustainable urban development and emergency architecture. www.masteremergencyarchitecture.com

Mecanoo is a multi-award-winning Dutch architecture practice renown for its focus on context, materials, attention to detail and sustainability. Founded in Delft in 1984, Mecanoo initially focused on social housing projects in urban renewal areas before expanding to complex, multi-purpose buildings and urban developments. Mecanoo comprises a multidisciplinary staff of over ninety creative professionals working across the disciplines of urban planning, landscaping, architecture and interior design. Mecanoo's founder, Francine Houben, lectures internationally on the need for socially and ecologically responsible design – the ethos of her practice. www.mecanoo.nl

Médecins Sans Frontières (MSF; Doctors without Borders) is the world's leading independent organization for medical humanitarian aid. Through a global team of more than 24,000 field staff, MSF provides worldwide assistance during and after disasters. An MSF crisis team comprises a high proportion of national staff and approximately 10 per cent international staff, including doctors, nurses, administrators, epidemiologists, laboratory technicians, mental health professionals, logistics and water and sanitation experts. In 1999 MSF was awarded the Nobel Peace Prize. www.msf.org.au

Open Architecture Network: *See WorldChanging*

Participatory Development Programme in Urban Areas (PDP) is a programme of the Egyptian–German development cooperation to improve the living conditions of the urban poor of Greater Cairo through improvements to environmental conditions and public and civil society service delivery. PDP is implemented by the Egyptian Ministry of Planning and International Cooperation with support from the Deutsche Gesellschaft fur Internationale Zusammenarbeit (GIZ). www.egypt-urban.net

Partners in Health (PIH) is a non-government organization committed to community-based healthcare approaches. It was founded in Boston in 1987 by Jim Kim, Ophelia Dahl, Paul Farmer, Todd McCormack and Thomas J. White to support activities started in Haiti. Since its inception, PIH has expanded into twelve countries with the aim of caring for those most in need, alleviating the causes of disease, and sharing knowledge with other countries and non-government organizations. PIH also invests in partnerships to improve access to food, shelter, clean water, sanitation, education and economic opportunities on the basis that fighting disease means fighting poverty. www.pih.org

Project H is a grassroots network committed to using design to achieve social change in local communities. Founded by Emily Pilloton, this American not-for-profit organization supports youth-led public design projects to transform communities and improve education from kindergarten through to the end of high school. The 'H' represents the organization's core values: humanity, habitats, health, happiness, heart and hands. www.projecthdesign.org

Public Architecture is a San Francisco-based non-government organization that identifies and resolves practical problems of human interaction within the built environment, and functions as a catalyst for public discourse through education, advocacy and the design of public spaces and amenities. Founded in 2002 by John Peterson of Peterson Architects, Public Architecture represents a new model for architectural practice by repositioning the architect as problem-identifier. Public Architecture actively identifies problems that require innovative design solutions and approaches to clients and funding. Public Architecture also seeks to institutionalize pro bono architectural practice through their The 1% Program, in which firms pledge 1 per cent of their billable hours to pro bono service. www.publicarchitecture.org

publicinterestdesign.org is a website about a growing movement at the intersection of design and service that comprises community design, humanitarian design and pro bono design. Established by John Cary in 2011, the website seeks to share news and opportunities with stakeholders of the public interest design movement to increase communication within and about the movement. www.publicinterestdesign.org *Also see: John Cary*

RedR Australia is a humanitarian agency for international emergency relief, providing skilled people and training to help communities rebuild and recover in times of crisis. RedR Australia is a Standby Partner to five UN agencies. During a humanitarian crisis, a global network of Standby Partner organizations provides additional support to frontline UN response efforts. RedR Australia was established in 1992 by an engineer, Jeff Dobell, who called on his peers to apply their skills to disaster relief. Today, RedR Australia deploys more than 700 people to over seventy countries. RedR Australia is part of the international RedR network of nationally accredited organizations, each sharing a common vision and mission. RedR is represented in the UK, India, Sri Lanka, New Zealand and Malaysia. www.redr.org.au

Rural Studio is an undergraduate programme of the School of Architecture, Planning and Landscape Architecture at Auburn University. Established by D.K. Ruth and Samuel Mockbee in 1993, this off-campus design/build programme provides students with a hands-on educational experience while also supporting the people in West Alabama's Black Belt region. Based on the philosophy that design is for everyone, the studio is undertaking increasingly large and complex community-oriented projects. Rural Studio has completed 150 projects and helped educate over 600 'citizen architects'. www.ruralstudio.org

Shelter after disaster (1978) is the seminal book on post-disaster housing, written by Ian Davis, an architect and now Emeritus Professor at the Centre for Development and Emergency Practice, Oxford Brookes University. Davis' review of contemporary and historic provision of post-disaster housing in developing countries draws attention to the failures of many architectural proposals for 'emergency housing', heavily criticizing untested, so-called universal solutions for their lack of consideration for context and their expense.

The Shelter Centre is a non-government organization registered in Geneva, Switzerland that supports the humanitarian housing sector by establishing collaborations, consensus and capacity. Founded in 2004 in Cambridge, UK, the Shelter Centre helps organizations involved in transitional settlement and reconstruction after conflict and natural disaster, from the emergency phase through to lasting solutions. The Shelter Centre develops and maintains strategic and policy guidelines, technical guidelines, technical training, community of practice services and a global forum for the sector. The Shelter Centre partners with UN bodies, the Red Cross, international organizations, non-government organizations, academic and research groups and donors. Funding is provided by DFID, bilaterally or multilaterally. www.sheltercentre.org

The Sphere Project brings a wide range of humanitarian agencies together to improve the quality of humanitarian assistance and the accountability of humanitarian actors to their constituents, donors and affected populations. The Sphere Handbook, *Humanitarian charter and minimum standards in humanitarian response*, is one of the most widely known and internationally recognized sets of common principles and universal minimum standards in life-saving areas of humanitarian response. Established in 1997, the Sphere Project is not a membership organization. Governed by a Board composed of representatives of global networks of humanitarian agencies, the Sphere Project today is a vibrant community of humanitarian response practitioners. www.sphereproject.org

Stefan Behnisch Architects (Behnisch Architekten) is a multi-award-winning German architectural practice with offices in Stuttgart, Munich, Boston and Los Angeles. Founded in 1989 by Stefan Behnisch, the practice has maintained a design philosophy which privileges the social dimension of architecture and which has gained a reputation for expert experience in sustainable architecture. www.behnisch.com

John F.C. Turner is a British architect renowned for his extensive writing on housing and community organization. Turner is a key self-help housing theorist: in a radical break with contemporary thinking, he argued housing was best provided and managed by those who live in it, rather than being centrally administered by the state. His ideas were informed by experiences in the squatter settlements of Peru, where he studied and advised on reconstruction and slum upgrading programmes in 1957–1965. Turner presented this thesis in several seminal books, including *Freedom to build: Dweller control of the housing process* (1972) and *Housing by people: Towards autonomy in building environments* (1976).

UN-Habitat (or the United Nations Human Settlements Programme) is the UN agency for human settlement. Mandated by the UN General Assembly, it promotes socially and environmentally sustainable urban areas with the goal of providing shelter for all. UN-Habitat's programmes assist policy makers and local communities to tackle human settlement and urban issues and devise implementable, lasting solutions. With a strategic vision aimed at achieving cities without slums, the agency's work is guided by the UN Millennium Declaration, and particularly Millennium Development Goal No. 7 (to improve the lives of at least 100 million slum-dwellers by 2020) and Target 10 (to reduce by half the number of people

HUMANITARIAN AGENCIES
AND PEOPLE

without sustainable access to safe drinking water). UN-Habitat's four-pillar strategy comprises: advocacy of global norms, analysis of information, field testing of solutions and financing. www.unhabitat.org

Urban-Think Tank (U-TT) is an interdisciplinary design practice committed to high-level research and design of contemporary architecture and urbanism. Founded in 1993 in Venezuela, U-TT aims at increasing the understanding of the informal city and delivering innovative practical solutions through the combined skills of architects, civil engineers, environmental planners, landscape architects, and communication specialists through its offices in Caracas, Sao Paulo, New York and Zurich. In 2007, founder Alfredo Brillembourg and co-director Hubert Klumpner established the Sustainable Living Urban Model Laboratory (SLUM Lab) at Columbia University, USA. In 2010, the work of U-TT was recognized by the Ralph Erskine Award. www.u-tt.com

Voluntary Architects' Network (VAN) is a non-government organization that assists in the organization of post-disaster aid in the construction field. Established in 1995, VAN is the brainchild of award-winning Japanese architect Shigeru Ban. VAN has gained a reputation for its innovative use of paper, particularly recycled cardboard paper tubes, in projects to house disaster victims. A book titled *Shigeru Ban: Voluntary Architects' Network* (2010) details VAN's accomplishments. www.shigerubanarchitects.com

World Vision International is a Christian relief, development and advocacy organization committed to working with communities to overcome poverty and injustice. Founded in 1950, World Vision International is involved in short-term emergency relief projects, long-term sustainable community development, and working with communities and policy makers at the national, regional and global level to establish awareness of poverty and address the unjust systems associated with it. www.wvi.org

WorldChanging is a collaborative online open-source community committed to improving the built environment through design innovation and sustainability. WorldChanging, as the first website to offer open source architectural documentation, seeks to link communities with architects, designers and other stakeholders of the built environment to help them solve problems. The initiative is the brainchild of Architecture for Humanity (AFH) and grew out of frustration with the difficulties in sharing ideas and collaborating to address post-disaster housing needs. AFH leveraged their prestigious 2006 TED Prize to establish the Open Architecture Network (OAN) and in 2011 they acquired WorldChanging and merged it with OAN. www.openarchitecturenetwork.org *See also: Architecture for Humanity*

INDEX

Page numbers in italic indicate figures; page numbers in bold indicate the list of humanitarian agencies and people.